The Biography of
Mahommah Gardo Baquaqua:

His Passage from Slavery to Freedom
in Africa and America

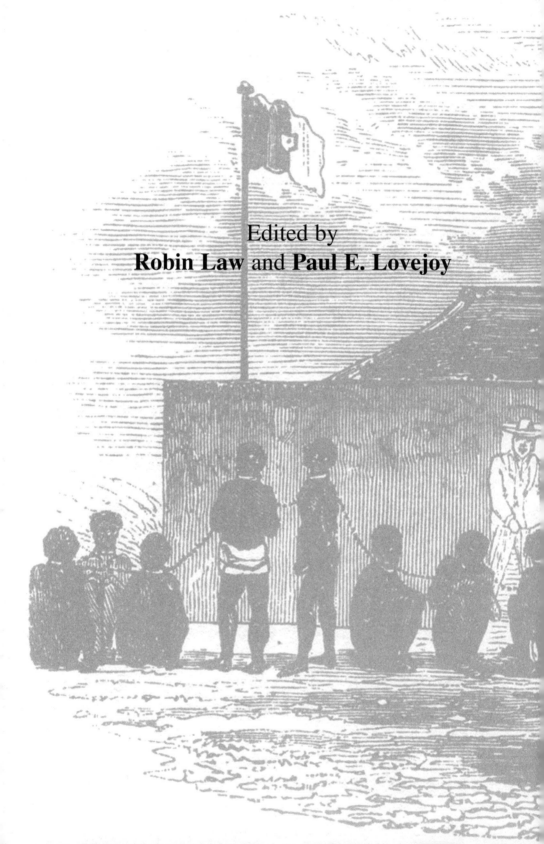

Edited by
Robin Law and **Paul E. Lovejoy**

The Biography of Mahommah Gardo Baquaqua:

His Passage from Slavery to Freedom in Africa and America

Ⓜ Markus Wiener Publishers
Ⓦ Princeton

For information write to:
Markus Wiener Publishers
231 Nassau Street, Princeton, NJ 08542

Photos courtesy of Paul Lovejoy

Library of Congress Cataloging-in-Publication Data

The biography of Mahommah Gardo Baquaqua: his passage from slavery
to freedom in Africa and America/edited by Robin Law and Paul E. Lovejoy.
   Includes bibliographical references and index.
   ISBN 1-55876-247-7 (hc)
   ISBN 1-55876-248-5 (pbk)
   1. Baquaqua, Mahommah Gardo.   2. Slaves—America—Biography.
   3. Slaves—Africa—Biography.   4. Free African-Americans—Biography.
   5. Djougou (Benin)—Biography.   6. Pernambuco (Brazil)—Biography.
   7. Rio de Janeiro (Brazil)—Biography.   8. Haiti—Biography.
   9. New York (N.Y.)—Biography.   10. Chatham (Ont.)—Biography.
   I. Law, Robin, II. Lovejoy, Paul E.
   E444.B2 B56 2001   2001
   909'.0496081'092—dc21   2001026981

Printed in the United States of America on acid-free paper.

Dedicated to the People of Djougou

TABLE OF CONTENTS

MAPS

ILLUSTRATIONS

(Forbes and possibly an agent of a British firm trading there) in Forbes, *Dahomey and the Dahomans*, i, 103, 112.

PLATE 8 (*page 147*). Ouidah: the French fort, c. 1856: the European factories were the only buildings in Ouidah at this period with windows; after an illustration by Repin in *Le Tour du Monde*, and reproduced in Richard Burton, *A Mission to Gelele: King of Dahome* (London, 1966) 80.

PLATE 9 (*page 150*). Ouidah: 'The Slave Chain' observed on 16 March 1850, in Forbes, *Dahomey and the Dahomans*, i, 100, 117.

PLATE 10 (*page 151*). Isidoro de Souza: here a portrait of the leading slave trader in the mid-1840s at Little Popo, west of Ouidah, from which Baquaqua may have been embarked; from a painting, c. 1822, in Pierre Verger, *Flux et reflux de la traite des Nègres entre le Golfe de Bénin et Bahia de Todos os Santos du XVIIe au XIXe siècle*, Paris (1968).

PLATE 11 (*page 152*). Bight of Benin: loading slaves in c. 1849, Church Missionary Intelligencer, 7:2 (1856) and also Church Missionary Gleaner (1874), 114.

PLATE 12 (*page 155*). Pernambuco: Recife waterfront in 1859; in Ferrez, *Photography in Brazil*, 160.

PLATE 13 (*page 157*). Pernambuco: perhaps Olinda, pictured here in 1860, with Recife in the distance, in Gilberto Ferrez, *Photography in Brazil* (trans., Stella de Sá Rego, Alburquerque, N.M., 1984), 164.

PLATE 14 (*page 162*). Rio de Janeiro: as taken in 1850 by F. Pustkov.

Plate 15 (*page 165*). Rio de Janeiro: passengers seeking 'excelentes comodos' in traveling to New York were invited to the office of the *Lembrança*, 93 Rua Direita, as advertised in *Jornal do Commercio* (Rio de Janeiro), 17 April 1847.

PLATE 16 (*page 168*). New York City Hall: where Baquaqua appeared in Court, from an illustration of 1838, I.N. Pheleps Stokes Collection, N.Y. Public Library, also in Lockwood, *Manhattan Moves Uptown*, 2.

PLATE 17 (*page 172*). New York City: view of the East River in 1852, in *The Renascence of City Hall; Commemorative Presentation Rededication of City Hall, The City of New York, July 12, 1956* (New York, 1956), 84. The Lembrança docked at the foot of Roosevelt Street, opposite Brooklyn Heights.

PLATE 18 (*page 174*). New York City: view of lower Manhattan, c. 1842–5, New York Historical Society, New York City, in Charles Lockwood, *Manhattan Moves Uptown: An Illustrated History* (Boston, 1976), 4.

PLATE 19 (*page 178*). Haiti: panorama of Port-au-Prince in 1870; in Samuel Hazard, *Santo Domingo Past and Present with a Glance at Hayti* (London, 1873).

PLATE 20 (*page 179*). Rev. William L. Judd, with Baquaqua: from the frontispiece, A.T. Foss and Edward Mathews, *Facts for Baptist Churches* (Utica, 1850).

PLATE 21 (*page 186*). New York Central College: New York Central College Collection, Cortland County Historical Society, Cortland, N.Y.

PLATE 22 (*page 187*). Cyrus P. Grosvenor: President of the College (1849–50) and also editor, Christian Contributor and Free Missionary (1845–50); from a photograph at the Lamont Memorial Free Library, McGraw, N.Y.

PLATE 23 (*page 188*). McGrawville: 'If you write to me sent [= send] to McGrawville, Cortland, Co., N.Y.' (letter to George Whipple, Brooklyn, 10 August 1853); downtown McGrawville, as seen in the early 1860s, as photographed by G.L. Holden, dentist and photographer, Lamont Memorial Free Library, McGraw, N.Y.

PLATE 24 (*page 215*). Sudan map: contemporary map based on information gathered in c. 1849 from Muslims in Brazil; see 'Carte du Soudan d'après les Négres esclaves a Bahia' [c. 1843], Francis de Castelnau, Renseignements sur l'Afrique Centrale et sur une nation d'hommes a queue qui s'y trouverait, d'après le rapport des Négres du Soudan, esclaves a Bahia (Paris, 1851).

PLATE 25 (*page 240*). Letter from Baquaqua, apparently to George Whipple: 'tell me when the vessal will go to Africa', 14 September 1853 (American Missionary Association Archives, Amistad Research Center, Tulane University, New Orleans).

PLATE 26 (*page 247*). Gerrit Smith: 'I do not exspected to write to you to Washington' (Letter to Smith, Chatham, Canada West, 25 May 1854), referring to Smith's election to Congress as a radical abolitionist; photograph in Octavius Brooks Frothingham, *Gerrit Smith: A Biography* (New York, 1909), frontispiece.

PLATE 27 (*page 248*). Chatham, Canada West: King Street, looking west from 5th Street, 1860, Courtsey of the Chatham-Kent Museum, 85.27.2.15, N674, Bk. 2#15.

ACKNOWLEDGMENTS

All academic research is collaborative, but some is more collaborative than usual. Such is the case of this new edition of Baquaqua's biography, which is part of a wider program of research that focuses on the "Nigerian" hinterland and its role in the development of the African diaspora, centered at York University, Toronto, Canada (http://www.yorku.ca/nhp), which is affiliated with the UNESCO Slave Route Project and supported by various institutions, including York University and the University of Stirling. The Social Sciences and Humanities Research Council of Canada provided financial assistance through its Major Collaborative Research Initiative Program, which enabled the research for this project to be conducted in the context of this much broader program. We owe a considerable debt to the numerous colleagues, among whom we count our students, who assisted in our research into Baquaqua's life, and who in one way or another have participated in the larger program of collaborative research.

The initial stages of research were conducted in northern Bénin in April 1999, when both Law and Lovejoy attended a conference in Parakou, organized by Obarè Bagodo, and visited Djougou. We would like to thank Obarè Bagodo, Zakari Dramani-Issifou, Nassirou Arifari Bako, Albarka Soulleymane, Alfa Houssane Djarra, Sani Alaza, and Denise Brégand for information on Djougou (Baquaqua's home town) and the region of Borgu, its languages and cultures. Elisée Soumonni was especially helpful in the Bénin phase of research; Silke Strickrodt checked numerous details in Britain, especially on the West African background. Ibrahim Hamza assisted with Hausa terminology and Charles Tshimanga assisted us with Fonds Person in Paris.

For Baquaqua's time in Brazil, Silvia Hunold Lara shared her own preliminary research, providing us with leads to pursue in North America; Manolo Florentino, Alberto da Costa e Silva, José Cairus, and Mariza de Carvalho Soares tracked down information in Rio de

Janeiro and repeatedly checked our accuracy on details; Marcus J.M. de Carvalho assisted with the Pernambuco section, while Stuart Schwartz, Mary Karasch, José Curto, João Reis, and Robert Krueger provided useful information and ideas as well. Lovejoy undertook additional research in Brazil in January 2001 in consultation with these specialists.

Our research in North America has relied on a number of people who generously assisted us in tracking down leads. We would like to thank especially Catherine Hanchett for generously providing assistance on the history of New York Central College, including access to her unpublished work on the College and Baquaqua's years there; Catherine Barber, Cortland County Historian, for newspaper references; Anita Wright, Curator, Cortland County Historical Society, for checking details on Mahommah's life in McGrawville and Freetown Corners; Mary Kimberly of the Lamont Memorial Free Library in McGraw, N.Y., for assistance; Karen Sundland and Stuart Campbell of the Samuel Colgate Historical Library in Rochester, N.Y., for access to materials on the American Baptist Free Mission Society and Central College, and Kwabena Akurang-Parry for locating Baquaqua's letters in the Amistad Collection at Tulane University. David Bebbington provided us with information on the wider Baptist background of the Free Mission Society. Carolyn Fick helped us on the Haitian background; Gwen Robinson provided us with information on William P. Newman and Chatham; Shannon Prince and Bryan Prince searched the Buxton records; and Julia Winch introduced us to the world of free African-Americans in the U.S.A. in the 1850s, especially the Purvis and Forten families who had children at New York Central College when Baquaqua was there. Cheryl Lemaitre assisted in collecting information on the American Baptist Free Mission in Canada, upstate New York, and Haiti; and Thorald Burnham checked publishing details in Detroit, followed up leads in Cortland, Syracuse, and McGraw, and tracked down missing information on the Haitian period.

The project would not have been conceived or initiated without the pioneering work of Allan Austin, whose important but much neglected edition of primary texts on enslaved Muslims first drew our attention to Baquaqua: see Allan Austin (ed.), African Muslims in Ante-Bellum America: A Sourcebook (New York & London, 1984). Finally, we have benefited from the assistance of Catherine Coquery-Vidrovitch, Donald Wright, Monica Schuler, Len Wong, Eugene Onutan, Brenda McComb, Muhammad Bashir Salau, and Behnaz Mirzai Asl. During the final stages of writing Law held a Lady Davis Visiting Professorship in conjunction with a Visiting Fellowship at the Harry S. Truman Research Institute, the Hebrew University, Jerusalem, and Lovejoy was awarded the Canada Research Chair in African Diaspora History.

We have dedicated this edition of Baquaqua's story to the people of Djougou who knew nothing of Baquaqua but who were willing to share local information that helped us to repatriate his memory as well as to establish his place in the African diaspora. May his memory enrich their understanding of their own history, the history of the Republique du Bénin, West Africa, and the Black Atlantic.

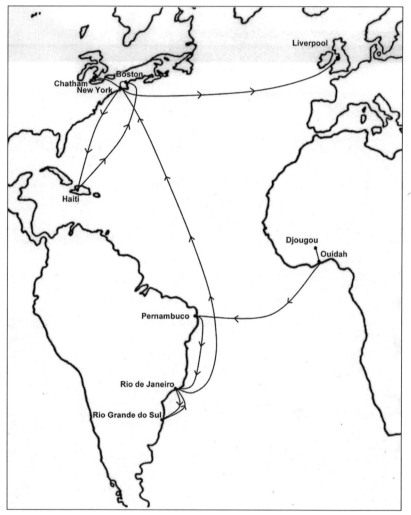

MAP 1. Itinerary of Mahommah Gardo Baquaqua.

INTRODUCTION:
THE INTERESTING NARRATIVE OF
MAHOMMAH GARDO BAQUAQUA

In 1854, George E. Pomeroy and Co. of Detroit, Michigan, published a pamphlet entitled *An Interesting Narrative. Biography of Mahommah G. Baquaqua, A Native of Zoogoo, in the Interior of Africa (A Convert to Christianity,) with a Description of That Part of the World; including the Manners and Customs of the Inhabitants.*[1] The subject of this biography, Mahommah Gardo Baquaqua,[2] had been born in Africa (the "Zoogoo" of the title being, as argued later, the city of Djougou, in the north of the modern Republique du Bénin);[3] enslaved and exported through the most important slave port in West Africa, the notorious Ouidah (Whydah), in the kingdom of Dahomey; and taken to Brazil, where he was a slave, first, of a baker in Pernambuco, and then of a ship's captain in Rio de Janeiro. Miraculously, as it seems, he was able to escape from slavery while in New York City in 1847, subsequently spending two years in Haiti, under the protection of the American Baptist Free Mission Society in Port-au-Prince. He returned to the United States in late 1849 to enroll in New York Central College, in McGrawville, where he was a student from 1850–53. At the time of writing his biography, he was living in Chatham, Canada West (Ontario), which at the time was one of the main termini of the Underground Railroad from the U.S.A. In early 1855, six months after the *Biography* was published, he moved

---

1. Cited in footnotes hereafter as *Biography*. Note that references to this work are given according to the pagination of the original 1854 edition, which is also indicated (in bold type, within square brackets) in the text as reproduced in the present work.

2. We generally refer to him subsequently by his third name, Baquaqua, as this seems to have been recognized as his surname in North America (he himself, for example, signing some of his letters as "M.G. Baquaqua"). In America, it may be noted, he was regularly addressed and referred to by his first name, Mahommah, although in Africa, from the evidence of the *Biography* (pp. 33, 40) he was called by his second name, Gado.

3. The Republique du Bénin (to be distinguished from the African kingdom of that name, which is in modern Nigeria, to the east) was until 1975 known as Dahomey.

1

to Britain, where he remained until at least 1857, the date that he dropped out of sight.

The pamphlet, sixty-six pages in length, includes two distinct parts: as specified on the title page, the first is "A Description of that Part of the World [i.e., Zoogoo/Djougou], including the Manners and Customs of their Inhabitants, their Religious Notions, Form of Government, Laws, Appearance of the Country, Buildings, Agriculture, Manufactures, Shepherds and Herdsmen, Domestic Animals, Marriage Ceremonials, Funeral Services, Styles of Dress, Trade and Commerce, Modes of Warfare, System of Slavery, &c.," which are described in five brief chapters (pp. 1–25); while the second gives an account of "Mahommah's Early Life, His Education, His Capture and Slavery in Western Africa and Brazil, His Escape to the United States, from thence to Haiti (the City of Port au Prince), His Reception by the Baptist Missionary there, the Rev. W. L. Judd, His Conversion to Christianity, Baptism, and Return to His Country, His Views, Objects and Aim," all this in a single long chapter, which comprises well over half of the whole work (pp. 25–66). Also included in the second section are two poems: "Lines Spoken by Mahommah," by Miss Kezia King, Baquaqua's teacher at Central College, and "Prayer of the Oppressed," by the African-American poet James M. Whitfield (1822–71), of Buffalo, New York.[4] The cover of the book, reproduced as an illustration in this edition, also carries an engraving of Baquaqua by Detroit artist J.G. Darby, said to be taken from a daguerreotype photograph by Moses Sutton.[5]

In purpose, Baquaqua's biography was part abolitionist tract, illustrating the evils of slavery and the slave trade through his personal

---

4. The latter poem was originally published in James Whitfield, *America, and Other Poems* (Buffalo, 1853): 61–63. For Whitfield's contribution to African-American literature, see Joan R. Sherman, "James M. Whitfield: Poet and Emigrationist: A Voice of Protest and Despair," *Journal of Negro History* 57:2 (1972): 173, and Howard H. Bell, "Introduction," in M.R. Delany and Robert Campbell, *Search for a Place: Black Separatism and Africa, 1860* (Ann Arbor, 1969): 6, 11.

5. Allan Austin, *African Muslims in Ante-Bellum America: A Sourcebook* (New York and London, 1984), 645n.

experience of them. But it was also propaganda for his intended return to Africa as a Christian missionary, concluding with an explicit appeal for funds for this objective in its final sentence: "Should a call be given to him to return at once to the land of his birth, he will cheerfully respond, and is sure friends will not be wanting to aid him in his benevolent purpose" (p. 65).

From one perspective, this work was merely one of several biographies of former slaves published in the U.S.A. around this period, of which the most distinguished was that of Frederick Douglass, which had appeared nine years earlier.[6] Baquaqua's biography, however, was unusual in various respects. First, as noted above, he was at the time of publication resident in Canada rather than in the U.S.A. In this, his case was not altogether unique: around the same time, Benjamin Drew and other abolitionists were collecting biographical accounts of fugitive slaves from the U.S.A. in Canada West (as Ontario was then known), a selection of which was published in Boston two years later.[7] Although Baquaqua's period of residence in Canada was brief (no more than a year), it is nevertheless perhaps legitimate to categorize his *Biography* as a previously unknown title belonging to the genre of Canadian prose, as well as to the literature of blacks in America.[8]

Second, Baquaqua had been a slave not in the U.S.A., but in Brazil; in fact, his arrival in the United States in 1847 was the occasion of his escape from slavery, and his subsequent period of resi-

---

6. Frederick Douglass, *Narrative of the Life of Frederick Douglass, an American slave, written by himself* (Boston, 1845, and frequently reprinted). The literature on slave narratives in the United States is extensive, but see Yuval Taylor, ed., *I Was Born a Slave: An Anthology of Classic Slave Narratives*, 2 vols. (Chicago, 1999); William L. Andrews, ed., *African American Autobiography: A Collection of Critical Essays* (Englewood Cliffs, NJ, 1993); and John W. Blassingame, ed., *Slave Testimony: Two Centuries of Letters, Speeches, Interviews, and Autobiographies* (Baton Rouge, 1977).

7. Benjamin Drew, *A North-Side View of Slavery. The Refugee: or the Narratives of Fugitive Slaves in Canada, Related by Themselves, with an Account of the History and Condition of the Colored Population of Upper Canada* (Boston, 1856).

8. For a discussion of the Canadian connection, see Paul E. Lovejoy, "Slavery and Memory in an Islamic Society: Whose Audience? Which Audience?" (paper presented at the conference 'Historians and their Audiences: Mobilizing History for the Millennium,' York University, Toronto, 13–15 April 2000).

dence and travel in North America (late 1849 to early 1855) was restricted to the northern States of the U.S.A. and Canada West, where slavery was no longer legal. As an extended first-hand account of the experience of slavery in Brazil, his account is indeed unique, being the only known Brazilian slave narrative.[9] It is also unusual and hence invaluable as an account of the impressions of the United States of a black person from outside the country.

Third, and most importantly, whereas other ex-slave narratives of this period (including those from fugitives in Canada collected by Drew) were by persons born into slavery in the U.S.A., Baquaqua had been born in Africa; and indeed well over half of the *Biography* (41 of 66 pages) deals with his life in Africa, prior to his transportation to Brazil. In this respect, it is likewise unique among nineteenth-century U.S.A. ex-slave narratives, which otherwise all come from American-born authors.[10] This reflects the fact that very few slaves were imported into the U.S.A. from Africa after the legal abolition of the slave trade there in 1808. The slave trade from West Africa to Brazil had also been technically illegal since 1815 (although this fact is not registered in Baquaqua's *Biography*), but suppression was not effective until 1850.[11] There had been earlier autobiographies of African-born former slaves, published in Britain in the eighteenth century, among which the most substantial and best-known is that of

9. See Robert Edgar Conrad, ed., *Children of God's Fire: A Documentary History of Black Slavery in Brazil* (Princeton, NJ, 1984), xix, 23–29; and Robert Krueger, "Milhões de Vozes, umas Pàginas Preciosas. As Narrativas dos Escravos Brasileiros," in Roger Zapata, ed., *Imàgenes de la Resistencia Indígena y Esclava* (Lima, 1990): 183–232.

10. 'Unique' at least among such narratives written in English. Another African-born Muslim (from Futa Toro, in modern Senegal), held in slavery in North Carolina, Umar ibn Said, wrote a brief autobiography in Arabic in 1831, of which a partial translation into English was published in 1854; see Allan Austin, *African Muslims Sourcebook,* 655–89; also see John Hunwick, "'I wish to be seen in our land called Afrika': 'Umar b. Sayyid's appeal to be released from slavery (1819)," forthcoming. An account by Mohammed Ali b. Said (alias Nicholas Said) of Borno has also survived, although Said was taken as a slave to North Africa, ultimately gaining his freedom in Russia, and traveling to the United States to enlist in the Union army in the Civil War; see "A Native of Bornoo," *The Atlantic Monthly* 19 (October 1867): 485–95.

11. See Leslie M. Bethell, *The Abolition of the Brazilian Slave Trade: Britain, Brazil and the Slave Trade Question 1807–1869* (Cambridge, 1970).

the abolitionist activist Olaudah Equiano (1789);[12] and there are also some accounts by other persons who were enslaved and illegally exported from Africa in the nineteenth century, but who were liberated through the capture of their ships by the British navy's anti-slaving squadron, and, therefore, did not complete the Middle Passage or go on to experience slavery in the Americas, including that of the future Christian missionary Samuel Ajayi Crowther (1837).[13] But while these other biographies of enslaved Africans provide interesting comparative material, they do not diminish the value of Baquaqua's account as one of the very few recorded African voices in the history of the transatlantic slave trade; even less do they justify the almost total neglect which it has met until recently.

The pamphlet is reproduced here with extensive annotations intended to elucidate and assist evaluation of the text, principally through the citation of collateral material. The local African terms given in the text have been identified wherever possible (most are in Dendi, one of the major languages of the Djougou area); these identifications are summarized in a glossary. Wherever possible we have also identified place-names, and otherwise attempted to make sense of the various descriptions provided in Baquaqua's account of his life in Africa. In this we have been assisted by various local authorities on the Dendi language and society in Djougou, including Albarka Soul-

12. *The Life of Olaudah Equiano, or Gustavus Vassa, the African, written by himself* (London, 1789; also frequently reprinted). Also see Vincent Carretta, ed., *Unchained Voices: An Anthology of Black Authors in the English-Speaking World of the Eighteenth Century* (Lexington, 1996); and Philip D. Curtin, ed., *Africa Remembered; Narratives by West Africans from the Era of the Slave Trade* (Madison, 1967).

13. Published as an Appendix in *Journals of the Rev. James Frederick Schön and Mr. Samuel Crowther, who ...accompanied the Expedition up the River Niger in 1841* (London, 1842): 289–316. For other examples, see Sigismund Wilhelm Koelle, *Polyglotta Africana* (Graz, 1963 [1854]): 1-21. There are also cases of persons enslaved in Africa, but not sold into export, whose accounts have survived, such as Dorugu and Maimaina, who were emancipated by Heinrich Barth and taken to Europe in 1855. For their accounts, see Anthony Kirk-Greene and Paul Newman, eds., *West African Travels and Adventures: Two Autobiographical Narratives from Northern Nigeria* (New Haven, CT, 1971) and James Frederick Schön, *Magána Hausa. Native Literature, or Proverbs, Tales, Fables and Historical Fragments in the Hausa Language, to which is added a Translation in English* (London, 1885): 10–111, for Dorugu's account in Hausa.

leymane, Alfa Houssane Djarra, and Sani Alaza;[14] we also consulted Nassirou Arifari Bako of the Université Nationale du Bénin and Zakari Dramani-Issifou of the Université de Paris VIII, a linguist from Djougou.[15] For Baquaqua's later life in America, we have drawn upon available secondary literature which illuminates the wider context of his career and for the period 1847-55 in the U.S.A. and Haiti, upon contemporary newspapers and material in the printed reports of the Annual Meetings of the American Baptist Free Mission Society and in the unpublished archives of the American Missionary Association and the Gerrit Smith papers which document his own individual activities.[16]

In addition to the 1854 text, this edition also includes, as appendices, the texts of various letters and other documents that are specifically about or penned by Baquaqua. These comprise three affidavits recorded in New York in 1847 that describe, through translation, the dispute over Baquaqua's fight for his emancipation; six letters (or relevant sections thereof) from Rev. William Judd of the American Baptist Free Mission in Haiti and his wife Nancy to Cyrus Grosvenor, the editor of the *Christian Contributor and Free Missionary* (published in the latter journal in 1847–48), which relate Baquaqua's stories about his African past, his experience of Brazilian slavery, and his conversion; and letters written by Baquaqua himself (or attributed to him) to various people between 1848 and 1854. Two of these let-

---

14. Interviews conducted by Robin Law and Paul E. Lovejoy, April 1999.

15. See also Nassirou Arifari Bako, "La Question du peuplement dendi dans la partie septentrionale de la République du Bénin: le cas du Borgou," (Mémoire de Maîtrise, Université Nationale du Bénin, 1989); and Zakari Dramani-Issifou, "Routes de commerce et mise en place des populations du Nord du Bénin," in *Le Sol, la parole et l'écrit. Mélanges en hommage à Raymond Maun*, vol. 2 (Paris, 1981): 655–72.

16. Material on the American Baptist Free Mission Society (hereafter, ABFMS) and Central College was consulted at the American Baptist Samuel Colgate Historical Library, Rochester, New York. In addition to the *Christian Contributor and Free Missionary* and *The American Baptist*, the Colgate Library holds the printed annual reports of the Annual Meetings of the ABFMS (the Annual Reports of the Board of the Society presented to these meetings being also published in *The American Baptist*). The American Missionary Society archives are in the Amistad Collection, Tulane University, New Orleans, Louisiana. The Gerrit Smith Papers, Special Collections, Syracuse University Library, Syracuse, New York, contain additional material on Central College.

ters were published in the *Christian Contributor and Free Missionary* in 1848; two more appeared in *The American Baptist* in 1850–51; eight dating from 1853–54 are preserved in manuscript in the Amistad Collection at Tulane University in New Orleans; and three in the Gerrit Smith Papers, Syracuse University. Finally, there is the text of the only contemporary review of the *Biography* which has been traced, published in *The American Baptist* in 1854. Also included, as an illustration, is a second pictorial representation of Baquaqua, a photograph showing him with the Rev. Mr. Judd, which appeared in a book entitled *Facts for Baptist Churches*, published in 1850, with the caption, "American Baptist Free Missionary for Hayti Teaching Mahommah."[17] This additional material is valuable not only in supplementing the account of his later life as given in the *Biography*. The Judds' letters in 1847–48 also report statements by Baquaqua about his early life in Africa which sometimes conflict with information in the *Biography*; explanation and resolution of these contradictions is a major concern of this Introduction. Finally, various illustrations, most of which date from the period of Baquaqua's journeys, are included, with explanatory captions, to elaborate the text.

Authorship and Composition

The question of the authorship of the pamphlet is open to some dispute. The book as published was avowedly a collaborative production, involving Baquaqua and an editor, named on the title page as Samuel Moore, whom Allan Austin has identified with Samuel Downing Moore, a Unitarian minister and abolitionist who had emigrated to the U.S.A. from Ireland, and lived in Ypsilanti, in eastern

17. A. T. Foss and Edward Mathews, *Facts for Baptist Churches* (Utica, NY, 1850), frontispiece.

Michigan. How and when the two men met is not known.[18] The text of the *Biography* makes clear that it was written after Baquaqua had left the U.S.A. for Canada, which was probably in late January or February 1854, and the text had been completed by 4 July of the same year, when Baquaqua reported in one of his extant letters that it was "ready for the press," and he was seeking assistance in meeting the costs of printing.[19] It was published by 21 August, when a copy was deposited, for purposes of copyright, in the Clerk's Office of the United States District Court of Michigan, this latter date being recorded in a handwritten note on the cover of this copy, now preserved in the Detroit Public Library (shown in the illustration included here).[20] Where Baquaqua and Moore collaborated on the writing—whether in Canada West, or Baquaqua traveled to meet Moore in Michigan—is also not known; Baquaqua was in Detroit in early July, as noted above, but this was in order to see an already completed manuscript through the press. As far as is known, Moore and Baquaqua were not otherwise associated with each other.

The question arises, therefore, to what extent was Baquaqua himself responsible for the authorship of the pamphlet? Is it a biography or an autobiography? Whose voice are we in fact hearing? The principal study of Baquaqua's biography previously published, by Allan Austin, implicitly treats the book as Moore's rather than Baquaqua's, and is more generally dismissive of Baquaqua's intellectual abilities (though not much less so about Moore's).[21] This, however, seems to

18. For Austin's identification, see *African Muslims Sourcebook*, 590, 645n. Little is known about Moore, other than the claim on the cover of the *Biography* that he had published the *North of England Shipping Gazette* (not otherwise traced), presumably before moving to North America. He also claimed to be the author of "several popular works" and editor of "sundry reform papers," which have likewise not been identified. Moore is mentioned in "The Unitarian Ministers of Ireland and American Slavery," *The Liberator*, 12 May 1848. For his abolitionist views, see also Samuel Moore, "A Protest," *The Liberator*, 29 February 1856; and his letter to William Lloyd Garrison, *The Liberator*, 4 December 1857.

19. Letter of Baquaqua to Gerrit Smith, 4 July 1854 (reproduced in this edition as Appendix 3, no. 15).

20. The clerk who recorded the copyright was W. David King; the copy in the Detroit Public Library was brought to our attention by Silvia Hunold Lara.

21. Allan Austin, *African Muslims in Antebellum America: Transatlantic Stories and Spiritual Struggles* (New York, 1997; cited hereafter as *Transatlantic Stories*): 160–61. Austin refers to "the naïveté of both men."

the present editors to misconceive the process of composition, as indicated by the internal evidence of the book itself. On the title page, it is in fact Baquaqua who is identified as "the author," although the text is also said to have been "written and revised from his own words" by Moore. "Written" here evidently means "written down" rather than "composed," the implication being that Moore put into writing an account given orally by Baquaqua—an inference which is confirmed by the wording of some passages in Moore's Preface to the book (pp. 5, 7).

This interpretation is also supported by a short review of the book (the only contemporary notice of it which has been traced), which was published in *The American Baptist* in November 1854, and which explicitly credits Baquaqua rather than Moore with authorship, describing it as "an autobiography, but revised and prepared for publication by Samuel Moore."[22] The review was almost certainly written by the editor of *The American Baptist*, Warham Walker, who must be presumed to have been familiar with the circumstances of the production of the *Biography*, since he knew Baquaqua well. He had earlier published two of Baquaqua's letters in his journal, and both men had attended Annual Meetings of the American Baptist Free Mission Society, of which Walker was a Trustee. Walker and Baquaqua also served together on the African Mission Committee of the Society in 1853.

It may be noted, however, that in the Preface to the book Moore describes himself as the "compiler" of the work (p. 5), seemingly implying a more active role than merely "reviser" of a dictated text. The resolution of this apparent contradiction is to be found in a study of the contents of the book itself, which as noted above fall into two distinct parts. The first part, which gives a general account of Baquaqua's homeland in Africa, is basically written in the third person, though with occasional illustrative direct quotations from Baquaqua.

---

22. *The American Baptist*, 2 November 1854. The full text of this review is reproduced as Appendix 4.

The second part, which gives an account of Baquaqua's own life, in contrast, is mainly written in the first person, although with occasional third-person interpolations. The first-person mode becomes especially dominant when the text arrives at what is signaled as "the most interesting portion of Mahommah's story," namely his enslavement in Africa, sale into export, and subsequent experiences in the Americas, which is explicitly stated to be given "in nearly his own words" (p. 34). It seems reasonable to conclude that Moore was indeed a "compiler" with regard to the first section of the book, organizing material supplied by Baquaqua into a coherent whole; but a "reviser" with regard to the second section, editing a narrative dictated by Baquaqua.

It should be stressed further that in an entrepreneurial or legal, as opposed to a narrowly literary sense, the book was clearly Baquaqua's rather than Moore's. The text itself makes clear that it was the former who took the initiative in its production: "I came to the conclusion that the time had arrived when I might with propriety commit to paper all that has been recounted in this work" (p. 65). The letter which Baquaqua wrote reporting the completion of the text in July 1854 indicates that Moore was only a hired assistant, whom Baquaqua paid for his services ("English man [sic] wrote it for me. I pay him for do it").[23] Consistently with this, on the title page of the book it is explicitly described as "printed for the Author, Mahommah Gardo Baquaqua by Geo. E. Pomeroy and Co.," which suggests that the publisher recognized his authorship; and this legal authorship is confirmed on the reverse page, giving copyright information, where the work is recorded as registered in the United States District Court of Michigan under Baquaqua's own name.

This is not to deny that there are particular sections of the text which represent the voice of Moore rather than of Baquaqua. Some passages, including many of the elaborated instances of abolitionist rhetoric, are distinguished by a more pretentiously literary style and

---

23. Letter to Gerrit Smith, Detroit, 4 July 1854 (see Appendix 3, no. 15).

embellished with bits of poetry and other quotations, and these almost certainly represent Moore's hand. Moreover, even beyond such straightforward editorial interpolations, there are places where the composite character of the work seems to have resulted in errors and confusion, arising from imperfect communication between Moore and Baquaqua, on points that the latter should have known well. The *Interesting Narrative,* it may be suggested, is all the more interesting because of this ambiguity as to whether it is biography, autobiography, or in fact something else: a co-authored work that is part biography of Baquaqua and part descriptive account of his homeland, in whose production Moore served as scribe, in the process sometimes getting details wrong.

Consideration of authorship of the work should also take account of a collective dimension, arising from Baquaqua's close relationship with his mentors in the American Baptist Free Mission Society and its supporting churches. Among those who contributed to Baquaqua's evolution into authorship were the Rev. Mr. Judd, mentioned in the title page of the *Biography,* and his wife Nancy, under whose guidance he was converted in Haiti; Warham Walker of *The American Baptist,* as noted above; and also Cyrus P. Grosvenor, editor of the *Christian Contributor and Free Missionary* and President of New York Central College where Baquaqua was educated. The *Biography* was preceded, as has been seen, by the publication of letters written by and about Baquaqua in the journals edited by Grosvenor and Walker; and a brief biographical notice of him, including an account of his baptism in Haiti, had been published, together with the photograph of Baquaqua receiving instruction from the Rev. Mr. Judd, in the book *Facts for Baptist Churches,* published for the American Baptist Free Mission Society in 1850.[24]

One of Baquaqua's Baptist mentors in particular, Cyrus Grosvenor,

---

24. Foss and Mathews, *Facts for Baptist Churches*, 392–93 (most of which is reproduced in the *Biography*, pp. 59–60); also reprinted by Austin, *African Muslims Sourcebook*, 638–39. This biographical note has no independent value as a source, being entirely derived from earlier printed accounts, mainly in the *Christian Contributor and Free Missionary*.

may well have played a role in the planning of the publication of the *Biography*. Grosvenor also knew Baquaqua especially well; as editor of the *Christian Contributor and Free Missionary*, Grosvenor had published a series of letters from Judd and his wife on Baquaqua and the Haitian mission, as well as letters by Baquaqua himself, during 1847–50; and as President of New York Central College, he was responsible for admitting Baquaqua as a student in early 1850, and personally welcomed him to the College. He also knew Canada West, where Baquaqua was to settle. He spent "several weeks of missionary service" there for the American Baptist Free Mission Society during the summer of 1853, after the Annual Meeting of the Society in Utica, New York, which both he and Baquaqua attended; this would presumably have included a visit to Detroit, where the *Biography* was to be published, since the Free Mission there was linked administratively to the Mission in Canada West.[25] Although these links to Baquaqua's biography are only circumstantial, they suggest the possibility that Grosvenor might have played some role at least in the preparatory stages of its production.

Whatever Grosvenor's role, it should be noted that during 1853, after completing his education at Central College, Baquaqua himself had been involved in fund-raising for a projected Baptist mission to Africa, in which he himself was to serve. His desire to return to Africa as a missionary and his appeal for funds for this purpose are reiterated in the *Biography*. Although the book was published in his own name (and this reflected a degree of estrangement from the Free Baptists by 1854, as noted later), it seems likely that it was originally conceived for publication, in effect, on behalf of the American Baptist Free Mission Society, and in particular in support of its efforts to raise funds for the African Mission.

Moreover, it is clear that Baquaqua's story of his life had taken

---

25. See ABFMS, 11th Annual Meeting, Albany, New York, 7–8 June 1854; for the administrative link between the Free Mission in Detroit and Canada West, see ABFMS, Ninth Annual Meeting, Montrose, Pennsylvania, 2–4 June 1852.

shape, in oral if not in written form, over several years prior to being written up for publication in 1854. He had told parts of his story on many occasions. When he arrived in Haiti in 1847, Nancy Judd noted that he remembered not only incidents in his own individual life in Africa, but also "the productions and manner of cultivating them ... [and] some of the laws of his country"; and after his conversion in 1848 he delivered an oration of thanks to God at a Baptist prayer meeting, first in his "native tongue" and then in English, which consisted of a summary of his experiences, from enslavement in Africa, through slavery in Brazil and liberation in New York, to conversion in Haiti.[26] As Mrs. Judd reflected, in a letter to Cyrus Grosvenor published in the *Christian Contributor and Free Missionary*, "O how many, many deeply interesting circumstances, I have gathered already of his former history, if I had time to write and you room to publish, which I feel could not fail to be read with the deepest interest."[27] So it may well be that the idea of a book on Baquaqua's life originated with her. Likewise in the U.S.A., when Mrs. Judd introduced Baquaqua at New York Central College in 1850, she "related some incidents connected with his history and conversion," which one of her audience judged "truly interesting and affecting."[28] Subsequently, Baquaqua took over the role of narrator himself: in 1853, when he was involved in fund-raising for the projected African mission in Pennsylvania, he is reported to have "made several attempts to give a sketch of the manners, customs &c. of his native country, and of his being kidnapped and sold into slavery, &c. &c."[29] The *Biography* as published may therefore be considered a written ver-

26. Letters of Mrs. N.A.L. Judd to Cyrus Grosvenor, 8 October 1847 and 21 July 1848, in *Christian Contributor and Free Missionary*, 19 January and 30 August 1848 (reproduced in this edition as Appendix 2, nos. 1, 5).

27. Letter of Mrs. N.A.L. Judd to Cyrus Grosvenor, 24 March 1848, in *Christian Contributor and Free Missionary*, 17 May 1848 (see also Appendix 2, no. 3).

28. Letter of J. Scott, McGrawville, 22 January 1850, in *Christian Contributor and Free Missionary*, 7 March 1850.

29. Letter of A.L.P [Albert L. Post], Montrose, Pennsylvania, July 1853, in *The American Baptist*, 28 July 1853.

sion of what Baquaqua had been saying on the Baptist lecture-circuit.

However, although the presumption that the project of the *Biography* originated in Baquaqua's involvement with the Baptist Free Mission Society is strong, by the time of its actual publication in the summer of 1854 his relations with the Society had deteriorated. This may account for the fact that the editor whose assistance Baquaqua sought, Samuel Moore, was from outside the Free Mission circles in which he had moved in New York State, being not a Baptist, but rather a Unitarian from Ireland. Likewise, although it is not known how Baquaqua met his publisher, George E. Pomeroy, who among other things was the owner of the *Detroit Tribune*: he had no known connection with the Baptist Free Mission Society and was in fact Presbyterian.[30] However, Moore was a known Abolitionist, and Pomeroy did publish at least one other abolitionist tract in 1854, and that tract was co-authored by James Whitfield, whose poem was included in the *Biography*.[31] Therefore, it can be supposed that Baquaqua somehow was referred to both Moore and Pomeroy, and perhaps to Whitfield's poem, through the abolitionist network.

A possible link was the "Rev. William" mentioned in Baquaqua's letter written on 4 July 1854, when he was in Detroit arranging publication of the *Biography*, who is possibly to be identified with the Rev. William King, the Presbyterian minister at Buxton, Canada West, and if so had presumably accompanied Baquaqua from Canada to Detroit.[32] The fact that both King and Pomeroy were Presbyterians may have been a factor, if the identification of "Rev. William" is cor-

---

30. George Eltweed Pomeroy, b. 16 September 1807, founded an express company between Albany and Buffalo, New York, in 1841 that eventually became Wells Fargo, selling out to his brother in 1844. He then founded the *Detroit Tribune*, residing in a palatial home in Clifton, Michigan, to the west of Detroit. In later years, he lived in Toledo, Ohio, where he died on 12 January 1886; see Albert A. Pomeroy, *Geneology of the Pomeroy Family* (Toledo, OH, 1912), 453–54; and Friend Palmer, *Early Days in Detroit* (Detroit, 1906), 194–97.

31. M.T. Newsome, ed., *Arguments, Pro and Con, on the Call for a National Emigration Convention, to be held in Cleveland, Ohio, August, 1854, by Frederick Douglass, W.J. Watkins, and James M. Whitfield, With a Short Appendix of the Statistics of Canada West, West Indies, Central and South America* (Detroit, 1854).

32. Letter to Gerrit Smith, Detroit, 4 July 1854 (see Appendix 3, no. 15).

rect. The "Rev. William" was clearly known to Gerrit Smith, to whom this letter was addressed. That Gerrit Smith was another important figure in Baquaqua's life at this time is certain; the letter of 25 May announcing Baquaqua's troubles with the Free Mission Society is addressed to Smith, as is the letter of 4 July soliciting a loan to meet the costs of printing the *Biography*. Smith, too, had Presbyterian connections; he had been brought up in a Presbyterian household, but as an adult and political activist, he was not affiliated with any religious denomination, consciously fashioning himself as nondenominational and founding a "free" church in Peterboro, New York. His connections with the Baptist Free Mission were strong; he attended the Baptist-run Hamilton College (1814–18) and supported the Baptist Free Mission in founding New York Central College in McGrawville, which opened in 1849. He also hosted the semi-annual meeting of the American Baptist Free Mission at his home in Peterboro, New York, in 1851 (and which Baquaqua attended). In addition he maintained strong links with many of the important abolitionists, including those in Canada West, whatever their religious affiliation.[33] Since Smith was more widely connected than Baquaqua's erstwhile Baptist sponsors, it was perhaps through him that Baquaqua was introduced to his editor and his publisher in Michigan. However this may be, it was Smith whom Baquaqua approached, when he found that he could no longer count on the Free Mission Society for financial support in publishing the *Biography*.[34]

33. Gerrit Smith (1797–1874) was a wealthy landowner, reformer, and philanthropist. In addition to his vast land holdings in upstate New York, Smith also invested in banking, railroads and canals. He was active in various nondenominational reform movements, including temperance, bible and tract societies, and the Sunday school movement, as well as various anti-slavery organizations. As noted, he was a leading benefactor of Central College. He also granted land to blacks and anti-slavery whites from his holdings in upstate New York. He was elected to the House of Representatives in 1852, resigning his seat in August 1854, returning to politics in 1856 as the presidential candidate for the Liberty Party, and in 1859 providing clandestine financial support for John Brown's abortive raid on Harper's Ferry, Virginia; see E.P. Tanner, "Gerrit Smith: An interpretation,"(paper presented at the annual meeting of the New York State Historical Society, Lake Placid, New York, 1923): 22–37; and Ralph Volney Harlow, *Gerrit Smith, Philanthropist and Reformer* (New York, 1939). Also see Robin Winks, *Blacks in Canada*, 2nd edition (Monteal & Kingston, Ont., 1997): 179–80, 254.

34. Letter to Gerrit Smith, dated Chatham, Canada West, 25 May 1854 (see Appendix 3, no. 14).

Authenticity

Baquaqua's arrival in New York in 1847 and the ensuing legal proceedings were reported in local newspapers and the abolitionist press
elsewhere, while the subsequent period of his residence in Haiti and
the U.S.A. is extensively documented in American Baptist sources.
For this later period, in fact, the supplementary documentation is
fuller than the account given in the *Biography*; although there are differences of emphasis and nuance, the additional material is comple-
mentary to rather than contradictory to the *Biography*, and tends
broadly to confirm its accuracy. For the period in Africa and Brazil
before 1847, there is no such additional material relating to Baquaqua's individual life, and the account in the *Biography* can be evalu-
ated only in the light of more general, contextual information; but
here again, in the view of the present editors, Baquaqua's account is
generally consistent with what we think we know of conditions in his
homeland of Djougou, in the kingdom of Dahomey through which he
was exported, in the Middle Passage across the Atlantic, and in Brazil
where he was held in slavery.

The question is complicated, however, by the fact that some of the
details of Baquaqua's life recorded in the earlier American Baptist
sources in Haiti contradict what is said in the later *Biography*. Although the more significant of these discrepancies are discussed at
length, either in this Introduction or in annotations to the text, a statement of the editors' general approach to such cases may be offered
here. In principle, it has seemed to us that the *Biography* is normally
to be preferred to the earlier accounts, on the grounds that Baquaqua
himself exercised greater control over its contents, which are, therefore, more likely to represent his own perceptions. By contrast, the
version of his account recorded by the Judds in Haiti involved prob-
lematic processes of translation. When he arrived there in 1847, as
Mrs. Judd noted, Baquaqua spoke Portuguese in addition to one or
more African languages, but not English or French, beyond "a very
few sentences in broken English, which he learned on his passage out
here." The Judds were therefore initially not able to communicate

with him directly, but depended upon an intermediary, an African-American called Jones, who himself spoke only "but little Portuguese." Because of this, as Mrs. Judd acknowledged, "he could not, of course, learn so much as he would have done, had he been able to have conversed with him more freely."[35] Only three weeks later, admittedly, her husband claimed that Baquaqua had "so far advanced in English that I have been able to learn from him precisely his former residence in Africa," but since (as will appear below) Judd's understanding on this question is among the points contradicted in the later *Biography*, some skepticism seems in order.[36] In these circumstances, it seems likely that many of the discrepancies between the *Biography* and the earlier statements of the Judds reflect misunderstandings on the latter's (or Jones') part. This is not to deny that Baquaqua himself may have changed his story over time, or sought to conceal or obscure certain elements in it, but this explanation is invoked sparingly, and only when plausible reasons for such shifts can be adduced.

Baquaqua's Early Life in Africa

Baquaqua was born, according to the *Biography,* in the city of "Zoogoo," situated inland from the kingdom of Dahomey (in what is today southern Bénin), through which he was transported into transatlantic slavery. Although the identification of his homeland has caused confusion among some modern commentators,[37] it in fact pre-

---

35. Letter of Mrs. N.A.L. Judd, 8 October 1847. In the *Biography* (p. 57) Baquaqua actually says that Jones spoke Spanish, rather than Portuguese, implying a further linguistic obstacle.

36. Letter of Rev. W.L. Judd to Cyrus Grosvenor, 28 October 1847, in *Christian Contributor and Free Missionary*, 22 December 1847 (see also Appendix 2, no. 2).

37. Richard Brent Turner concludes erroneously that Baquaqua was born in northern Ghana; see *Islam in the African-American Experience* (Bloomington: Indiana University Press, 1997): 41. Kwame Anthony Appiah and Henry Louis Gates, Jr., eds., *Microsoft Encarta Africana 2000* (Redmond, WA, 2000) have his birthplace as Angola. Similarly, Robert Edgar Conrad proposes that "Zougou" is to be identified with Soulougou in Burkino Faso (formerly Upper Volta); see *Children of God's Fire* (Princeton, NJ, 1984): 23. This was also initially the opinion of Krueger; see *Milhões de Vozes*, 214, although corrected in *Biografia e narrativa*, 11.

sents no serious difficulty. There are actually two distinct towns of this name in the general area indicated (both within modern Bénin): Djougou, situated some 185 km. north of Abomey, the capital of Dahomey; and Zougou, near Kandi, another 200 km. northeast of Djougou. Despite the different spellings nowadays conventional, both of these names represent transcriptions of the same word, *zugu*, meaning "forest" in Dendi.[38] From the details of Baquaqua's account, especially his route to the coast after enslavement, it is clear that it is the more southerly town (which was also the more important of the two) from which he originated.[39] His description of "Zoogoo" also confirms the identification with Djougou; although some aspects of it would also apply to other towns in the region, some details are more specifically localized, notably the titles he gives for the "gatekeepers" of the town (p. 15), most of which correspond to those of chiefs of wards of Djougou.

Baquaqua's reminiscences of his early life in Africa include both memories of particular events in his own individual career and general observations on the "manners and customs" of his homeland. In reading the text, it is, therefore, important to make a distinction between the authenticity of specific details in Baquaqua's life and the extent to which his account enhances our understanding of the West African society in which he was born. His recollections come to us, of course, as edited by Moore (or alternatively, on certain points, as reported by the Judds). Given these means of transmission, it is not surprising that there is some confusion in his account, especially in relation to his childhood and family. The principal previous commentator on the *Biography*, Allan Austin, has stigmatized the general ethnographic data in it as "usually unreliable."[40] To the present edi-

---

38. "Zugu" remains the local pronunciation of the name of Djougou. The village near Kandi, in Borgu, is referred to as Zougou Kpantorosi to distinguish it from Djougou, which is known as Djougou Wangara (personal communication, Elisée Soumonni).

39. The identification of Baquaqua's birthplace with Djougou was correctly made by Austin, *African Muslims Sourcebook*, 645n.

40. Austin, *Transatlantic Stories*, 161.

tors, on the contrary, allowing for the vagaries of transmission of his information, and to the extent that it can be checked, the picture of life in nineteenth-century Djougou which it presents seems both plausible and invaluable. Baquaqua's recollections both confirm our general knowledge of trade and politics in the interior of this part of West Africa, and also add important details which extend our previous knowledge. When put into context his account of economy and society in Djougou fleshes out the history of the town, and of the wider networks of long-distance trade in which it was involved.

It must be conceded that interpretation and assessment of Baquaqua's account is made more difficult by the limitations of the evidence on Djougou in the first half of the nineteenth century available for comparison. Although Djougou was, as the *Biography* makes clear, a partially Islamic society (and Baquaqua himself was from a Muslim family), in which some people were literate in Arabic (p. 27), no Arabic manuscript material relating to the town during the nineteenth century appears to survive. Moreover, as the *Biography* notes (pp.14–15), Djougou itself had not yet been visited by any European traveler, so that there are also no contemporary European accounts of the town during Baquaqua's lifetime. The earliest first-hand European accounts of Djougou date from the late nineteenth century, the most substantial (and therefore the most often cited in the annotation in this edition) being that of the German Heinrich Klose in the 1890s.[41] Even more recent ethnographic literature on Djougou is limited; a major study of the town projected by the late Yves Person was unfortunately never completed, and, although his rough drafts and notes for this work are preserved, they are in a fragmentary and disorganized condition, for the most part very difficult both to read and interpret.[42]

---

41. Heinrich Klose, *Le Togo sous drapeau allemand (1894–1897)*, trans. by Phillippe David (Lomé, 1992): 367–69.

42. Fonds Person, Bibliothèque de Centre de Recherches Africaines, Paris. We wish to thank Charles Tshimanga for his assistance in obtaining the material on Djougou in this collection. We have cited primarily one typescript of Person which is in relatively finished form, entitled "Zugu, ville musulmane."

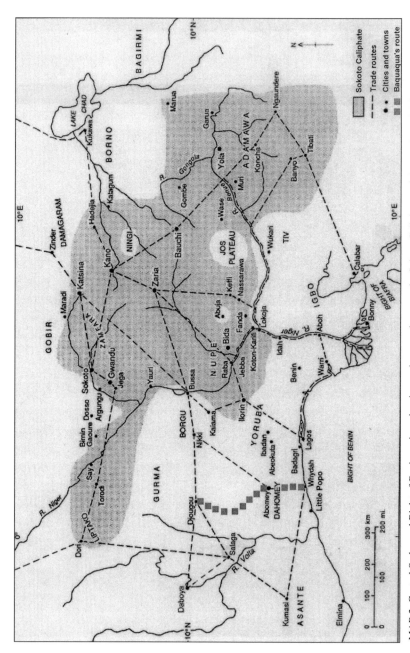

MAP 2. Central Sudan and Bight of Benin region, showing trade routes between the Sokoto Caliphate and Asante through Djougou (the route to the coast taken by Baquaqua).

Djougou was, however, both politically and commercially integrated into wider regional networks, and was especially closely linked to the country of Borgu to the east. As the *Biography* notes (p. 9), the king of "Zoogoo" was tributary to the king of "Berzoo" (more correctly, "Bergoo"), i.e., Borgu; the reference is probably specifically to the ruler of Nikki, 170 km. east of Djougou, which was conventionally regarded as the capital of Borgu. Borgu is much better documented than Djougou. Although no contemporary accounts are available of Nikki itself until the late nineteenth century, Hugh Clapperton and Richard and John Lander traveled through eastern Borgu (visiting the towns of Kaiama, Wawa, and Bussa) between 1826–30 and left extensive descriptions of the area.[43] Borgu is also better served in terms of more recent ethnography, especially the massive study of its political organization by Jacques Lombard and the analysis of its commercial community by Denise Brégand.[44] Given the considerable influence from Borgu upon the institutions and culture of Djougou, and the fact that Baquaqua's account deals in part with his family's involvement in the wider world rather than focusing narrowly upon Djougou, this material relating to Borgu can also be drawn upon, albeit with caution, in elucidating his text.

It may be noted that Allan Austin, in his earlier commentaries on the *Biography,* extensively cited the contemporary account of the Scottish explorer John Duncan, on the assumption that the latter passed close to, if not actually through, Baquaqua's homeland in his travels.[45] Duncan certainly traveled through Dahomey on his way northwards from the coast in 1845, around the same time (in fact,

---

43. Hugh Clapperton, *Journal of a Second Expedition into the Interior of Africa* (London, 1829); John Lander, *Records of Captain Clapperton's Last Expedition to Africa* (London, 1830); Richard Lander and John Lander, *Journal of an Expedition to Explore the Course and Termination of the River Niger* (London and New York, 1832).

44. Jacques Lombard, *Structures de type "féodal" en Afrique noire: étude des dynamismes internes et des relations sociales chez les Bariba du Dahomey* (Paris, 1965); and Denise Brégand, *Commerce caravanier et relations sociales au Bénin: les Wangara du Borgou* (Paris, 1998). For the history of Borgu, see also Richard Kuba, *Wasangari und Wangara: Borgu und seine Nachbarn in historische Perspectif* (Hamburg, 1996).

45. John Duncan, *Travels in Western Africa in 1845 & 1846*, 2 vols. (London, 1847).

probably shortly after) Baquaqua was being taken in the opposite direction, into slavery in America; and his account can be usefully drawn upon to document the conditions of the latter's journey to the coast and embarkation for his transatlantic voyage. But it has been demonstrated that the most northerly section of Duncan's travels, which would have taken him into and probably through the Borgu region, is in fact an invention; although probably to some degree based upon information about Borgu obtained orally in Dahomey, it cannot be considered a reliable source for the purpose of comparison with Baquaqua's account.[46]

The precise date of Baquaqua's birth is uncertain, possibly as early as 1824 and certainly not later than 1831. When he arrived in Haiti in late 1847, he was thought to be aged about sixteen, implying that he was born c. 1831: this was both the conclusion of Jones, who introduced Baquaqua to the American Baptist Free Mission in Port-au-Prince and who had interviewed him at length on the voyage out from Boston; and was confirmed by the Rev. Mr. Judd and his wife, at least to the extent that they did not dispute this estimate.[47] By the time of his baptism in the following year, the Rev. Mr. Judd had adjusted his estimate of Baquaqua's age slightly upwards, thinking that he was then aged about eighteen; and the implied birth date of 1830 was reproduced in the short biographical account of Baquaqua published in 1850.[48] Consistently with this second estimate (or maybe merely derived from it), Baquaqua is listed in the U.S.A. census of 1850 as aged 20.[49] Given that he spent around two years in slavery in Brazil

46. See Marion Johnson, "News from nowhere: Duncan and Adofoodia," *History in Africa* 1 (1974): 55–66; Robin Law, "Further light on John Duncan's account of the 'Fellatah Country' (1845)," *History in Africa*, 28 (2001).

47. Letters of Mrs. N.A.L. Judd, 8 October 1847; Rev. W.L. Judd, 28 October 1847.

48. Letter of Rev. W.L. Judd, 21 July 1848, in *Christian Contributor and Free Missionary*, 23 August 1848 (see Appendix 2, no. 4); Foss and Mathews, *Facts for Baptist Churches*, 392. Our thanks to Thor Burnham for locating Judd's letter.

49. 1850 U.S. Census, Cortland Country, New York, Town of Cortlandville, Village of McGrawville, August 1850. Also see Catherine M. Hanchett, "New York Central College Students," New York Central College Collection, Cortland County Historical Society, Cortland, New York (1997).

before arriving in the U.S.A. in 1847, this would make him aged no more than fifteen at the time of his enslavement and export from Africa. However, Samuel Moore in the *Biography* reports that Baquaqua believed himself to be about 30 in 1854 (p. 9), making him some six years older, and aged around 21 when he left Africa. The details of his life as given in the *Biography*, which included a long-distance trading journey (to Daboya, in modern Ghana, to the west) and a period of service as a bodyguard to a local ruler prior to his enslavement and transportation to Brazil, seem to support an earlier date for his birth.

In the 1830s and early 1840s, to which Baquaqua's account relates, Djougou was one of the most important towns between Asante (in modern Ghana) to the west and the Sokoto Caliphate (modern northern Nigeria) to the east, two of the largest states in West Africa in the middle of the nineteenth century. Its importance within regional commercial and political networks is reflected in references to it (as "Zogho") in material collected from foreign Muslims resident in Kumasi, the capital of Asante, by the British Consul Joseph Dupuis in 1820, although these hearsay reports are vague and seemingly (at least as regards Djougou's military and political power) exaggerated.[50] Djougou played a central role in the trade between Asante and the Sokoto Caliphate. During the long dry season, large caravans of 1,000 or more merchants and porters, and comparable numbers of donkeys, passed through Djougou, often staying for a short period on each leg of the journey. They carried kola nuts and gold from Asante, and European imports brought from the Gold Coast, eastward towards the Sokoto Caliphate, and returned with salt, natron, textiles, spices, leather products, livestock, slaves, and other goods from the

---

50. Joseph Dupuis, *Journal of a Residence in Ashantee* (London: 1824); Robin Law, "'Central and Eastern Wangara': an indigenous West African perception of the political and economic geography of the Slave Coast, as recorded by Joseph Dupuis in 1820," *History in Africa* 22 (1995): 281–305.

Caliphate and neighboring Borno.[51] This trade was dominated by merchants from Kano, Katsina, and other towns in the Sokoto Caliphate, who spoke Hausa and often identified as such. In fact, however, the merchant families that controlled the trade had diverse origins, including immigrants to Hausaland from Borno to the northeast, the southern Sahara and Sahel, and even from North Africa.

Baquaqua's family was heavily involved in this trade and is to be identified with the Muslim merchant community of Djougou, which was known as Wangara, its members speaking Dendi as their first language.[52] Baquaqua's account does not use either of the terms Wangara or Dendi, but the list of numerals given at the beginning of the *Biography* (pp. 3–4), which is presumably in his native language, as well as many of the terms given in the bulk of the text, are identifiable as Dendi. Dendi, it should be stressed, was not the language of the indigenous inhabitants of the Djougou area, who were Yowa (Pila-Pila), whose language is Yom.[53] Djougou was in fact a highly multilingual community. Its royal family was of Gurma origin (from further north),[54] speaking (at least originally) yet another language. As noted earlier, it was also closely linked both commercially and politically with Borgu to the east, where the dominant language was Baatonu (Bariba); and Baatonu linguistic influence is evident in the title system of the town.[55] Moreover, Hausa as well as Dendi was

---

51. The route was one of the most important in West Africa in the nineteenth century; see Paul E. Lovejoy, *Caravans of Kola: The Hausa Kola Trade, 1700–1900* (Zaria, Nigeria, 1980); Lovejoy, "Polanyi's 'Ports of Trade': Salaga and Kano in the Nineteenth Century," *Canadian Journal of African Studies* 16 (1982): 245–78. Also see Charles William Berberich, "A Locational Analysis of Trade Routes of the Northeast Asante Frontier Network in the Nineteenth Century" (Ph.D. diss., Northwestern University, 1974): esp. 108–109, 241–42.

52. See esp. Brégand, *Commerce caravanier*. For the Wangara in a broader historical and geographical context, see also Paul E. Lovejoy, "The role of the Wangara in the economic transformation of the Central Sudan in the fifteenth and sixteenth centuries," *Journal of African History* 19 (1978): 173–93.

53. For a discussion of the Yowa and their diverse origins, see Person, "Zugu, ville musulmane."

54. Not Bariba (Baatonu), as assumed by Austin, *Transatlantic Stories*, 162.

55. Baatonu (pl. Baatombu) is the indigenous name for the people of Borgu; Bargawa (people of Borgu) is the Hausa name for the people and the region, while Bariba is the Yoruba and Dahomian term. In eastern Borgu (Bussa and Wawa) a distinct language, Boko, is spoken.

widely spoken as a commercial language throughout the Borgu region, including Djougou itself, as noted by Klose in the 1890s;[56] while Arabic was of course the language of literate culture within the Muslim community.

How many of these languages Baquaqua himself might have spoken is uncertain. In a letter of 1854, stressing his qualifications to serve as an interpreter for projected missions to Africa, he mentioned only the Arabic and "Zogoo" (Djougou, i.e., presumably Dendi) languages as those which he spoke.[57] It is difficult to believe, however, that he did not also know Hausa and probably also some Baatonu, since the former (as will be seen) was the ancestral language of his mother's family, as well as being widely spoken in commerce, while his father originated from Borgu, where the latter was the dominant language. Presumably anybody growing up in Djougou also knew Yom; Baquaqua most certainly did if (as he claims) he was employed in the palace of a local ruler, where the language in use would have been the local, and not the commercial tongue. Although Djougou, from its commercial and cosmopolitan character, was an extreme case, a degree of multilinguality was common throughout West Africa; a factor which has perhaps been underestimated in considerations of "ethnicity" among African-born slaves in the Americas, for many of whom, including Baquaqua, a choice among alternative ethnic identities was evidently available.[58]

Despite sharing a common language and the Islamic religion, the Wangara, like the Hausa merchants who dominated the caravan trade, traced their roots to many different origins. This complexity is captured in Baquaqua's account. Jones, who accompanied Baquaqua from Boston to Port-au-Prince in September 1847, learned from

56. Klose, *Le Togo sous drapeau allemand*, 390.
57. Letter of Baquaqua to George Whipple, 22 January 1854 (see also Appendix 3, no. 13).
58. Paul E. Lovejoy, "Cerner les identités au sein de la diaspora africaine, l'islam et l'esclavage aux Amériques," *Cahiers des Anneaux de la Mémoire*, 1 (1999): 249–78; and Lovejoy, "Ethnicity, religion and the mirage of identity: Mahommah Gardo Baquaqua's journey to the Americas," in Mohammed Ennaji and Paul E. Lovejoy , eds., *Liberté, identité, intégration et servitude* (Rabat, forthcoming).

Baquaqua that, "His father and mother were of different tribes."[59] The *Biography* confirms and elaborates: "He states his parents were of different countries, his father being a native of Berzoo, (of Arabian descent) and not very dark complexioned," while "his mother being a native of Kashna and of very dark complexion, was entirely black" (p. 9). The reference to "Berzoo" (i.e ., Borgu), almost certainly alludes to Nikki, the most important city in Borgu to the east, whose king was recognized by various other towns, including Djougou, as the capital of a loose confederation. Baquaqua's father's claim to "Arabian descent" suggests that he belonged to the group known as *shurfa*, of North African, perhaps Moroccan, origin, claiming descent from the Prophet Muhammad, who were prominent in long-distance commerce in the region.[60] His mother's birthplace, "Kashna," on the other hand, is Katsina, in Hausaland, further east across the River Niger.

On Baquaqua's origins and ancestry, however, there are discrepancies between the *Biography* and the earlier statements of the Judds. When he first arrived in Haiti in 1847, he was understood to claim that he himself was from Katsina, no mention being made of Djougou: "He is from the city of Kashina, of the tribe Houssa"; circumstantial corroboration being apparently provided by the claim that he "remembers well the Yaoors, the next nation west of the Houssas [i.e., Yauri, on the River Niger]" and "says he is acquainted with the city of Kano," the leading commercial center in Hausaland.[61] After Baquaqua's conversion in the following year, when his return to Africa as a missionary was mooted, Judd still understood that he was "from the city of Kachna," and it was likewise to Katsina that he was understood to hope to go: he "dreams often of visiting Kachna, … and being kindly received by his mother."[62] The simplest explanation of this contradiction is that the Judds misunderstood statements about

---

59. Letter of Mrs. N.A.L. Judd, 8 October 8, 1847.
60. For a discussion of *shurfa* (Hausa: *sharifai*) in Borgu and Hausaland in the late eighteenth and early nineteenth centuries, see Lovejoy, *Caravans of Kola*, 58–59, 68–69, 70–71, 73n.
61. Letter of Rev. W.L. Judd, 28 October 1847.
62. Letter of Rev. W.L. Judd, 21 July 1848.

Baquaqua's mother's origins as referring to himself; that they misunderstood at least part of what he told them is demonstrated by the fact that in 1847 they thought that his "native language" was Arabic, whereas the *Biography* shows it was only a second language, his first being Dendi. Moreover, Baquaqua had probably not been to Yauri and Kano; certainly no such claim is made in the *Biography*, although this recounts his travels to the west of the Djougou region, to Daboya in Gonja, then a tributary of Asante. His knowledge of the Hausa region more probably reflects what was known in his family and more generally in Djougou. By 1853, it may be noted, Baquaqua's patrons in the American Baptist Free Mission Society had grasped that the home to which he wished to return was in fact Djougou ("Zougo").[63]

However, it is quite possible that Baquaqua's close relationship with his mother (noted in the *Biography*, p. 26) led him to identify himself with her family, and hence as Hausa. This identification with his mother may have been intensified by the fact that his father had apparently died before he left Africa; this, at least, was understood by the Judds in 1847, and although not explicitly confirmed in the *Biography*, is consistent with the fact that he repeatedly referred to his feelings of loss with regard to his mother (and sometimes also his brother and sisters), but never his father.[64] In the light of his father's presumed death, it is also conceivable that he believed his mother might have gone back to live in Katsina, so that he might have to look for her there rather than in Djougou. However, it seems likely that Baquaqua's self-identification as Hausa also reflected his experience in Brazil, where he would have found few if any fellow slaves from

63. ABFMS, Tenth Annual Meeting, Utica, New York, 1–2 June 1853.
64. Letter of Rev. W.L. Judd, 28 October 1847, where it is stated that "his father died before he left." For reference to Baquaqua's feelings for his mother, see *Biography*, pp. 35, 39; also e.g., letter of Baquaqua to Hepburn, n.d. [November 1848] (see Appendix 3, no. 1). On some occasions, he referred to his brother and sister(s) as well as his mother: letters of Baquaqua to Cyrus Grosvenor, 14 November 1848, and to George Whipple, 25 September 1853 (see Appendix 3, nos. 1 and 9); letter of A.L. Post, July 1853, in *The American Baptist*, 21 July 1853.

Djougou (or even from the Borgu region more generally),[65] but there was a substantial Hausa (and Muslim) community in Rio de Janeiro with which he could have associated. This is indeed suggested by a remark of the Rev. Mr. Judd in 1847, that Baquaqua's recollection of the Arabic language might have been reinforced by "his intercourse with other slaves from the same country," which Judd, as has been seen, understood to be Hausaland.[66]

Details of Baquaqua's family in the *Biography* confirm its membership in the merchant community of Djougou. His father is said to have been a "traveling merchant," who was once "a wealthy man," although he had subsequently lost "the greater part of his property" and was left "comparatively poor" (p. 21); Mrs. Judd in 1847 reported that Baquaqua's father had dissipated his wealth through "intemperance and gambling," but this is difficult to square with Baquaqua's later insistence in the *Biography* on his father's Islamic piety and is probably a confusion on her part.[67] Baquaqua himself subsequently undertook a long-distance journey for purposes of trade, traveling to Daboya in Gonja to the west as a porter of grain (p. 30). His mother's family was also involved in craft production and commerce. Her

65. Some slaves from Borgu are documented (under the name "Bariba") in Brazil, in the province of Bahia: for references, see Robin Law and Paul Lovejoy, "Borgu in the Atlantic Slave Trade," *African Economic History* 27 (1999): 69–92. But the Bariba are not included among the "nations" of African-born slaves in Rio de Janeiro, listed by Mary Karasch, *Slave Life in Rio de Janeiro 1808–1850* (Princeton, NJ, 1987): 11–21, 371. Mrs. Judd in 1847 understood that Baquaqua was purchased in Rio de Janeiro by the ship's captain Clemente da Costa "together with another of his countrymen": letter of 8 October 1847. No such statement is made in the *Biography*, though this does report that he met another slave from Djougou in the coastal port of Ouidah, before himself he was shipped to Brazil, but implies that this other man remained behind in Africa (p. 40). Maybe Mrs. Judd misunderstood a reference to this man; or alternatively, by a "fellow-countryman" Baquaqua here meant simply someone also born in Africa.

66. Letter of Rev. W.L. Judd, 28 October 1847. For the Hausa community in Rio de Janeiro, see Karasch, *Slave Life in Rio de Janeiro*, 284–85; and for the preservation of the Arabic language among Muslims in Rio, also ibid., 219; and Alberto da Costa e Silva, "Buying and Selling Korans in Nineteenth Century Rio de Janeiro," Conference on Rethinking the African Diaspora: The Making of a Black Atlantic World in the Bight of Benin and Brazil, Emory University, Atlanta, Georgia, 1998.

67. Letter of Mrs. N.A.L. Judd, 8 October 1847. In the *Biography*, Baquaqua stresses that Muslims did not drink alcohol (p. 24).

brother, Baquaqua's uncle, is described as "a very rich man, who was blacksmith to the king [presumably of Djougou]"; for a time Baquaqua was apprenticed to him and learned "the art of making needles, knives, and all such things" (p. 26). From Baquaqua's own account, this uncle was a generic metalsmith rather than strictly a "blacksmith," working in gold, silver, and copper as well as iron, and making bracelets and rings as well as tools. This also involved him in the caravan trade to Asante, since he used to travel to Salaga, also in Gonja, at this time the principal market for foreign merchants trading to Asante, to purchase metals for his craft; he even owned property in Salaga, which was inherited by Baquaqua's mother on his death (pp. 27–28).

These details of Baquaqua's mother's family's business activities and marital connections reveal the history of long-distance trade in new ways. His maternal kin may have been connected with one of the important merchant houses of Katsina, and as Heinrich Barth reported in the 1850s, most of those families were Wangarawa (the Hausa term for Wangara);[68] the likelihood that his mother was from a Wangarawa family is increased by its connection with craft production, specifically metal-working, including silver-smithing. Or they may have been related to immigrants from Borno who had moved to Katsina in the early nineteenth century or earlier. By the early nineteenth century, many merchant families from Katsina traced their ultimate origins to Borno and were known in Hausa as Beriberi or Kambarin Beriberi.[69] Hence the identification with Katsina conforms with what we know about the history of this period, but that identification also raises other questions relating to remoter origins. The far-flung links which Baquaqua's mother's family maintained stretched the full length of the "kola route." The family traced its origins to

---

68. Heinrich Barth, *Travels and Discoveries in North and Central Africa,* vol. 1 (London and New York, 1859): 479.

69. Paul E. Lovejoy, "The Kambarin Beriberi: The Formation of a Specialized Group of Hausa Kola Traders in the Nineteenth Century," *Journal of African History* 14, no. 4 (1973): 648–49.

Katsina and presumably maintained its connections there, and also operated out of Djougou, with a base in Salaga; its marriage alliance with another prominent merchant from Nikki is also characteristic of the way in which this commercial diaspora operated.[70]

The *Biography* also demonstrates the strong identification with Islam characteristic of the Wangara commercial diaspora. Baquaqua's father is described as a devout Muslim, who performed his prayers scrupulously (pp. 9–10). His mother was clearly also a Muslim, though on this there is some discrepancy of testimony. The *Biography* implies that she was no more than a nominal Muslim, indeed effectively "of no religion at all," since she "did not care much about the worshipping part of the matter" (p. 26); but in fact, it was normal in many Muslim societies for women to take little part in public worship at the mosque, so that the imputation of lack of piety seems misplaced, and perhaps due to the editor Moore rather than to Baquaqua himself. Mrs. Judd earlier described Baquaqua's mother, rather than his father, as "strict in her observance of her prayers and the ceremonies of her belief," and understood that it was she who had taught Baquaqua the Islamic prayers.[71] But in view of the directly contradictory statements in the later *Biography*, it is possible that, here again, she somehow misinterpreted remarks by Baquaqua about his father as relating to his mother, although it is possible also that his mother shared the responsibility for making sure that he learned his prayers.

References to other members of the family confirm its allegiance to Islam. An elder brother of Baquaqua was an Islamic scholar. He told the Judds in 1847 that "his oldest brother was well educated, could read and write the Arabic with fluency";[72] the *Biography* like-

---

70. For a parallel instance, see the case of another enslaved Muslim, Abu Bakr al-Saddiq (born c.1794) who also had a Katsina mother, although he was born in Timbuktu, the home of his father; see Ivor Wilks, ed., "Abu Bakr al-Siddiq of Timbuktu," in Curtin, *Africa Remembered*, 159–60; and Austin, *African Muslims Sourcebook*, 553, 555.

71. Letter of Mrs. N.A.L. Judd, 8 October 1847. For the importance of Islam to the merchant community of Borgu, including Djougou, see Brégand, *Commerce caravanier*, and Osséni Ouorou-Coubou, "L'Islam en pays baatonu au xix siècle" (Memoire de Maîtrise en Histoire, Université Nationale du Bénin, 1997).

72. Letter of Rev. W.L. Judd, 28 October 1847.

wise states that "His brother was a staunch Mahommedan and well learned in Arabic," and teacher in a Quranic school in which Baquaqua himself was (briefly) enrolled (p. 27). This brother also served "the king" (presumably of Djougou) as a "fortune teller," indicating that he had been trained in the Islamic science of divination. The provision of such religious services, as well as commerce, could involve long-distance travel; and his brother is said to have traveled to "Bergoo" (i.e., Nikki) to the east and to Daboya to the west, in the latter case explicitly as adviser to the local ruler. It was while his brother was at Daboya that Baquaqua himself went there; and when he was taken prisoner in a local war his brother arranged his redemption from captivity (pp. 29–31).

The *Biography* also refers to an uncle of Baquaqua who served as "officiating priest" at ceremonies of "public worship" held in the evenings during Ramadan, the Islamic month of fasting, on property that belonged to Baquaqua's grandfather (p.10). Whether this was the same person as his mother's brother who is described elsewhere as a smith, or a different person, perhaps a paternal uncle, is not made clear. Baquaqua's description of this uncle's role suggests that he may have been the imam of a mosque, although probably not that of the central mosque in Djougou, who is distinguished later in the same passage as the "chief priest" (p.11); or perhaps more likely, the prayers were held in the family's private household, although open to the general public. In either case, the family's prominence within the Djougou Muslim community is evident.

According to the *Biography*, Baquaqua's father intended him also to be trained as an Islamic scholar, and placed him in his brother's Quranic school; but Baquaqua "not liking school very much" went instead to live with his uncle, to be trained as a metalsmith. His father later (seemingly after the uncle had died) sent him back to school, but he "soon ran away [again]." As Baquaqua comments, he "did not progress very well in learning, having a natural dread of it" (pp. 26–27). This is consistent with what he told the Rev. Mr. Judd in Haiti in 1847: "He says they put him to his books very closely, but loving play, he used to leave home clandestinely." Judd was nevertheless impressed with Baquaqua's knowledge of Arabic, although it is doubtful whether Judd himself knew much Arabic, and was therefore in a position to make an informed assessment.[73] Three words written in Arabic in one of Baquaqua's surviving letters are the only evidence of his fluency. The words are not written in a practiced hand. Baquaqua apparently was attempting to write *bismi'llah al-rahman*, but managed only a garbled *bismi'llah al-ra[hman]*, with the bracketed part omitted.[74] Nonetheless, his description of his education demonstrates the extent to which the Djougou Muslim community conformed to the pattern of Islamic learning along the Muslim-dominated trade routes of West Africa.

The Islamic community in Djougou, although distinct from the (originally non-Muslim) ruling establishment, maintained reciprocal links of service and patronage with it: the roles of his brother as diviner/adviser and of his uncle as blacksmith to "the king," presumably of Djougou, were noted above. But Baquaqua also claimed a closer relationship, by kinship, with one local ruler, although the precise nature and significance of this connection are unclear. Mrs. Judd in 1848 observed that "we are convinced from many circumstances and incidents, which he has related from time to time, that their parents, particularly his mother, were related or some way connected with the prince, or chief of the country where he lived."[75] This is confirmed in the *Biography*, which states that his mother was "related" to "our king" (p. 31)—in this case, from the context, not the king of Djougou, but that of a neighboring subordinate town: perhaps Soubroukou, to the southwest.[76] Given her foreign origin (from Katsina), the relation-

73. Ibid.

74. Letter of Baquaqua to George Whipple, 26 October 1853 (see Appendix 3, no. 11).

75. Letter of Mrs. N.A.L. Judd, 24 March 1848.

76. The *Biography* gives this ruler's title as "Massa-sa-ba" (pp. 31–32); although this is explained here as a generic title, applied to all subordinate rulers, informants in Djougou recognized it (in the form *masasawa*) as the title of the ruler of Soubroukou specifically (fieldwork in Djougou, April 1999).

ship was presumably by marriage; or perhaps the reference is to a form of clientage, she being taken under the protection of the king after the deaths of her husband and brother.

This connection with a local ruler had a significant influence on Baquaqua's career. On his return from visiting his brother (and undergoing captivity and redemption) in Daboya, he was taken into this king's service, by implication through the influence of his mother. He describes his position in the royal court as that of "a Che-re-coo, that is a kind of bodyguard to the king," which he claims was the third-ranking office after the king himself (p. 31). This certainly represents *tkiriku* (alternatively, *tyiriku*) which is not the title of a specific office but used generically of palace servants (who were usually, as noted later, slaves) throughout the Borgu region, including at Djougou.[77] On his own account, in this capacity he served as the king's messenger outside the palace and joined with other royal servants in requisitioning palm-wine and other provisions from the local peasantry; "we plundered for a living" (p. 32). It was presumably in this context that Baquaqua acquired a predilection for alcohol which, by his own account, occasioned his subsequent enslavement (pp. 34–35), and which persisted or recurred through his period in slavery in Brazil and into his early period in Haiti, until his conversion to Baptist Christianity there.[78] By thus enlisting in royal service (although this is not clearly signaled in the *Biography*), Baquaqua was in effect abandoning the commercial and Islamic circle of his family and entering the military and implicitly non-Muslim world of the local rulers; his account thus illuminates an additional aspect of the social history of nineteenth-century Djougou.

The name "Mahommah Gardo Baquaqua" is entirely credible for a person from the background indicated in the *Biography*. The first name is, of course, as the Judds in 1847 recognized, a local West African form of the Arabic name Muhammad and advertises his fam-

---

77. See Lombard, *Structures de type "féodal,"* 67; also fieldwork in Djougou, April 1999.
78. For subsequent references to his drunkenness, see *Biography*, pp. 46, 50–51, 54, 57–58.

ily's allegiance to Islam.[79] The second name, more properly Gado, is one given in both the Dendi and Baatonu languages (and also in Hausa, the language of Baquaqua's mother's family) to a son born next after twins; and the *Biography* confirms that Baquaqua was "the next born after twins," although without explaining the connection to his name (p. 26).[80] This seems to be the name by which he was usually known in Djougou, assuming the greeting he received from a former acquaintance, also a slave, whom he met in Ouidah was typical (p. 40). The third name, Baquaqua, however, has not yet been identified. It was not recognized by informants in Djougou in 1999; although since both his parents originated from elsewhere, this is perhaps not surprising. As Baquaqua himself notes in the *Biography* (p. 14) "Ba-" is a common prefix to titles in the Borgu area, as in that of Ba-Kparakpe, the official at Djougou (and also in some other towns in the area) who served as intermediary between the local king and the Wangara community; it literally means "father" (in Baatonu, the language of western Borgu, rather than in Dendi). There was also a title in Nikki, '*yan kwakwa*, which was that of the official responsible for overseeing the caravanserai, and this may be a possible derivation. Although it does not appear that this title was used at Djougou, it (or some variant of it) might have been held by Baquaqua's father, who came from Nikki.[81] Alternatively, the name might have a Hausa, rather than a Baatonu derivation, Hausa being not only the language of Baquaqua's mother and uncle, but also spoken in all the Muslim communities along the trade routes between the Sokoto Caliphate and Asante. The prefix "Ba-" is also common in Hausa, for the singular form of terms that denote place of origin, such as Bakano, Bakatsine,

79. Letters of Mrs. N.A.L. Judd, 8 October 1847; Rev. W. L. Judd, 28 October 1847.
80. We wish to thank Obarè Bagodo for information on the use of Gado as a name in Borgu. For its use in Hausa, see G.P. Bargery, *A Hausa-English Dictionary and English-Hausa Vocabulary* (London: 1934), 341.
81. Kuba, *Wasangari und Wangara*, 336; following Musa Baba Idris, "The Role of the Wangara in the Formation of the Trading Diaspora in Borgu," Conference on Manding Studies, SOAS, London, 1972.

Bazazaggi, or Bazamfara (someone from Kano, Katsina, Zaria or Zamfara, respectively), or ethnicity, such as Bahaushe, Bayaraba or Ba'agali (for Hausa, Yoruba or Agalawa). However, 'kwakwa' or 'k'wak'wa' does not refer to any known place or ethnic designation. Although the name 'sounds' authentic, it cannot be precisely pinned down.

Baquaqua's Enslavement in Africa

Baquaqua's account of his enslavement is confusing. In the first place, there are contradictions between what he said to (or at least, was reported as saying by) the Judds in Haiti in 1847–48 and the account in the later *Biography*. Secondly, in the *Biography* itself he claims that he was enslaved twice, first in Daboya, in central Gonja, to the west, and then somewhere near Djougou under circumstances that are not well explained. What relationship, if any, there was between these two experiences is also not clear.

In 1847 he apparently told the Judds that he was kidnapped while playing truant from Quranic school; or in a slightly different formulation, he "was taken captive when a child, while playing at some distance from his mother's door." In this first version, he is evidently assumed to have been taken for sale at the coast immediately after his enslavement, taking only "several weeks" in the journey south.[82] By the time of his conversion in 1848, however, their understanding of his story had been modified in an important respect, Mrs. Judd then reporting that "it seems, by what he has informed us lately, that he was several years a slave in Africa," before being sold at the coast.[83] This second version was also reproduced in the brief biographical notice of Baquaqua published in 1850, which reported that he was

---

82. Letters of Rev. W.L. Judd, 28 October 1847; Mrs. N.A.L. Judd, 8 October 1847.

83. Letter of Mrs. N.A.L. Judd, 24 March 1848. Cf. also letter of Rev. W.L. Judd, 21 July 1848, which reports that he "says he was a slave for some time on the coast of Africa"; this last phrase should probably be understood to mean simply "in Africa," rather than literally "on the coast."

"clandestinely seized upon, and reduced to slavery" at an "early age," and "for some time he was held in this condition in Western Africa" prior to being transported to Brazil.[84]

In the *Biography* Baquaqua provides two stories of his enslavement. The first, as noted earlier, was in Gonja, to the west, which he visited during a civil war arising from a disputed succession to the throne. He was captured by an army which sacked the town of Daboya; he was ransomed from captivity by his brother, then in the service of the local ruler (pp. 30–31). This was probably in the early 1840s, when a succession dispute in Gonja provoked intervention by its overlord Asante to the south, who sent an army into Gonja. Gonja may well have been Baquaqua's captors. His brother was presumably in the service of Nyantakyi, one of the rival claimants to the royal skin (upon which the paramount ruler of Gonja sat) who was then based at Daboya.[85] Once freed, his brother sent him back home, where he enlisted as a "bodyguard" in the palace of a local ruler, possibly that of Soubroukou. In the second enslavement, which occurred after "a considerable length of time" spent in this royal service, Baquaqua claims that he was kidnapped after a drunken party, and sold south into slavery (pp. 34–35); this is said to have happened at "Zaracho," apparently Yarakeou, a village to the southwest of Soubroukou. He explains his enslavement as due to deception, he having believed that his hosts were his friends, and implies that he was the victim of a deliberate conspiracy rather than a random kidnapping, inspired by jealousy of the position of power to which he had risen.

There are thus two major areas of contradiction. First, the Haitian accounts claim that he was enslaved as a child, whereas the *Biography* implies that he was a young adult, since he was employed at the time as a palace messenger, and had earlier undertaken a long-distance trading journey as a porter. Second, the later Haitian

84. Foss and Mathews, *Facts for Baptist Churches*, 392.
85. Cf. Ivor Wilks, *Asante in the Nineteenth Century* (Cambridge, 1975): 275–79. The Asante army returned from Gonja in 1844, after a campaign which had lasted three years.

accounts assert that after his enslavement he spent "several years" in slavery in Africa, before being taken for sale at the coast, whereas in the *Biography* he is taken directly to the coast after his kidnapping at "Zaracho". It may be noted that Baquaqua, or least his editor Samuel Moore, was evidently conscious of these inconsistencies, since in reproducing the published account from 1850 in the *Biography* (p. 59), the first two sentences which directly contradicted his later version were omitted.

In part, these contradictions may reflect difficulties of communication between Baquaqua and his reporters, especially in Haiti before he learned English. Hence, the earlier statements that he was enslaved as a child may represent merely misunderstanding by the Judds; the later *Biography* reports both that Baquaqua used to play truant from Quranic school and that he was kidnapped while away from home, but presents these as two separate episodes. It may also be the case that the first kidnapping near Daboya occurred after he had ran away (evidently, for the final time) from Quranic school. In this case, the Judds may have conflated the two separate incidents of enslavement recorded in the *Biography*, according to which he was redeemed, not sold to the coast, after this first enslavement.

The aspect of the earlier accounts which seems most difficult to explain away as mere misunderstanding is the assertion that he spent some considerable time as a slave in Africa, prior to being sold to the coast for export. However, a possible resolution of this problem is suggested by the *Biography*'s account of his life in the period between his two enslavements. When he returned home after being captured and (allegedly) redeemed in Gonja, as has been seen, he is said to have enlisted in the service of a local ruler as a palace servant, or *tkiriku* ("Che-re-coo"). The status of *tkiriku*, however, was normally a servile position in Borgu, though it could also include criminals attempting to escape justice by enlisting as palace servants.[86] If indeed

---

86. Lombard, *Structures de type "féodal" en Afrique noire*, 112.

Baquaqua was a *tkiriku*, therefore, this probably means that he had either been enslaved and failed to explain this condition in his text, or was taken on in this capacity as a fugitive from justice or for other reasons to his discredit that are also not explained. Conceivably, after his enslavement in Gonja, he had passed somehow directly (by sale or flight) into the status of *tkiriku*, rather than through redemption and voluntary enlistment, as the *Biography* claims. However this may be, his status as *tkiriku* implies that he was not, at the time of his seizure for sale to the coast, legally free and certainly raises the possibility that there are further details which he may have chosen to suppress. It seems likely, therefore, that the earlier report of his having spent some time held in slavery in Africa relates to this period as a palace servant. Baquaqua's suppression of his period of slavery in Africa in the *Biography* might have been motivated merely by the desire to present his own circumstances in the most favorable light. It is possible, however, that in the U.S.A. he had become aware that defenders of the slave trade and of slavery in the Americas commonly sought to justify them on the grounds that those taken were already enslaved in Africa, so that the trade involved merely the transfer of slaves from one continent to another, rather than the enslavement of free persons; and he may have wished to prevent his own case being cited in support of anti-abolitionist propaganda.

Unlike his reported earlier experience in Gonja, on this second occasion he was not ransomed but instead traded southward into Dahomey, changing hands among several successive owners along the way. His route southwards, via towns which he calls "Ar-oozoo," "Chir-a-chur-ee" and "Cham-mah" (pp. 35–36), is readily traceable on any modern map, once more confirming the authenticity of his account: these names representing Alejo, Krikri and Tchamba, all situated to the south-west of Yarakeou, the first within modern Bénin and the latter two across the border in the Republic of Togo. It was apparently originally intended to keep him in slavery locally, at a place called "Efau," probably in northern Dahomey, where he did in fact stay for "several weeks"; but he was visibly unsettled and thought likely to attempt to escape, and was therefore sold on to the coast (p. 38). He was taken to a coastal port which he calls "Gra-fe," which is Glehue, the local name for the town better known as Ouidah (Whydah), the principal port of Dahomey, from where he was taken along the coastal lagoon for embarkation onto a slave ship (pp. 39–41). His account here is consistent with other contemporary evidence, that the blockade maintained at this time by the British navy's anti-slaving squadron made it difficult to load slaves at Ouidah, and that therefore they were commonly moved along the lagoon either eastward to Porto-Novo or Badagry or westward to Agoué or Little Popo.[87] Unfortunately, Baquaqua does not specify in which direction he was moved along the lagoon, so that it is impossible to determine from which coastal port he was eventually shipped.[88] If it was to the west of Ouidah, however, and if (as suggested below) he was shipped in 1845, arriving in Brazil at the end of March of that year, it may be noted that the Scottish traveler John Duncan was exploring the lagoons west of Ouidah at around this same time. It is even possible that he was on a canoe seen by Duncan taking slaves to the westwards on 18 February 1845; and even if not, Duncan's account provides a useful eyewitness account of the conditions under which Baquaqua would have traveled.[89]

From Slavery in Brazil to Freedom in the United States

From West Africa, Baquaqua was taken into slavery in Pernambuco, in northeastern Brazil. While the date of his transportation can only be calculated approximately, the first certainly fixed date in his life is April 1847, when he left Brazil on a voyage to New York,

87. For the role of the lagoon route in the slave trade in this region more generally, see Robin Law, "Between the sea and the lagoons: the interaction of maritime and inland navigation on the pre-colonial Slave Coast," *Cahiers d'études africaines* 29 (1989): 209–37.

88. But see the annotation to the main text (n. 201), for the argument that he is more likely to have gone west, and, therefore, to have embarked from Agoué or Little Popo.

89. Duncan, *Travels in Western Africa*, i, 110–11.

where he arrived in late June and was ultimately able to claim his freedom. A year later, he told the Rev. Mr. Judd that he had spent "nearly two years" in slavery in Brazil, which would place his arrival there in the first half of 1845.[90] Our effort to identify the ship he was on relies on this chronology.

The general conditions of the slave trade to Pernambuco in this period are described in a report of a British agent there in 1846:

> The mode in which the African Slave Trade was formerly conducted in this port, has now...assumed a new feature. Instead of the larger classes of vessels, varying from 150 to 300 tons burthen each, a smaller kind is now employed, of from 45 to 60 tons, named, 'Maria,' 52 tons admeasurement, 'Maraquinhas [Mariquinhas],' 52, 'Déliberacao [Deliberação],' 54, two 'Diligencias,' of 54 and 55, and the 'San Domingos [São Domingos].' of 56 tons burthen; these insignificant-looking craft, rigged with boom, main, and fore-sails only, sail fast, are of light draught of water, and built low, that they may more easily escape detection; their complement of crew varies from eight to 14 men, who are engaged by the run, and whose interests are solely contingent on the voyage being prosperous, are always on the alert.[91]

These ships carried from 150–300 slaves in miserable conditions well described by Baquaqua in the *Biography* (pp. 42–44) and in his earlier reports to the Judds.

Very likely one of the vessels named in this report is that which transported Baquaqua. Most of the ships delivering slaves to Pernambuco in this period, however, are reported to have come from Angola

90. Letter of Rev. W.L. Judd, 21 July 1848; this information is repeated in Foss and Mathews, *Facts for Baptist Churches*, 392, which is in turn reproduced in the *Biography*, p. 59; see further discussion in annotation to the latter (n. 288).

91. PP, Slave Trade 1846, Class B, no. 361, Mr. Goring to Earl of Aberdeen, Pernambuco, 16 May 1846.

or elsewhere in West-Central Africa, rather than from West Africa. While there were six ships that brought slaves to Pernambuco from the Bight of Benin in 1844, their voyages seem too early for Baquaqua.[92] During 1845, the only recorded landing of slaves which might have been Baquaqua's was a ship coming from an unspecified African location (which is also, unfortunately, itself unnamed), which put in at Macaro, near the Island of Itamaraca, north of Recife, the capital of Pernambuco, on 31 March 1845. According to the British report, this ship brought 163 slaves, of whom thirty were sold to persons in the neighborhood (at 250 *milreis* per head), and eleven were given to the local authorities as a bribe, while the remaining 122 were initially "disposed of, and secreted in the adjacent Engenhos [sugar estates]," although many of them were later taken into Recife for sale.[93] Baquaqua's account (p. 44) likewise reports that his ship put in outside "the city" (i.e., Recife), but this was normal practice at this time, in order to evade the attentions of the British navy; more circumstantial is the detail that after embarkation he too was initially taken to a farm, and only later into Recife. This identification is advanced only tentatively, since there may well have been other shipments of slaves from West Africa to the Recife area of which no record has survived; but it is consistent with the details given in Baquaqua's account, sketchy as this admittedly is.

Unlike in Bahia or Rio de Janeiro in this period, persons newly

92. According to the Portuguese consul in Recife, these ships flew the Brazilian flag and were registered as trading with São Tomé and Principe, but actually went to "Benin, Onim [Lagos] and Ajudá [Ouidah]." The ships were described as "small" by comparison with the large ships used to transport enslaved Africans from Angola (Torre do Tombo, Consulado de Portugal em Pernambuco, caixa 3, Joaquim Batista Moreira ao Ministro dos Negócios Estrangeiros, 10 de dezembro de 1844). According to Marcus J.M. de Carvalho, who generously provided this reference, the Portuguese consul did not mention any ships coming from the Bight of Benin in 1845, but the consul was primarily concerned with tracking ships flying the Portuguese flag, not Brazilian ships, despite his observations in 1844, and hence the failure to report any Brazilian ship movements in 1845 does not mean that there were none.

93. PP, Slave Trade 1846, Class B, no. 173, Consul Cowper to Earl of Aberdeen, Pernambuco, 2 March 1846, with inclosure 1, List of arrival of vessels suspected of being employed in the Slave Trade from the Coast of Africa to the Province of Pernambuco, during the Year ending December 31, 1845.

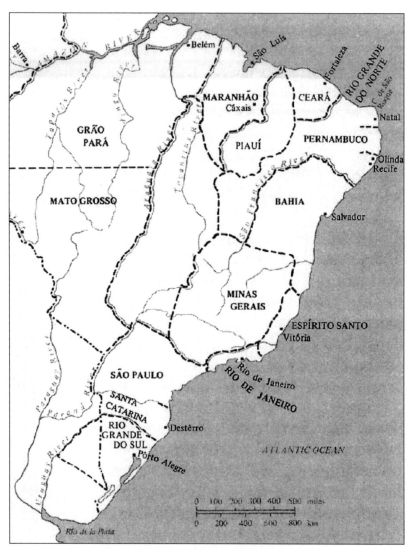

MAP 3. Brazil–Pernambuco, Bahia, Rio de Janeiro, Rio Grande do Sul.

imported from Africa such as Baquaqua formed a relatively small minority of the slave population of Pernambuco. In 1844, the population of Pernambuco was 618,950, of whom 83,854 were slaves, and among the slaves only 22,233 were Africans (13,596 males and 8,637 females), and of the people brought from Africa, it is unlikely that more than 10 per cent were from the Bight of Benin, and fewer still from the far interior.[94] Baquaqua was sold to a baker who lived in a town outside Recife, perhaps Olinda, 10 km. to the north, or one of the parishes (*povoados*) located on the Capibaribe River, which flows into the ocean in Recife's harbor.[95] Although most slaves ended up on sugar estates or cotton plantations, there was a sizeable urban slave population in Pernambuco, as in Bahia and Rio de Janeiro. The British Consul in Pernambuco thought that the conditions of slaves working on the sugar and cotton estates were particularly bad, the slaves there being "generally ... treated worse than beasts," but that "the condition of the urban slaves is superior."[96] According to his own testimony, however, Baquaqua worked under harsh conditions in Pernambuco, which prompted him to run away on one occasion, and

94. PP, Slave Trade 1844, Class B, inclosure in no. 265, "Probable Amount of the Population of the Province of Pernambuco—1844." According to Vergolino, most African-born slaves listed in post-mortem inventories for Pernambuco in the nineteenth century were reported to have come from west-central Africa, with only a small percentage designated "gentio costa", apparently referring to West Africa generally, "Nago," "Mina," or "Benin"; see José Raimundo Oliveira Vergolino, 'A demografia excrava no nordeste do Brasil: o caso de Pernambuco—1800/1888' (texto para discussão No. 383, Departamento de Economia, Universidade Federal de Pernambuco, March 1997): 20. On slavery in Pernambuco, see also Marcus J.M. de Carvalho, *Liberdade: Rotinas e Rupturas do Escravismo, Recife, 1822–1850* (Recife, 1998)" 73–90; Carvalho, "Le "Divin Maître": Esclavage et liberté à Recife dans les année 1840," François Crouzet, Denin Rolland, and P. Bonnichon, eds., *Pour l'histoire du Brésil* (Paris, 2000): 435–49.

95. Olinda, the capital of Pernambuco during the Dutch period, is situated at the mouth of the Rio Beberibe. Baquaqua's reference to the tide in the river in which he attempted to drown himself, as well as the relative proximity to Recife ("Pernambuco"), suggests this possibility, but the parishes (*povoados*) near Recife, particularly Várzea, Poço da Panela, or Monteiro, are also possible. These *povoados* were located on the Capibaribe River, which flows into the ocean in Recife's harbor. Other towns in Pernambuco were inland or far from Recife, or both; see Carvalho, *Liberdade: Rotinas e Rupturas do Escravismo*, 21–22; and Carvalho, "Os Caminhos do Rio: Negros Canoeiros no Recife na Primeira Metade do Século XIX," *Afro-Ásia* 19–20 (1997): 75–93.

96. PP, Slave Trade 1844, Class B, no. 265, Cowper to Earl of Aberdeen, 1 January 1844.

to attempt suicide on another (pp. 44–47). In this regard, Baquaqua's testimony seems to confirm the impression gained from other sources, that urban slavery in Pernambuco (as elsewhere in Brazil) might involve a wide range of treatment but with slaves often moving independently through the towns and countryside pursuing a trade or craft.[97] In any event, he was eventually sold south to Rio de Janeiro, moving from one urban setting to another.

His purchaser in Rio de Janeiro was a ship's captain, who is not named in the *Biography*, but identified in other evidence as Clemente José da Costa, captain and part owner of the ship *Lembrança* ("Remembrance"), the co-owner being Antonio José da Rocha Pereira.[98] During the period when he was owned by Costa, Baquaqua himself was known by the Portuguese name of José da Costa. He served on board the *Lembrança* as a cabin steward, making two voyages south along the coast of Brazil, to Rio Grande do Sul and the island of Santa Catarina (pp. 48–49). On 24 April 1847, the *Lembrança* sailed from Rio de Janeiro for New York, carrying a consignment of coffee, as well as a few passengers, including an English man who, as later recalled in the *Biography* (p. 54), encouraged Baquaqua to think of his freedom. There were two other slaves on the ship: Maria da Costa, who as her name suggests was also owned by Captain Costa, and José da Rocha, who belonged to Costa's partner, Antonio José da Rocha Pereira. Maria helped Costa's wife, who

97. See Carvalho, "Negros Canoeiros no Recife," 78–93. On the harshness of the slave regime in the 1840s, also see Peter L. Eisenberg, *The Sugar Industry in Pernambuco, 1840–1910* (Berkeley, 1974): 172, 173.

98. See affidavit of Clemente da Costa, New York, n.d. [12 July 1847], printed in *National Anti-Slavery Standard*, 2 November 1847 (reproduced in this edition as Appendix 1, no. 1). The registration of the *Lembrança* has not been located in a search of the archives in Rio de Janeiro and Rio Grande do Sul, where the ship was known to have traded. Clemente José da Costa is a common name, and so far has not been further identified (personal communication, Alberto da Costa e Silva). Antonio José da Rocha Pereira, born in Porto, Portugal, has been identified through a post-mortem inventory conducted in 1871 at the request of his wife, Maria Roza Leite Pereira, and his son, José Maria Fernandes. By the time of his death, he had emancipated three of his slaves who had reached fifty years of age (Januario Angola, Fernando Mina, and Felicidade Mina). He left the remainder of his slaves, whose names are not specified, to his three daughters. (We wish to thank Manolo Florentino for this reference.)

accompanied her husband on his voyages and who at the time was a new mother. On 27 June 1847, the ship arrived in New York.[99]

In New York, at the dock at the foot of Roosevelt Street, on the East River, local abolitionists, organized loosely as the New York Vigilance Society, approached the *Lembrança*, initiating a legal tug-of-war over the fate of Baquaqua, José da Rocha and Maria da Costa. At the urging of these local abolitionists and prompted by severe beatings, Baquaqua, along with his two fellow-slaves, sought the "freedom" that he speaks about so poignantly in his *Biography*. After attempts by Baquaqua to jump ship had failed, their abolitionist friends filed a writ of *habeas corpus* requiring delivery of the three slaves to the Court of Common Pleas of New York. At the first hearing Maria da Costa indicated that she wanted to return to the ship, and thereafter the case involved only the two men. The case of the two "Brazilians" came to the attention of the local press in New York. The case was well covered in the New York *Daily Tribune*, the *Herald*, the *Express*, and the *National Anti-Slavery Standard*.[100] Despite this notoriety, Baquaqua and Rocha did not have an easy time gaining their freedom; they were put in the jail on Eldridge Street, pending the out-

---

99. For details of the voyage see, in addition to the *Biography*, the affidavit of Clemente José da Costa, [12] July 1847; and notice of the arrival of the *Lembrança* in *New York Daily Tribune*, 28 June 1847. In New York, J.L. Phipps and Co. handled the consignment of coffee. An advertisement for passengers on the *Lembrança*, promising "excelentes comodos," was published in *Jornal do Commercio* of Rio de Janeiro, 17 April 1847, instructing interested individuals to inquire on the first floor, 93 Rua Direita (Rua Primeiro de Março), the main street in Rio. The Brazilian Consul-General in New York, Luiz Henrique Ferreira d'Aguiar, wrote to the Ministry of Foreign Affairs (Saturnino de Souza e Oliveira), on 8 September 1847 (Arquivo Histórico do Itamaraty, Rio de Janeiro: 258–3–5, page 81): "Reading in a Rio de Janeiro newspaper that the coffee imported by this country (the United States) will have to pay a duty tax of 20%, I want to inform you that the Brazilian ships and their cargoes receive in the Union the same privileges accorded to the American ships. Therefore, the Brazilian coffee is admitted free of duty, as was recently the case of the coffee brought by the Brazilian ships 'Lembrança' and 'Albina.'" (We thank Manolo Florentino and Alberto da Costa e Silva for these Brazilian references to the *Lembrança*, and José Cairus for the identification Rua Direita with Rua Primeiro de Março.)

100. The case was also followed in Brazil; see *Diário do Rio de Janeiro*, 4 October 1847, translating a report from the New York *Express*. Robert Edgar Conrad notes this reference to the *Lembrança* incident in New York, but does not identify Baquaqua as one of the slaves on board; see *World of Sorrow: The African Slave Trade to Brazil* (Baton Rouge, 1986):117.

come of the case.[101] Unfortunately for the two men, on 17 July, Judge Charles P. Daly ruled that they should be returned to the ship, on the grounds that they were members of its crew, and their return was therefore required under the terms of treaty of reciprocity between Brazil and the U.S.A. governing the desertion of crew members; technically, their status as slaves was not a factor in this decision.[102] Their local supporters then appealed to the New York Supreme Court. Through an interpreter and with the assistance of their abolitionist friends, the two men filed an affidavit, which is reproduced here in an appendix.[103] But their identity as crew was confirmed in a second legal decision by Judge Henry P. Edwards, who ruled on 5 August that Judge Daly had been correct in his judgment, and, therefore, remanded the two men to the custody of the captain of the ship.

In turn this decision was to be appealed, but before yet another judge could hear the case, Baquaqua and José da Rocha miraculously disappeared from the jail on Eldridge Street on the night of 9 August. The jailer admitted that he had fallen asleep and left the keys to the cell on his desk.[104] Whether or not the warden sympathized with Baquaqua and his fellow fugitive is not clear, but the two men were able to reach Boston, passing through Springfield. As a Springfield newspaper reported, the two men had "arrived in that town a few days since by the 'underground railway' and proceeded the same route next morning on their way to a land of liberty." The mystery as to how they escaped was explained by the claim that "this road runs directly under the prison in New York, and that the slaves had let themselves down through a stone trap-door into one of the peculiar cars which

101. *National Anti-Slavery Standard*, 29 July 1847. Baquaqua's own account of these judicial proceedings is sketchy, probably reflecting limited understanding, due to his lack of knowledge of English (*Biography*, pp. 55–56).

102. *National Anti-Slavery Standard*, 15 July 1847. For Daly's ruling that the three fugitives had to return to the ship, see ibid., 22 July 1847.

103. Their affidavit, together with a second one by Captain Costa submitted on this occasion, were published in the *National Anti-Slavery Standard*, 2 September 1847 (see Appendix 1, nos. 2–3).

104. *New York Daily Tribune*, 10 August 1847, and *National Anti-Slavery Standard*, 12 August 1847.

regularly pass over this mysterious thoroughfare."[105] Their case was known among abolitionists in Boston, where *The Liberator* had reported the case, and hence Baquaqua and Rocha were easily taken care of.[106]

Baquaqua and the Baptist Free Mission

Four weeks later, Baquaqua and Rocha left for Haiti, a land where, as the *Biography* notes (p. 57), since the Revolution of the 1790s, blacks were free. They arrived in Port-au-Prince, the capital of Haiti, some time during September 1847. On the voyage out they befriended Mr. Jones, an African-American, who had links with the American Baptist Free Mission in Port-au-Prince. On arrival in Port-au-Prince, Baquaqua first went to work for another African-American emigré, but he did not treat him as well as Baquaqua believed to be fair, and eventually turned him out. Baquaqua claims then to have been at another low point in his ongoing odyssey, hampered as he was by not speaking French, and he sought solace in drink (p. 58). But he had either maintained or now renewed his contacts with Jones, who introduced Baquaqua and Rocha to the Rev. William Judd at the Baptist Free Mission, in early October 1847.[107] Thus began an association with the Free Baptists that transformed Baquaqua's life, resulting in his conversion and baptism, and later his education in the U.S.A. His association with the Mission gave him access to a network of Baptist abolitionists in New York, Pennsylvania and Canada West, ultimately leading to the publication of his biography. Soon after meeting the Rev. Mr. and Mrs. Judd, and Mrs. Judd's sister Electa Lake, who shared their home, Baquaqua was living in their house, serving as

105. The Springfield *Gazette*, quoted in *New York Daily Tribune*, 23 August 1847.

106. *The Liberator*, 16 July 1847, noted the case of the Brazilian slaves, and on 20 August 1847, reprinted a lengthy report from the *National Anti-Slavery Standard* on Judge Edward's decision.

107. Mrs. Judd, writing on 8 October, says that he had been taken into the protection of the mission "within a few days": letter of Mrs. N.A.L. Judd, 8 October 1847.

their cook.[108] From the beginning there was a meeting of minds, and very quickly a strong bond developed, reinforced on Judd's side by the hope that if Baquaqua were converted he might become a missionary to his own people in Africa.

With the Judds' encouragement, Baquaqua also seized the opportunity to acquire an education in English. As Mrs. Judd reported, within a few days of his arrival, he "expresses a very strong desire to obtain an education ... He very eagerly embraces every opportunity to read; and among us all, he manages to get several lessons into [a] day, generally."[109] Thereafter, Baquaqua studied English and otherwise ingratiated himself into the hearts of the Judd household. In March 1848, he experienced conversion to Christianity, and in July was baptized into the Baptist church.[110] After conversion, he continued his education, concentrating on reading the Bible and learning to write in English.[111] This interest in education soon brought him to the attention of Cyrus Grosvenor, the editor of the *Christian Contributor and Free Missionary*, then being published in Utica, N.Y., to whom Baquaqua wrote a letter which was printed in that journal in December 1848. As this letter makes clear, Baquaqua hoped to continue his education in the U.S.A.: "I want to go to the United States very much, and go to school and learn to understand the Bible very well," preparatory to going back to Africa as a missionary.[112] Grosvenor used the occasion of the publication of this letter to issue an appeal for "one rich man" to sponsor Baquaqua's education in America.[113]

---

108. Letter of Mrs. Judd, 24 March 1848.

109. Letter of Mrs. N.A.L. Judd, 8 October 1847.

110. Baquaqua's conversion is described in the letter of Mrs. N.A.L. Judd, 24 March 1848, and also noted in ABFMS, Fifth Annual Meeting, Utica, New York, 10-11 May 1848. His baptism is described in the letter of the Rev. W.L. Judd, 21 July 1848 (quoted in Foss and Mathews, *Facts for Baptist Churches*, 393; and from there also in the *Biography*, pp. 50–51); apparently it took place on Sunday, 16 July.

111. Letter of Mrs. N.A.L. Judd to Cyrus Grosvenor, 13 November 1848, in *Christian Contributor and Free Missionary*, 27 December 1848 (see Appendix 2, no. 6).

112. Letter of Baquaqua to Cyrus Grosvenor, 14 November 1848.

113. "Remarks," appended to letter of Mrs. N.A.L. Judd, 13 November 1848, in *Christian Contributor and Free Missionary*, 27 December 1848.

The American Baptist Free Mission Society, to which Baquaqua was attached in Haiti between 1847–49, was unusual in that its egalitarian ideals rejected discrimination on the basis of either race or gender. The Free Mission Society was an outgrowth of the Free Will Baptist movement, which had broken with the main body over the issue of abolition in 1843, only rejoining the parent church in 1870.[114] The Free Mission undertook work among Native Americans in the U.S.A. and among fugitive slaves in Canada West who had fled the United States on the Underground Railroad, as well as launching the mission in Haiti, to which Baquaqua by good fortune was introduced.[115] It also founded New York Central College, opened in 1849, where Baquaqua was later a student. The Baptist Free Mission was also in favor of a mission to Africa; indeed, it had initiated its mission in Haiti, in part, in the hope of recruiting personnel there for missionary work in Africa. For this purpose Baquaqua seemed to be a providential gift. Baquaqua himself quickly warmed to the idea of returning to Africa, which he expressed as early as March 1848, and (as will be seen) frequently repeated thereafter.

Baquaqua, of course, responded to the religious commitment of his Baptist mentors, whose reports on his conversion no doubt primarily project their own concerns and perceptions rather than those of Baquaqua himself. However, there are fortunately a number of stories, including reports of Baquaqua's own comments, which allow some assessment of how he interpreted his commitment to Christianity, considering his Muslim background in Africa. In Djougou, as has been seen, Baquaqua had belonged to a devoutly Muslim family,

114. See Edward Mathews, *Review of the Operations of the American Baptist Free Mission Society* (Bristol, 1851). The convention which founded the American Baptist Free Mission Society at Tremont Chapel in Boston on 4 May 1843, issued a pledge that became the doctrinal basis of the movement and its commitment to abolition, temperance and conversion. The pledge is published in *The American Baptist*, 29 April 1850, among other places. Free Missionists were strong in parts of New England, upstate New York, Pennsylvania, Ohio, and Wisconsin.

115. The Haïtian mission had been established by the Rev. William Jones in 1845; Judd had succeeded him there earlier in 1847.

even if his own commitment to the tenets of Islam was less stringent than that of his father or brother; in addition to dropping out of Quranic school, he also indulged in alcoholic drinks, which was by his own account the occasion of his enslavement, despite his own recognition, stated in the *Biography*, that Muslims "use no kinds of intoxicating drinks on any occasion" (p. 24). As a slave in Brazil, he had also received some rudimentary instruction in the Roman Catholic religion, although he was retrospectively dismissive of its superficiality: "we were taught to chant some words which we did not know the meaning of" (p. 45).

Prior to his conversion, in his conversations with Jones on the voyage from New York to Haiti and after arrival there, they had discussed "his ideas of God, &c., of the soul, of heaven, &c." Baquaqua had apparently indicated his continuing adherence to Islam: "His name for God is Allah"; and tried to convey to Jones his concept of the soul through an analogy with a person's shadow. He also expressed disapproval of alcoholic drinks; "He is, also, strongly opposed to intemperance. When Mr. Jones explained to him the object of our Temperance Pledge, he expressed himself very ready to have his name attached to it."[116] Given his own indulgence in alcohol earlier, in Brazil as well as in Africa, and indeed his admitted lapses in this respect in Haiti later, prior to his definitive conversion, this last should perhaps be understood in terms of an assertion of the Islamic prohibition, to which Baquaqua as a Muslim in principle subscribed, rather than a statement about his personal conduct. But in any case, a degree of convergence between Islam and Baptist Christianity is evident, which must be presumed to have facilitated his subsequent conversion.

The account of Baquaqua's conversion in March 1848 given by Mrs. Judd is conventional enough in stressing his growing consciousness of his own sinfulness and of the presumed evidence of God's providential intervention in his life hitherto: "Mahomah sin so

116. Letter of Mrs. N.A.L. Judd, 8 October 1847.

much, O too much … God very good for Mahomah—not let him die."[117] Mrs. Judd understood him to be "referring to his sins in Africa, as well as since." The later *Biography* indicates that it was specifically his behavior when employed as a palace servant whose "wickedness" he retrospectively repented, referring mainly to his activities in looting provisions from the local peasantry (p. 32), but perhaps also to his indulgence in alcoholic drinks. It is noteworthy, however, that Baquaqua saw the problem of sin in collective as well as individual terms, as affecting the society in Africa from which he had come as well as himself specifically: "[H]e had been thinking about Africa; and how bad the people were there. (This he would never admit until lately.) 'Now I see the people very bad in Africa.'" In the night after this conversation, "he dreamed of being there [in Africa]," and the next day announced his wish to go back to Africa to preach Christianity there. Although the Judds assumed that Baquaqua's dream of home related to his realization of the "wickedness" of African society, and its consequent need of Christian salvation, it is surely not overly cynical to suggest that nostalgia for his homeland, very likely crystallized by the stimulus of the Judds' persistent urging on him of the idea of returning there as a missionary, played a central role in his conversion. Certainly, Baquaqua's commitment to education and to the Christian church was consistently linked thereafter to the project of returning home.

After his conversion, Baquaqua seems to have internalized the Christian teaching that the Muslim religion to which he had adhered (at least nominally) in Africa was, rather than a variant of the worship of the same "True God," a false faith—at least, unless the numerous references in the *Biography* to Muhammad as a "false prophet" are to be attributed to his editor Samuel Moore, rather than to Baquaqua himself. There are, nevertheless, some indications that his attitude to Islam remained ambivalent. One was his retention of the name Mahommah, which oddly is nowhere commented upon in the Free

117. Letter of Mrs. N.A.L. Judd, 24 March 1848.

Baptist sources, despite its obvious (and indeed, recognized) significance as a badge of religious affiliation. It is also noteworthy that the brief reference to his conversion in the *Biography* again stresses the issue of temperance, on which Baptist and Islamic teaching converged: "after my conversion to Christianity I gave up drinking and all other kinds of vices" (p. 58). There is also an intriguing story, reported by Mrs. Judd, of a conversation which Baquaqua had with a Spanish Roman Catholic in Haiti, in which he derided the latter's veneration of a crucifix: "this God wood, eh? ... Well you take e little wood—make a God—go pray for God, eh? ... Oh! Your God not say e nothing ... O Mr. _____ very bad, [to] have wooden God. God not like it."[118] Here again, although the Judds understood Baquaqua's anti-Catholicism as evidence of the strength of his Baptist faith, an alternative reading might be that his commitment to Christianity was sometimes compatible with the retention of things Muslim. Condemnation of wooden idols was a central feature of Islam, which may have influenced the argument that he pursued. In this way, perhaps, Baquaqua was able to find some resolution of the predicament of being born a Muslim, but being saved by Christians.

In October 1849, just over two years after arriving in Haiti, Baquaqua departed for New York, arriving there apparently on 25 November. He was accompanied on this voyage by Mrs. Judd and her sister Electa Lake, who was returning to the U.S.A. for reasons of health. In the *Biography* (pp. 58–59) Baquaqua says he was sent out of Haiti to avoid being drafted into the militia; and the contemporary account of Mrs. Judd confirms that there were fears that "he might be arrested and pressed into the army."[119] This threat presumably relates to the protracted war in which President Soulouque of Haiti (who had

118. Letter of Mrs. N.A.L. Judd, 21 July 1848.
119. Letter of Mrs. N.A.L. Judd, 4 December 1849, in *Christian Contributor and Free Missionary*, 3 January 1850. In late 1849, the *Journal of Commerce* (as reported in the *New York Daily Tribune*, 13 December 1849) noted that Emperor Faustin Soulouque had "almost unlimited power for increasing the military," thereby providing confirmation that such fears of conscription were wide spread and well founded.

proclaimed himself Emperor Faustin I earlier in 1849) was currently engaged on the Spanish side of the island of Hispaniola.[120] But this circumstance can only have determined the precise timing of his return to the United States; the overriding reason for this return, which had been projected since the previous year, was to advance his education, with a view to returning to Africa as part of a mission.

After a brief stay in New York, as reported by Mrs. Judd, she, her sister, and Baquaqua proceeded by steamer to Albany, from where they "took the cars" to Fort Plain and then went by stagecoach to the sisters' parental home in Milford. They also visited Meredith, in near-by Delaware County, where the Rev. Mr. Judd had been pastor for seven years. They had now entered the Baptist and abolitionist networks of the United States, and everywhere they stayed and visited they solicited donations to support Baquaqua in his future educational career. As Mrs. Judd observed, "They manifested a deep interest in Mahommah … [in] every family where we visited, and this interest was manifested by giving him money, or substantial articles of clothing, &c."[121] According to the *Biography*, Baquaqua remained four weeks in Milford, before moving from there to Meredith, "amongst the Free Missions," where the subject of his further education was discussed, and to his relief, "they agreed at once [to] undertake the task of educating me" (p. 62). This probably refers to a meeting of the Board of the American Baptist Free Mission Society, which was attended by Baquaqua, together with Mrs. Judd and her sister, and where he spoke about his desire to return to Africa as a missionary.[122] Further efforts were made to raise funds for him; in the following year, the Annual Meeting of the Free Mission Society expressed its thanks to the Free Mission Society of Franklin, New York, for having

120. For Faustin Soulouque's period of rule in Haïti, see James G. Leyburn, *The Haitian People* (New Haven, 1966): 91–93 and contemporary reports in *Christian Contributor and Free Missionary*, *New York Daily Tribune*, and *National Anti-Slavery Standard*.
121. Letter of Mrs. N.A.L. Judd, 28 March 1850, in *Christian Contributor and Free Missionary*, 18 April 1850.
122. ABFMS, Seventh Annual Meeting, Bristol, Ontario Co., New York, 5–7 June 1850.

"kindly [come] forward and ministered to his needs."[123] This was not
to be Baquaqua's last fund-raising mission. Later he also visited other
towns where abolitionists were prominent, often for the purpose of
raising money for his education and then increasingly to sponsor his
return to Africa. Baquaqua's tour of the Free Baptist network introduced him to abolitionists throughout upstate New York, especially in
Syracuse, Utica, and McGrawville, and later also in eastern Pennsylvania.

Between 1850–53, Baquaqua attended New York Central College
in McGrawville. This institution had been established in December
1848, and opened for students in September 1849. The College was
located in the finger lake district of upstate New York. As an abolitionist institution established by the American Baptist Free Mission
Society, Central College admitted women as well as blacks. Its char-
ter stated the basic commitments of the Free Baptists, "unchangeably
pledged to the morality of Anti-slavery; and…the unity, equity, and
brotherhood of the human race." The College was also committed
"equal advantages in literary, scientific, moral and physical education" for women.[124] Baquaqua, with Mrs. Judd and her sister, arrived
at Central College in McGrawville on 16 January 1850; a letter from
the latter records the dinner held for their reception, at which the
President of the College, Cyrus Grosvenor, and Baquaqua himself
both spoke; she praised the commitment to equality, without respect

123. Ibid.
124. Central College closed its doors in 1861, primarily because its benefactor, Gerrit
Smith, refused to provide additional financing unless the College was reorganized, but efforts
to appoint suitable candidates to run the institution failed. For a history of the College, see
Kenneth R. Short, "New York Central College: A Baptist experiment in integrated higher education, 1848–61," *Foundations: A Baptist Journal of History and Theology* 1 (1962): 250–56;
Seymour B. Dunn, "The early academies of Cortland County," *Cortland County Chronicles*, I
(1957): 71–76; Albert Hazen Wright, ed., "Cornell's Three Precursors: I. New York Central
College" (Studies in History No. 23, Pre-Cornell and Early Cornell VIII, Ithaca, 1960); Cathe-
rine M. Hanchett, "'Dedicated to Equality and Brotherhood': New York Central College, C.P.
Grosvenor, and Gerrit Smith," (paper presented at the Madison County Historical Society,
Oneida, New York, 16 February 1989).

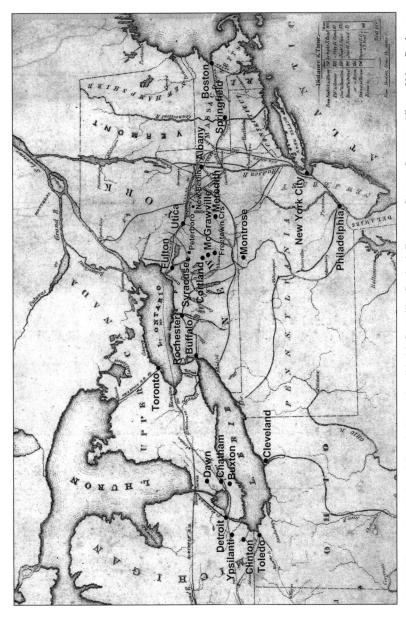

MAP 4. Upstate New York and Canada West: Meredith, McGrawville, Cortland, Freetown Corners, Syracuse, Albany, Utica, Rochester, Fultonville, Peterboro, Buffalo, Toronto, Detroit, Buxton, Windsor, Clifton, Montrose, Toledo, Cleveland, Philadelphia, New York, Springfield, Boston.

to gender, race or authority, which she witnessed during the event.[125] Br. J. Scott of the Baptist Church, Elgin, Illinois, was in attendance at a prayer meeting in the College on the following night, Saturday 17 January, and reported that Mrs. Judd and her sister had "brought a colored youth with them, named Mahommah." He understood that "He is a native of Africa, and was kidnapped by some of the natives of America [sic] ... He is to be a student here; and will probably, some time or other, bear the glad tidings of salvation to central Africa."[126]

Baquaqua joined the College in the middle of its first year in operation, the school having opened the previous September. He was enrolled in the Primary Department, the preparatory school for the College.[127] His teacher, Miss Kezia King, wrote a report on her experience teaching his class, although she did not specifically mention Baquaqua.[128] She also wrote a poem which was to be recited by Baquaqua and which is quoted in the *Biography* (pp. 62–63). While he was there, Central College grew to about 200 students, half of whom were women. There were other blacks besides Baquaqua,

125. Letter of E.C. Lake, 18 February 1850, in *Christian Contributor and Free Missionary*, 7 March 1850.126. Letter of J. Scott, 22 January 1850, in *Christian Contributor and Free Missionary*, 7 March 1850.

127. Various documents which mention Baquaqua at Central College are on deposit in the New York Central College Collection, Cortland County Historical Society, Cortland, New York, specifically "Labor Lists of Males and Females," for January–June, September, and October 1850; the Commencement Program, 4 July 1850; and the Catalogues of the Officers and Students 1851–52 and 1852–53, which both list him as a student in the Primary Department. Unlike the advanced program, which was organized in three terms, instruction in the Primary Department was given in four sessions of twelve weeks each in the year, with one week vacation between the terms; the tuition fee being $4 per term. It should be noted that Frederick Douglass addressed commencement on 2 September 1853, although whether or not Baquaqua was in attendance is not clear. His surviving correspondence suggests that he was not in McGrawville at the time.

128. Kezia King is listed as teacher in the Primary Department in the *Catalogue of the Officers and Students of New York Central* College for 1851–52 and 1852–53. Her report to the Board of Trustees, Central College, 11 July 11, 1853, is in Miscellaneous Scrapbook & McGraw Schools and Central College, vol. 108, Cortland County Historical Society, Cortland, New York.

including Joseph Purvis, Robert Purvis and James Forten, the sons of prominent black families from Philadelphia.[129] There was one other student who had been born in Africa, John Lom Lagrow, from Senegambia, also enrolled in the Primary Department, with whom Baquaqua roomed for a time in during 1852.[130] Baquaqua's education continued to be financed by charitable donations, organized through the Free Mission Society; as the Board of the Society reported to its Annual Meeting in 1852:

> Eld. B.F. Remington in connection with brethren Silus Hammond and Ezra Thompson are a committee of the Board to oversee and make arrangements for that education which is necessary to prepare him for wider usefulness on his return [sc. to Africa]. Through their exertions, those of some others, and his own labors, enough has been obtained to meet his expenses to the present.[131]

129. For references to the students who attended Central College, see Catherine M. Hanchett, "New York Central College Students" (Cortland County Historical Society, 1997); also "After McGrawville: The Later Careers of Some African American Students from New York Central College" (paper presented before the Cortland County Historical Society, 26 February 1992); on the Forten family, see Julie Winch, "'You Know I am a Man of Business': James Forten and the factor of race in Philadelphia's antebellum business community," *Business and Economic History* 26, no. 1 (1997): 213–28; and Gary B. Nash, *Forging Freedom: The Formation of Philadelphia's Black Community, 1720–1840* (Cambridge, MA, 1988).

130. Lagrow joined the College in 1852. His place of residence is given as "Senegambia, Africa" in the *Catalogue of the Officers & Students* for 1852/3. He is said to have come from Africa two years earlier "as a cabin boy on a vessel"; he had lived the previous year with a family at Augusta, Maine, but had then been taken by J. E. Ambrose to Utica and then to Syracuse, where Gerrit Smith, the principal benefactor of Central College, "manifested a very deep interest in his welfare" and paid for his fare to McGrawville: letter of J.E. Ambrose to W. Walker, 27 July 1852, in *The American Baptist*, 5 August 1852. On 1 August 1852 Lagrow wrote to Smith asking for money to buy boots and a pair of pants, identifying himself as being "from Africa" (Gerrit Smith Collection, Special Collections, Syracuse University Library, Syracuse, New York). In a letter to Ambrose dated 17 July 1852, in *The American Baptist*, Lagrow wrote, "I wish to inform you that I am well, and well pleased with my school and place. I am boarding with Mr. Briggs on the College farm, and at work for him the most of the time that I labor. I think I am doing well in my studies, and think we have very good teachers, and I feel glad that I came here. I room with Mahommah, and find him a very pleasant companion…".

131. Ninth Annual Meeting, Montrose, Pennsylvania, as reported in *The American Baptist*, 24 June 1852.

However, Baquaqua also contributed to his own living expenses, for at least part of his time at Central College, by leasing and cultivating land locally.[132]

The *Catalogue of Officers and Students* of Central College for the years 1851/52 and 1852/53 lists Baquaqua's place of residence as McGrawville;[133] and the *Biography* indicates that he roomed in the College (p. 63). According to his roommate Lagrow, part of the time Baquaqua lived at the college farm.[134] However, he may have resided during part of this period at Freetown Corners, a few miles from McGrawville, or at least maintained connections there: two letters by him which were published in the *American Baptist* in 1850–51 were both written from Freetown; and later, at least, he was a member of the Baptist Church there.[135] He was also active in wider Free Baptist networks, partly in order to raise funds for his education. In September 1851 he spoke at the Semi-Annual Meeting of the Baptist Free Mission Society, held at Peterboro, New York, the home of Gerrit Smith, where a collection of $2.35 was made for his benefit.[136] And in June 1852 he attended the Annual Meeting of the Society, this time at Montrose, Pennsylvania, where "Mahommah, the converted Africa, led in prayer," after which a collection in aid of his education was taken up.[137]

At Central College, as earlier in Haiti, Baquaqua seems to have been an assiduous student, in contrast to his own reports of his earlier educational experiences in Djougou, where he had dropped out of school. When he spoke to the Board of the Free Mission Society in

132. Letter of Baquaqua to George Whipple, 6 January 1854 (see Appendix 3, no. 11).

133. The *Catalogue of Officers and Students* for these years are to be found in the Cortland County Historical Society, Cortland, New York.

134. Letter from Lagrow to Gerrit Smith, 1 August 1852 (Gerrit Smith Collection, Special Collections, Syracuse University Library, Syracuse, New York.

135. Letters of Baquaqua to W. Walker [?], 28 September 1850, 21 February 1851 (see Appendix 3, nos. 3, 4); and to George Whipple, 26 October 1853. The last letter states that he had been friendly with a white girl who was also a member of the Freetown Baptist Church, since "about three years ago," i.e., since autumn 1850, around the time of his first letter from Freetown Corners.

136. *The American Baptist*, 11 September 1851.

137. ABFMS, Ninth Annual Meeting, Montrose, Pennsylvania, 2–4 June 1852.

1850, it was noted that his English was still poor, although he was nevertheless positively received: "Though imperfectly acquainted with our language, his prayers and exhortations testify to every hearer that he had been truly taught of Christ."[138] During his time at Central College, the *Biography* claims that he "made very great progress in learning" (p. 62); and this is supported by an approving report of the Board of the Free Mission Society in 1853 that "his fidelity to Christ continues unchanged; [and] his progress in knowledge is encouraging."[139] Yet it is clear that he had continuing trouble with English, perhaps especially with the spoken word, although he wrote (in his extant letters) carefully and intelligibly, if ungrammatically. A report of 1853, after he had left Central College, refers to the "quite broken English" which he still spoke, although it also noted that "he improves [as] rapidly as could reasonably be anticipated in communicating his thoughts"; and he was clearly an effective speaker, to the extent that audiences liked him and warmed to his story, despite the deficiencies of his English.[140]

According to the *Biography* Baquaqua studied at Central College for "nearly three years" (p. 62), which indicates that he left around the end of 1852 or the beginning of 1853, in the middle of the academic session. The reason for his departure is not given, but it may be suspected that his performance was judged inadequate to proceed to more advanced study. After leaving Central College, according to the *Biography*, he initially continued his education in a school at Freetown Corners, also "under the direction of the missions" (p. 63); although no confirmation of this has been traced in Free Mission records. In the summer of 1853, however, as he later complained, his "friends" decided that his education should be discontinued or suspended, so that he could devote his time to fund-raising for the projected African mission in which he was intended to serve.[141] In June

138. ABFMS, Seventh Annual Meeting, Bristol, New York, 5–7 June 1850.
139. ABFMS, Tenth Annual Meeting, Utica, New York, 1–2 June 1853.
140. Letter of A.L.Post, July 1853, in *The American Baptist*, 28 July 1853.
141. Letter of Baquaqua to George Whipple, 8 October 1853 (see Appendix 3, no. 10).

1853, shortly after the Annual Meeting of the Free Mission Society in Utica, New York, which Baquaqua attended, the Society's Board charged him with touring Baptist Churches to solicit donations;[142] though on this, conversely, the *Biography* is curiously silent. The fund-raising campaign began in eastern Pennsylvania,[143] but Baquaqua soon returned to New York State. His surviving letters show that he was again resident in McGrawville by August 1853, although during August and September he successively visited Brooklyn, Syracuse and New Berlin; whether any of these visits were in connection with his fund-raising activities for the Free Mission Society is not indicated.[144]

Although Baquaqua moved within the Free Baptist network, he was also exposed to the ugly racist face of upstate New York. In the *Biography* he reports a series of incidents of harassment against him by fellow-students in McGrawville, which he believed were racially inspired: "I could not tell why they plagued me thus, excepting that did not like my color" (p. 63). His experience indicates that it was difficult for a black man even in supposedly abolitionist McGrawville. In a scandal which occurred during the period of his residence, William Allen, a black professor at Central College, became involved with one of his students, Mary King, a white girl from Fulton whose father was a minister and avowedly an abolitionist.[145] When Allen

142. This decision is reported retrospectively in ABFMS, Eleventh Annual Meeting, Albany, New York, 7–8 June 1854.

143. Letter of A.L. Post, July 1853, in *The American Baptist*, 28 July 1853.

144. Letters of Baquaqua to George Whipple, 10 August 1853 (from Brooklyn), 14 September 1853 (from Syracuse); to unnamed recipient, 18 September 1853 & to George Whipple, 25 September 1853 (both from New Berlin); and to George Whipple, 8 October 1853 (from McGrawville) (see Appendix 3, nos. 6–11).

145. For Allen's story, see William G. Allen, *American Prejudice against Colour: An Authentic Narrative, showing how easily the Nation got into an Uproar* (London, 1853); and his letters in Carter G. Woodson ed., *The Mind of the Negro as Reflected in Letters Written during the Crisis, 1800–1860* (New York, 1969): 282–90. Various letters and speeches of Allen and his wife are also published in C. Peter Ripley, ed., *The Black Abolitionist Papers. Volume I. The British Isles, 1830–1865* (Chapel Hill, 1985): 355–82; 423–26, 453–56. For an analysis, see Carleton Mabee, *Black Education in New York State* (Syracuse, 1979): 85–92. Also see Catherine M. Hanchett, "New York Central College and its Three Black Professors, 1849–1857," (paper presented at conference on "A Heritage Uncovered: the Black Experience in New York State," Elmira, New York, 22 April 1989). Allan Austin confuses Mary King, the women whom Prof. Allen married, and Baquaqua's teacher, Miss Kezia King; see *Transatlantic Stories*, 167.

went to visit her, he found himself exposed to the virulent hostility of the community, including the supposedly abolitionist King family, only Mary's sister remaining loyal to the couple. On 30 January 1853, a mob of local people drove Allen out of town; he was lucky that he was not lynched. He and Mary arranged to meet in New York, where they were married on 30 March, sailing from Boston for England on 9 April. In England, the couple was active on the abolitionist lecture circuit, also touring extensively in Ireland.[146] The Allen-King romance was condemned in much of the upstate New York press.[147]

Although Baquaqua does not mention the Allen-King affair, either in the *Biography* or in his extant letters, it seems likely that it had indirect repercussions in his personal life. Like Allen, Baquaqua also became close friends with a white girl, who was a fellow member of the Baptist Church at Freetown Corners and with whom he had become friends shortly after his arrival in McGrawville. Around June 1853, rumors began circulating that he intended to marry this girl. Despite his denials, her mother banned him from her household. In October of the same year, after further rumors that the couple intended imminently to marry, Baquaqua was warned not to attend the church at Freetown Corners because persons opposed to the supposed marriage might "do very bad to me." Faced with this explicit threat of violence, he observed that "I have to be very careful, I don't go out much … I have a great trouble with these wickit [wicked] people."[148] The pressure thus placed upon him to distance himself from his friend presumably reflected local recollections of the incident involving Professor Allen, which had occurred only a few months earlier.

By the latter half of 1853, indeed, it seems that Baquaqua was increasingly disillusioned with United States society. In August of that year, he asserted that, if he could not go to Africa, he would not stay in the U.S.A., "I did not like to stay in this country"; and again in September, "I think I shall not remain in the United States long";

146. Allen, *American Prejudice against Color*, 2, 86.
147. For a sample of press coverage, see the *Syracuse Star*, 1 February 1854; *Oswego Daily Times*, 3 February 1854; both cited in Allen, *American Prejudice against Color*, 53–56, 71–74.
148. See Baquaqua's letter to George Whipple, 26 October 1853.

instead, he said, he would go to Canada.[149] His letters indicate that he intended to leave McGrawville for Canada in late October;[150] and very likely he did, this being the visit to Canada for "a short time" mentioned in the *Biography* (p. 64). By January 1854, as his letters show, he was back in McGrawville;[151] but he presumably left definitively for Canada West soon afterwards. The *Biography* reports his very favorable impressions of Canada: "I was kindly received by all classes wherever I went ... I am thankful to God ... that I am now in a land ... where every man acting as a man, no matter what his color, is regarded as a brother, and where all are equally free to do and to say" (p. 64); the contrast with his experience in the United States, although implicit, is pointed.

In the *Biography* Baquaqua claims that he took out naturalization papers in Canada (which would technically have made him a British citizen) (p. 64). Although no records appear to have survived, it is likely that he was registered, as other fugitives from the United States were, for the purpose of providing him with documentation that could be used to foil would-be bounty hunters from the U.S.A. who occasionally tried to kidnap refugees and return them to their masters south of the border.[152] In Canada, he settled at Chatham, from where his only extant letter from Canada was written, in May 1854. Chatham, located on the Thames River and connecting via Lake St. Clair with Detroit, was the center of the largest concentration of black immigrants in southwestern Canada West.[153] Nearby Buxton, located

149. Letters of Baquaqua to George Whipple, 10 August & 8 October 1853.
150. Letter of Baquaqua to Whipple, 26 October 1853.
151. Letters of Baquaqua to Whipple, 6 & 22 January 1854.
152. Robin Winks, *The Blacks in Canada* (Montreal & Kingston, Ont., 2nd ed., 1997): 244–71.
153. Letter of Baquaqua to Gerrit Smith, 25 May 1854 (see Appendix 3, no. 14). At the time, there were approximately 800 blacks living in Chatham, and perhaps another 1,200 or more living in Buxton and other neighbouring communities; see Drew, *North-Side View of Slavery*, 234, 291; Winks, *Blacks in Canada*, 245; and Michael Wayne, "The Black population of Canada West on the eve of the American Civil War: A reassessment based on the manuscript census of 1861," in Franca Iacovetta, Paula Draper, and Robert Ventresca, eds., *A Nation of Immigrants: Women, Workers, and Communities in Canadian History, 1840s–1960s* (Toronto, 1998): 73. Also see John Kevin Anthony Farrell, "The History of the Negro Community in Chatham, Ontario" (Ph.D. diss., University of Ottawa, 1955).

a few kilometers south of Chatham, had been founded in 1849 as an all-black community of landowning farmers under the patronage of the Rev. William King, a Presbyterian minister and former slave owner. The black community at Dawn, to the north of Chatham, was established as a center of education and training under the leadership of Josiah Henson, allegedly the model for the Uncle Tom of Harriet Beecher Stowe's *Uncle Tom's Cabin*. As the commercial and trans-portation center, Chatham became one of the principal foci for the refugee population. In choosing to settle at Chatham, Baquaqua may have been using his connections in the Free Mission Society, since it was one of the places in Canada West where this body worked. However, the influence of the Free Mission in Society in Canada was now in decline; at this time it was winding up its management of the Dawn settlement, which was forced into receivership in 1854. The administration of the Dawn settlement had been fiercely criticized by the Rev. William Newman, also of the Free Mission Society, now based in Toronto. Newman, who had earlier volunteered to travel with Baquaqua to Africa to install the "Africa Mission," had met Baquaqua at the annual meetings of the Free Mission Society. Newman had let Baquaqua down by withdrawing from the African Mission, however, so Baquaqua may not have visited Newman in Toronto, but it is pos-sible that the paths of the two men crossed in 1854.

However, it is clear that Baquaqua's relations with the Free Mission Society had by now become somewhat strained, and it is likely that he developed other contacts, perhaps specifically through Gerrit Smith, who at the time was a Congressman from upstate New York and well known in Canada West through the Underground Railroad network, and with whom Baquaqua corresponded during his period of residence in Canada.[154] In his letter to Smith in May 1854, Baquaqua confides his anguish over the failure of the Baptist Free

154. For the Free Mission in Canada West, see ABFMS, Annual Reports; and Winks, *Blacks in Canada*, 231, 238. For Gerrit Smith's influence in Canada West, see Winks, *Blacks in Canada*, 179–80, 254.

Mission to fulfill its commitment to an African Mission, with which he had intended to be attached. With his hopes of returning to Africa undermined, he appears to have contemplated settling permanently in North America; he specifically requested assistance from Smith in buying land in Canada (probably at nearby Buxton which required that settlers be landowners). Alternatively, he suggested that he be granted land in New York State, presumably because he knew that Smith had been giving land to blacks and poor whites from his vast holdings in the Adirondack Mountains. However, evidently nothing came of this request. In July 1854, Baquaqua went to Detroit, to arrange the publication of the *Biography*, where he wrote again to Smith, this time soliciting his help in meeting the cost of printing.[155] Nonetheless, his letter makes it clear that he intended to return to Chatham, where he probably resided until January 1855, when he went to New York City to board a ship for England.

Baquaqua's Attempts to Return to Africa

From his association with the Free Baptists in Port-au-Prince, if not earlier, Baquaqua was destined to return to Africa. The Rev. Mr. Judd saw in him the prospect of a successful African Mission, and the training and guidance provided to Baquaqua was directed at achieving this end. Shortly after Baquaqua moved into his household in October 1847, Judd expressed his wish for the "speedy conversion of Mahommah," so that he might become "a missionary to his native land," which Judd (as noted earlier) then believed to be Katsina. What Judd had in mind was apparently that Baquaqua would serve as interpreter and local guide to an American missionary; he expressed the hope that the Baptists in the U.S.A. would be on the lookout for "a man properly qualified to accompany him," including having a knowledge of "Hebrew and Arabic."[156] Whether Baquaqua himself yet

155. Letter of Baquaqua to Gerrit Smith, 4 July 1854 (see Appendix 3, no. 15). On Smith's land grants to blacks, see Tanner, "Gerrit Smith," 29–30.
156. Letter of Rev. W.L. Judd, 28 October 1847.

shared this desire to return to Africa is not clear; but after his conversion in March 1848 he explicitly declared his interest in so doing. Mrs. Judd then reported that, "For the first time since he has lived with us, he expressed a desire to go back to Africa, to tell them about Jesus Christ," a wording which leaves unclear whether what was new was his desire to return home, or his intention to preach Christianity there. Again in July, shortly after Baquaqua's baptism, she observed that, "he appears to have an increasing desire for Africa, which we feel to encourage." Likewise, the Rev. Mr. Judd, reporting his baptism, said that he "talks much of Africa, and prays ardently that her people may receive the Gospel—dreams often of visiting Kachna [Katsina], accompanied by 'a good white man,' as he calls a missionary."[157] And in a letter to Cyrus Grosvenor later in 1848, Baquaqua himself declared: "By-and-by I want to go back to Africa, and see my friends and tell all the people about Jesus Christ."[158] Despite his own sustained efforts over several years and some support from the Free Mission Society, his desire to get back to Africa was not realized, at least by 1857, when he drops out of the historical record.

The project of education for Baquaqua in the U.S.A., as the *Biography* notes (p. 59), was explicitly conceived with the intention of training him for missionary work in Africa; he reiterated his commitment to the latter from time to time during his period of study at New York Central College. At the meeting of the Board of the Free Mission Society in 1850, for example, he spoke to this purpose:

His soul was full of the desire to return as a missionary of the gospel to Africa, the land of his birth and whence he was stolen. He feels that unless his mother and other relatives, of whom he makes frequent, mention, can learn of Christ, they are lost.[159]

---

157. Letters of Mrs. N.A.L. Judd, 24 March & 21 July 1848; Rev. W.L. Judd, 21 July 1848; Rev. W.L. Judd, 21 July 1848.

158. Letter of Baquaqua to Cyrus Grosvenor 14 November 1848.

159. ABFMS, Seventh Annual Meeting, Bristol, New York, 5–7 June 1850.

In a letter of 1851, he asked for prayers "that God will help me in my studies, and send me back to Africa, that I may tell my poor friends about the Saviour who died for our sins and rose again."[160] In 1852, when he attended the Annual Meeting of the Free Mission Society, he reiterated his desire to return home as a missionary: "how ardently he longed to make known to them the good news of salvation."[161]

The proposed African mission, and Baquaqua's intended role in it were regularly discussed by the Board of the Free Mission Society from 1848 onwards, as recorded in its successive Annual Reports to the Society. These make clear that what was envisaged remained that Baquaqua would act as an assistant to an American missionary, rather than operate on his own. In 1852 its Committee on the African Mission explicitly recommended that "the return of Mahommah [to Africa] be deferred until a suitable person be obtained to accompany him." During that same year, in fact, this problem appeared to have been solved, when William P. Newman, who was active in the Society's mission in Canada West, offered his services: "If it is the will of God, I am ready to go to Africa with Br. Mahommah and do what I can";[162] a "sister" whose name was withheld also volunteered for the mission to Africa. The Board of the Society noted that, "It is still the desire of Mahommah, the converted African, to return to the

---

160. Letter of Baquaqua to W. Walker [?], 21 February 1851.

161. This speech is referred to retrospectively in the Report of the following year's meeting: ABFMS, Tenth Annual Meeting, Utica, New York, 1–2 June 1853.

162. William P. Newman, an African-American from Ohio, wrote "The Colored People of Canada," for the *Christian Contributor and Free Missionary* (13 September 1848) and was secretary to the executive committee of the Dawn settlement in 1845, was pastor at the Second Baptist Church in Detroit in 1849, and otherwise "labored among the colored people of Canada West." He was a relentless critic of Josiah Henson and arguably undermined the development of the Dawn Settlement (*Christian Contributor and Free Missionary*, 20 June 1849; also see the *Kent Advertiser*, 4 July 1850). He became the pastor of the Baptist Church in Toronto in 1853 and was appointed editor of the *Provincial Freeman* in 1855. Newman and Baquaqua both addressed the semi-annual meeting of the American Baptist Free Missionary Society in Utica on 5 September 1851 (*The American Baptist*, 11 September 1851), and they probably met at other meetings of the Society. Newman was a frequent correspondent for *The American Baptist* between 1851 and 1855, whereupon he used the *Provincial Freeman* as his voice.

land of his nativity as a missionary of the Cross," and recommended that:

> In reference to an African mission, the Board are of the opinion, that, under existing circumstances, such as the want of means and information, Eld. Newman had better be appointed as a missionary to Africa; that he be recommended to visit the churches in behalf of the contemplated mission, and that he continue to collect funds until enough shall be raised to sustain him for at least two years after his arrival in Africa.[163]

For reasons which are unclear, however, the proposed linking of Newman with Baquaqua in the African Mission fell through; instead of going to Africa, Newman accepted the pastorate of the First Baptist Church in Toronto, which he took up in December 1852.[164] At the Annual Meeting of the Society in Utica, New York in June 1853, the Board had to report that still, "No suitable person has yet appeared ... to be joined with Mahommah in the attempt to introduce Christianity among his people at Zougo."[165]

At the 1853 Annual Meeting, Baquaqua was appointed, together with Albert L. Post of Montrose, Pennsylvania, and Warham Walker, the editor of *The American Baptist*, to the Society's Committee on the African Mission.[166] He was then employed in a more systematic campaign to raise funds for the projected mission, and for his own return to Africa. As reported by Post from Montrose in July 1853, Baquaqua "has spent a little time in this and a few neighboring places, collecting funds for the contemplated African mission ... the plan is to send him to such pastors of churches, or other religious persons, as will

163. ABFMS, Ninth Annual Meeting, Montrose, Pennsylvania, 2–4 June 1852; also reported in *The American Baptist*, 24 June 1852.
164. Newman's letter of 4 January 1853, in *The American Baptist*, 20 January 1853.
165. ABFMS, Tenth Annual Meeting, Utica, New York, 1–2 June 1853; *The American Baptist*, 28 July 1853.
166. Ibid.

take an interest in the mission to labor under their general direction."
Baquaqua's approach was to talk about his own life and the "manners, customs &c. of his native country," anticipating the content and
perhaps the form of the later *Biography*; it was probably in this context that the idea of publishing the latter was conceived. According to
Post, his talks went down well with his audiences, speaking "uni-
formly with interest to his hearers," despite the continuing deficiencies of his English; he had already raised $200 in money and
pledges.[167] At the same time, however, the Society's difficulties in
finding anyone to accompany Baquaqua to Africa persisted. On 1
September 1853, the Board instructed the African Mission Committee to "correspond with several individuals named, in regard to
their becoming Missionaries in Africa", but as the Board once again
reported to the following annual meeting in June 1854, "no such missionary has ... yet been secured."[168]

By the latter half of 1853, Baquaqua was beginning to become disillusioned with the Free Mission Society and skeptical of its ability to
secure his return to Africa. He thought that the Society's fund-raising
target was over-ambitious; they expected him to raise $5,000, appar-
ently within two years, which he did not think was possible. In a letter written in August 1853 (addressed to a third party, not to the
Society itself), he declared that he "did not think that my friends will
do anything in my mission."[169] By now, in fact, he was looking for an
alternative sponsor and made contact with the American Missionary
Association, a Congregationalist body based in New York City, with
whose Secretary, George Whipple, he corresponded between August
1853 and January 1854, in the hope of securing employment. In
August 1853 Baquaqua himself was in Brooklyn, apparently hoping
for a personal meeting with Whipple, though whether this took place
is not known.[170] The American Missionary Association had estab-

167. Letter of A.L. Post, July, 1853, in *The American Baptist*, 28 July 1853.
168. ABFMS, Eleventh Annual Meeting, Albany, New York, 7–8 June 1854.
169. Letter of Baquaqua to George Whipple, 10 August 1853.
170. Ibid.

lished the Mendi Mission, led by George Thompson, which returned
the surviving members of the successful slave revolt on the *Amistad*
to Sierra Leone in 1841. This mission had difficulty in maintaining its
numbers, and was reinforced in the early 1850s.[171] Baquaqua offered
his services for the Mendi Mission, apparently thinking that he might
be able to proceed from Sierra Leone to his home in Djougou: in one
of his letters he asked, "if I go with Br Thompson, do you think we
can try to found [= find] my Mother and Sister and Brother in
Africa?"[172]

The attitude of the American Missionary Association itself to this
approach is not directly documented, since we have only Baquaqua's
side of the correspondence, but his letters seem to be responding to a
series of objections or queries raised by Whipple, relating to his linguistic competence, personal conduct, and religious affiliation, and
also to the prospect of financial support from the Baptist Free Mission. Baquaqua pressed his qualifications as an interpreter, admitting
the limitations of his competence in English, but stressing his knowledge of the Arabic and "Zogoo [i.e., Dendi]" languages; the phrase of
Arabic which he included in one of his letters, noted earlier, was presumably intended to demonstrate his potential usefulness as a trans-
lator. However, he also offered, if he was not considered adequately
qualified to serve as a teacher or interpreter, to serve Thompson (as
he had Judd earlier) as a cook. Despite the evidently lukewarm
response of Whipple, Baquaqua initially expected to go to Africa with
the Mendi mission before the end of 1853: in August he wrote, "I
made my mand [= mind] to go to Africa this fall"; and in September,
"Please ... tell me when the vessel will go to Africa, if it will go in
October or December." But by January 1854, his hopes were reced-
ing into the remoter future: "I should like to know, if I will go to

---

171. Christopher Fyfe, *A History of Sierra Leone* (London, 1962): 222–23, 246, 285.
172. Letter of Baquaqua to George Whipple, 25 September 1853. Baquaqua's handwriting
is not clear in this letter, and he could have written "sisters" rather than "sister"; in the
Biography (p. 24), he reported that he had three sisters.

Africa, this year or next year."[173] In the end, he evidently gave up hope altogether and left for Canada.

It appears from this correspondence that Baquaqua initially approached the American Missionary Association without the knowledge of the Baptist Free Mission Society: as he admitted in August 1853: "I not gone [= going] to say anything about you or anybody else to my friends." Whipple evidently insisted that he should clear the matter with them, and in October he reported: "I have consulted some of my friends and no objection has been made as yet, to my going to Africa in connexion with the Mendi mission."[174] Nevertheless, it appears that some degree of distance now emerged in relations between Baquaqua and his Baptist sponsors. At the Annual Meeting of the Free Mission Society in June 1854, reference was made to the fund-raising activities for the projected African mission with which Baquaqua had been charged in the previous year:

> At the first meeting of the Board after the Anniversary, in June last, Mahommah G. Baquaqua was authorized to visit, under the supervision of a Committee appointed for that purpose, certain pastors, and to seek aid from them and their churches for the purpose of opening a mission in Africa. It is understood that he did thus visit, to some extent; but with what results is not definitely known to us.[175]

This makes clear that communication with Baquaqua, now at Chatham in Canada West, had become tenuous, if not broken down altogether. However, the somewhat coy wording of this report, by implication blaming Baquaqua for the lapse of contact, appears to conceal a more overt breach. Baquaqua himself, in his letter to Gerrit

---

173. Letters of Baquaqua to George Whipple, 10 August & 14 September 1853, 6 January 1854.
174. Letters of Baquaqua to George Whipple, 10 August & 8 October 1853.
175. ABFMS, Eleventh Annual Meeting, Albany, New York, 7–8 June 1854.

Smith in May 1854, was more robust in his expression, and explicit
in blaming the Society: "I am very sorry to inform you that the Free
Mission has kill[ed] the Africa Mission, and kill[ed] Mahommah
too… The Free Mission did not do right by me at this time."[176] This
evidently explains why the *Biography* was published under his own
name rather than, as might have been anticipated, under the auspices
of the Free Mission Society; it is indicative that when he needed money to finance the printing of the book a few weeks later, it was Smith
as a potential individual benefactor, rather than the Society, whom he
approached. The Annual Reports of the Society for 1854 and 1855
make no reference to the publication. However, *The American Baptist*
published a review of it in November 1854, hence it was known to its
readership at least.[177]

Baquaqua presumably hoped that the *Biography* would finally
elicit the necessary funds for his return to Africa. But the response
may have been disappointing; certainly the pamphlet does not seem
to have circulated widely or to have attracted much attention. In January 1855, evidently in frustration, Baquaqua decided to leave America for England, in the hope of getting from there to Africa. The
Annual Meeting of the American Baptist Free Mission Society, held
in New York City in May 1855, once again noted the lack of progress
in realizing the projected African mission, due to the failure to find
anybody willing to go. But it was reported that, in any case,

> In the mean time, Mahommah G. Baquaqua, the African con-
> vert, to whom the attention of the Society has been directed in
> the hope that he might one day become useful to such mission-
> aries, as an interpreter,—yearning for his home and kindred, and
> weary and heart-sick, of hope long deferred,—has gone, with
> such slender resources as he could collect, to seek his mother.
> He sailed from New York about the 30th January last, for

176. Letter of Baquaqua to Gerrit Smith (Appendix 3, no. 14).
177. *The American Baptist*, 2 November 1854 (text of review in Appendix 4).

PLATE 1 (page 72). Liverpool dock: "He sailed from New York . . . for Liverpool, —having letters of introduction to several persons . . ., from whom he expected counsel and aid in making his way to Africa" (ABFMS, Twelfth Annual Meeting, 1855); Shaw's Brow and St. George's Hall, Liverpool, 1849, in Ramsay Muir, *A History of Liverpool*, 2nd ed. (London: University Press of Liverpool, 1907), p. 313.

Liverpool,—having letters of introduction to several persons in the latter city, from whom he expected counsel and aid in making his way to Africa.[178]

It is not specified from whom in England Baquaqua hoped to secure assistance in returning to Africa. He may still have been working through Free Mission networks, since the Society had an agent in England, Edward Mathews, who had earlier published *Facts for Baptist Churches,* containing information on Baquaqua as well as the illustration of him with Rev. Judd; he was thus well acquainted with

178. ABFMS, Twelfth Annual Meeting, New York City, 9 May 1855. The Board reported that there had been further correspondence with "different brethren, on the question of their becoming, at some future time, missionaries to Africa, but nothing has been done with a view to present action."

Baquaqua's ambitions, if not also with him personally.[179] Though Mathews was based in Bristol rather than in Liverpool, where Baquaqua landed, Baquaqua may have hoped to contact him.[180] It is also conceivable that he was in touch with Professor Allen and his wife, formerly of New York Central College, who were now living in England, though likewise also in Bristol. Alternatively, however, it may be that, just as he had earlier approached the American Missionary Association, Baquaqua was hoping to enlist in an English-based mission to Africa; a likely candidate would have been the Baptist Missionary Society, one of whose missionaries, W.H. Webley, Baquaqua had known earlier in Haiti,[181] and which had maintained a mission in West Africa (at Doula, on the coast of Cameroun), in which it employed black personnel from Jamaica, since 1841. But if Baquaqua approached the English Baptists, he was evidently not enlisted for their Cameroun mission.[182] However, it may be that he was hoping to secure purely secular assistance, perhaps by paying or working for his passage on a commercial shipping service to Africa.

Despite his absence in England, Baquaqua remained in the thoughts of the American Baptist Free Mission Society, in connection

179. Mathews had been involved in the abortive Southern Mission of the ABFMS, retreating to England when conditions became unbearable in Kentucky in 1850; Edward Mathews, *The Autobiography of the Rev. E. Mathews, The "Father Dickson," of Mrs. Stowe's "Dred"* (London, 1853): 1–28; and R.J.M. Blackett, "William G. Allen: The Forgotten Professor," *Civil War History* 26 (1980): 39–52. Also see *The American Baptist*, 20 October 1853.

180. Mathews's appointment as the Society's agent in Britain had been renewed on an annual basis. At its 28 December 1854 meeting, the Board of Society "invited" Mathews "to return to this country early in the Spring," which means that it was possible for Baquaqua to have met him in England in early 1855; see the report of the ABFMS, Twelfth Annual Meeting, New York City, 9 May 1855.

181. Webley was based at Jacmel in southern Haïti and met Baquaqua in early November 1847, shortly after the latter's installation in the Judd household, when he suggested that, if the American Baptist Free Mission Society could not send Baquaqua as a missionary to Africa, the English Baptists might do so; see postscript, dated 5 November 1848, to letter of Rev. W.L. Judd, 28 October 1847. Baquaqua also accompanied Judd on a visit to Webley at Jacmel in 1849; see "Haitien Mission: W.L. Judd, Visit to Jacmel," in *Christian Contributor and Free Missionary*, 7 March 1849.

182. There is no reference to Baquaqua in Brian Stanley, *The History of the Baptist Missionary Society, 1792–1992* (Edinburgh, 1992).

with its continuing discussions of the projected African Mission. At the 1856 Annual Meeting, the Board noted that

> From the first the Society has proposed to itself a mission in Africa. It was hoped, ere long, that the providence of God, which strangely threw upon our hands Mahommah G. Baquaqua, a young native of Africa would open the way for the accomplishment of this much desired object. But hitherto efforts have seemed to be entire failures. Up to very recently, the door has seemed to be shut. It is now, however, evidently opened. Facts which have appeared in the Am. Baptist [*The American Baptist*], proving this, are worthy of a place in our report, and we give them hoping that they may awaken a suitable ardor in all to enter the field through that door.

The new opportunity to which the Board referred was a request for assistance from Baptists in Sierra Leone, which was also supported by George Thompson of the Mendi Mission, whom Baquaqua himself had previously approached. John J. Brown, acting pastor of the First Baptist Church in Freetown, Sierra Leone, whose membership consisted of African-American re-emigrants from Nova Scotia, had sent a plea for the Free Mission Society to send "a good minister" to take over leadership of the church. The Board expressed its customary hope that "neither the men nor the means may be wanting ... to establish and carry on this proposed mission," but once again no practical action resulted.[183] Whether the mention of Baquaqua in this context should be read as implying that he was still considered by the Society as a possible member of its African Mission is unclear; but given that the request from the Freetown Baptists was specifically for a minister, lack of the requisite training as well as his current distance may well have sabotaged any opportunity for him.

---

183. ABFMS, Thirteenth Annual Meeting, Norristown, Pennsylvania, 21–22 May 1856.

Meanwhile, Baquaqua's attempts to reach Africa from England were evidently also unsuccessful, since in 1857 he again approached the American Baptist Free Mission Society for assistance. The Board of the Society in February of that year noted an approach received from "Mahommah, the African educated in this country, now in England, expressing his desire to return and labor among his countrymen," but the decision on establishing such a mission was deferred for a year, and apparently no mission was ever sent.[184] We do not know what happened to Baquaqua after 1857.

Baquaqua's efforts to return to Africa were accompanied and supported by a self-conscious emphasis on his origins in that continent. At a prayer meeting after his baptism in Haiti in July 1848, as reported by Mrs Judd, after finding his English inadequate to express his feelings, he dramatically switched into his "native tongue," the effect of which Mrs. Judd found "thrilling."[185] Although on this occasion the action was presumably unpremeditated, Baquaqua subsequently exploited the dramatic effect of speaking in an African language deliberately: on his introduction to New York Central College in January 1850, as reported by Electa Lake, "Arabic and Indian [i.e., Native American] songs" were sung, the former presumably by Baquaqua, since this was followed by a conversation between him some "Indian" students of the College, "the former speaking in the Arabic and the latter replying in the Indian tongue, much to the diversion of all present."[186] Whether the language which he spoke on this and other occasions was really Arabic, of which his knowledge was probably limited to religious formulae, may be doubted; more likely, if he made an extended oration, it was in Dendi. At the commencement

184. *New York Free Mission Record*, 13 February 1857, which reports the meeting of the Board of the American Baptist Free Mission Society. We wish to thank Silvia Hunold Lara for this reference.

185. Letter of Mrs. N. A. L. Judd, 21 July 1848.

186. Letter of E. C. Lake, 18 February 1850, in *Christian Contributor and Free Missionary*, 7 March 1850. On 14 March 1850, the *Cortland County Express* of McGrawville noted that Baquaqua, who was referred to as "Mahoni" (i.e., Mahommah), spoke in "the Arabic" at public functions. (Our thanks to Anita Wright for this reference.)

ceremonies at the College later in 1850, Baquaqua again delivered "a speech in one of the African tongues."[187] It may also be noted that in the engraving on the cover of the *Biography*, Baquaqua is shown wearing African-style robes, in interesting contrast to the earlier photograph of him with the Rev. Mr. Judd, in which he appears in European dress. This evidently represents a further effort at promoting an exotic image of his African background.

No doubt there was an element of calculation in this emphasis on his identity as an African, since it was precisely his African origins which recommended him for employment by the Baptist Free Mission. But this employment in turn was attractive to Baquaqua precisely because it held out the prospect of his return to Africa. It may be suggested that a more positive assertion of his African roots was involved, and this is consistent with the fact, noted earlier, that the *Biography* is primarily a record of his life in Africa.

Reputation and Assessment

Statements in the *Biography* indicate that Baquaqua hoped to produce a second, longer version of the text. Samuel Moore's Preface states that, if Baquaqua succeeded in his ambition to go to Africa as a missionary, on his return he would re-issue the work "in a larger form, with the addition of matters that has [sic] either been entirely left out or curtailed for want of space," together with an account of his anticipated "success [sc. as a missionary] amongst his native race" (p. 8). A statement in the main text, probably also by Moore, indicates that it was specifically the African section of his life which Baquaqua intended to elaborate: "At some other time, should the public think fit to patronize these few stray sheets, it may be that a larger and more extensive volume may be issued," which would deal more fully with "everything within his knowledge of Africa and the Africans" (p. 34).

187. *The American Baptist*, 18 July 1850.

Whether he lived long enough to undertake this larger work, or sustained his interest in doing so, is not known; but if it was written, it does not appear to have survived. Regrettable as this is, we may be thankful for the remarkable and invaluable text which he did produce.

Despite its potential interest and value, however, Baquaqua's *Biography* has largely been ignored until recently within the corpus of biographical accounts of African-American slaves and their descendants in North America. In his own day, it appears that his hopes for public patronage of the work were not realized. The *Biography* appears not to have circulated widely, since copies of it are rare today;[188] and it does not seem to have been reviewed outside Free Baptist circles. The American Baptist Free Mission Society had a distribution network for publications, but it does not appear that Baquaqua's book was handled in this way.

One reason for this contemporary neglect may relate to Baquaqua's intention of returning to Africa, which by implication established him as a proponent of the emigrationist strategy in combating slavery and racism in North America. His identification of his own case with the wider emigrationist cause is suggested by his inclusion of James Whitfield's poem in the *Biography*, since Whitfield was a well-known emigrationist who dedicated his own collection of poems, from which this text was taken, published in Buffalo in 1853, to another leading emigrationist, Martin Delany.[189] Around the very time that Baquaqua was working on the *Biography,* Whitfield was engaged in a newspaper debate with Frederick Douglass, in which the former advocated the emigrationist and the latter the "nationalist" approach to the situation of blacks in the U.S.A.; the papers from this exchange were also published in Detroit by Baquaqua's publisher,

188. Copies are to be found in the Detroit Public Library, the New York Public Library, the Library of Congress, the University of Michigan, the American Antiquarian Society, Cornell University, the New York Historical Society, and Brigham Young University.

189. Whitfield, *America, and Other Poems*, vii-viii. In 1852 Martin Delany (1812–85) had begun to promote emigration to the West Indies; see his *The Condition, Elevation, and Destiny of the Colored People of the United States, Politically Considered* (Philadelphia, 1852).

George E. Pomeroy.[190] The debate focused on the proposal to hold a national convention in Cleveland in August 1854 to promote the cause of emigration, but the chosen destinations that were eventually discussed there included Canada, the West Indies, and Central America, but consideration of Africa was specifically excluded. Considering Baquaqua's overriding ambition to return to Africa, it is perhaps not surprising that he did not attend the Cleveland convention and thereby make contact with Whitfield, Delany, and others who organized it. Despite considerable disillusionment over the difficulties of the settlements of repatriated African-Americans in Sierra Leone and Liberia, emigration had continued to be discussed, but the 1854 convention in Cleveland demonstrated that it was not popular among many free African-Americans. Indeed, proponents of Liberia and other settlement schemes were decidedly on the defensive as the division between North and South widened.[191] It may be, therefore, that Baquaqua's book simply missed the fashion. Subsequently, the leading emigrationists once again began to look to Africa as a desirable location for colonies of former slaves and their descendants, and in 1859 Delany led an expedition to Yoruba country (southwestern Nigeria). Baquaqua would have been a logical candidate for the expedition, but perhaps (assuming he was still alive) was still outside the U.S.A., and again missed the opportunity.[192]

Baquaqua did not initially fare much better in modern academic study either of the history of Africa or of the African diaspora in the Americas. His *Biography* was not included in any of the standard

---

190. M. T. Newsome, ed., *Arguments, Pro and Con, on the Call for a National Emigration Convention, to be held in Cleveland, Ohio, August, 1854, by Frederick Douglass, W.J. Watkins, and James M. Whitfield, With a Short Appendix of the Statistics of Canada West, West Indies, Central and South America* (Detroit, 1854). Austin (*Sourcebook*, 643–44) speculates that Baquaqua's editor Samuel Moore was introduced to Whitfield when the latter visited Detroit trying to sell his poems, but Moore or Baquaqua could have been introduced to Whitfield's poetry through Pomeroy, who also published Newsome's book.

191. Howard H. Bell, "The Negro Emigration Movement, 1849–1854: A Phase of Negro Nationalism," *Phylon* 20 (1959): 132–42; Lamin Sanneh, *Abolitionists Abroad: American Blacks and the Making of Modern West Africa* (Cambridge, MA, 1999): 139–77.

192. For Martin Delany's role in the Niger River expedition of 1859, see *Official Report of the Niger Valley Exploring Party*, in Delany and Campbell, *Search for a Place*, 23–148.

anthologies of ex-slave narratives, down into the 1990s;[193] nor in Curtin's collection of narratives by specifically African-born slaves published in 1967.[194] In consequence of this obscurity, it was also ignored in historical studies for which it would have formed an invaluable source, including a study of the West African kola trade, in which his home town of Djougou played a central role, by one of the present editors published in 1980.[195] The text was brought to notice primarily through the efforts of Allan Austin, who included it in his collection of biographical material on African Muslims in the U.S.A. published in 1984; and discussed it further in his book on this subject in 1997.[196] The *Biography* was also independently rediscovered by historians of slavery in Brazil: the Brazilian portions of it were included in an anthology by Ann M. Pescatello in 1975, and his account of his enslavement in Africa and his description of the Middle Passage, in a documentary history of Brazilian slavery by Robert Edgar Conrad in 1984; the Brazilian sections were also published in Portuguese translation by Silvia Hunold Lara in 1988, and a Portuguese translation of the entire work, by Robert Krueger, was published in Brazil in 1997.[197] Only very recently, in consequence of this work of

193. See, for example, Blassingame,ed., *Slave Testimony*(Baton Rouge, 1977*)*; Taylor, ed., *I Was Born a Slave* (Chicago, 1999); Henry Louis Gates, Jr., ed., *The Classic Slave Narratives* (New York, 1987). Baquaqua is also not mentioned in William L. Andrews, Frances Smith Foster, and Trudier Harris, eds., *The Oxford Companion to African American Literature* (New York, 1997), nor in Rayford W. Logan and Michael R. Winston, eds., *Dictionary of Negro Biography* (New York, 1982).

194. Curtin, ed., *Africa Remembered*.

195. Lovejoy, *Caravans of Kola*.

196. Austin, *African Muslims Sourcebook*, 585-654; *Transatlantic Stories,* 157–71. The earliest modern reference to the biography is entry no. 1500 in Peter C. Hogg, *The African Slave Trade and its Suppression: A Classified and Annotated Bibliography of Books, Pamphlets and Periodical Articles* (London, 1973). The biography is also listed in Benjamin Nunez, *Dictionary of Afro-Latin American Civilization* (Westport, CT, 1980) and Mary Mace Spradling, *A Guide to Magazine Articles, Newspaper Articles, and Books Concerning Black Individuals and Groups* 3rd ed. (Detroit, 1980). It is also listed (but with no further discussion) among slave narratives of the era of the illegal slave trade by David Eltis, *Economic Growth and the Ending of the Transatlantic Slave Trade* (New York, 1987): 339, n.3.

197. "Mahommah G. Baquaqua: Recollections of a Slave's Life," in Ann M. Pescatello, ed., *The African in Latin America* (New York, 1975): 186-94; Conrad, *Children of God's Fire,* 23–29; Silvia Hunold Lara, "Biografia de Mahommah G. Baquaqua," *Revista Brasileira de História–São Paulo* 16 (1988): 269-84; and Mahommah Gardo Baquaqua, *Biografia e narrativa do ex-excravo afro-brasileiro* (trad. de Robert Krueger, Brasília, 1997). Also see Krueger, "Milhões de Vozes," 214–16.

republication, has Baquaqua's text begun to receive the attention which it deserves, being drawn upon for example in Mary Karasch's study of slavery in Rio de Janeiro (1987);[198] in Marcus J.M. de Carvalho's study of Pernambuco (1998);[199] in a study of the involvement of the Borgu region in the Atlantic slave trade, by the present editors (1999);[200] and, following Allan Austin's lead, in various studies of Islam and Muslims in the U.S.A.[201] The text has now also belatedly been drawn to the attention of people in his hometown of Djougou, Bénin, where it was altogether unknown until the present editors took a copy there, in order to discuss it with local authorities, in April 1999.

The interest of Baquaqua's *Biography* does not reside primarily in its literary merit, which is admittedly slight. In part, this reflects a conscious decision by the editor Samuel Moore to opt for "the plainest style" possible, in order to maximize accessibility to potential readers (pp. 6–7); he evidently had a readership among children specifically in mind, as a subsequent reference to "our young friends, who may read this work" indicates (p. 14). In terms of its narrative structure, the text is also somewhat rambling and shapeless. Part of the intended message of the story of his life was presumably, as Mrs. Judd observed of the speech which he made celebrating his conversion in Haiti in 1848, to show "the wonderful providence of God in his dealings with him";[202] but in practice, this potential organizing theme is only intermittently engaged with in the text. The *Biography* is also implicitly the story of Baquaqua's personal spiritual development, out of "heathen" wickedness into Christian faith, but this focus is also not consistently maintained, with the later Christian phase of his life treated only very summarily, and his actual conversion dis-

198. Karasch, *Slave Life in Rio de Janeiro*.

199. de Carvalho, *Liberdade: Rotinas e Rupturas do Escravismo, Recife*.

200. Law and Lovejoy, "Borgu in the Atlantic Slave Trade."

201. Turner, *Islam in the African-American Experience*, 40–41; Sylviane A. Diouf, *Servants of Allah: African Muslims Enslaved in the Americas* (New York, 1998): 42–45, 53, 203.

202. Letter of Mrs. N.A.L. Judd, 21 July 1848.

missed in a single sentence (p. 58). The editor Samuel Moore was evidently conscious of this deficiency, and inserted into the text a longer account of Baquaqua's baptism, taken from an earlier published account (pp. 59–60).[203] The principal value of the *Biography* is evidently rather as a historical source.

Considered as a historical source, the value of the *Biography* of course varies for different periods of the life which it recounts. As a source for the history of Djougou, a town of considerable importance within regional commercial and religious networks, it is uniquely valuable, not only as the only surviving narrative by an enslaved person exported from this area, but as the only first-hand account of any sort relating to the town in the first half of the nineteenth century. Beyond this, it represents an invaluable addition to the very limited number of narratives by African-born ex-slaves more generally. Its value in this respect is enhanced by the recent questions which have been raised about whether the author of the only other such narrative of comparable extent, Olaudah Equiano, was really born, as he claimed, in Africa.[204] But even apart from the issue of Equiano's authenticity, Baquaqua's account is on the face of it a better source, for whereas Equiano was, by his own account, aged only around eleven when he left Africa, and was recalling his early life there over thirty years later, Baquaqua, whatever his precise date of birth, had already entered the adult world before his enslavement and export (undertaking a long-distance trading journey, and spending some time as a palace servant), and recorded his account apparently within an interval of less than ten years.

The use of Baquaqua's biography as a historical source poses problems not only of its reliability, but of how far it can be taken as

203. Viz. From the Rev. W.L. Judd's letter of 21 July 1848, as reproduced in Foss and Mathews, *Facts for Baptist Churches.* We assume that this insertion was made by Moore, rather than by Baquaqua himself, because in the sentence introducing it "Mahommah" is referred to in the third person.

204. Vincent Carretta, "Olaudah Equiano or Gustavus Vassa? New Light on an Eighteenth-Century Question of Identity," *Slavery and Abolition* 20, no. 3 (1999): 96–105.

representative of the broader processes in which he became involved, a question which is perhaps especially critical in relation to the history of the transatlantic slave trade, and of slavery and the experience of free blacks in the Americas.[205] Taken in its entirety, Baquaqua's story was untypical; indeed, the particular trajectory of his life, from his origins in Djougou, through slavery in Brazil, liberation in the U.S.A., conversion in Haiti, education in the U.S.A., to residence in Canada and England, may well have been unique. Nevertheless, in its component segments, Baquaqua's case can be seen to fit into wider patterns, which enhances its value as a source beyond his individual biography, to serve to some degree as a representative example.

First, Baquaqua's *Biography* conforms to the dominant pattern of recorded slave voices, most of which are those of males. There was a predominance of males among slaves, and especially so among enslaved Muslims.[206] Although Baquaqua is not included in Curtin's anthology of voices from West Africa in the slave-trade era, his story conforms to the dominant theme of this collection, which is entirely male and largely Muslim.[207] Similarly, Austin's biographical material on enslaved Muslims in the Americas relates entirely to males.[208] Although the recent study of enslaved Muslims by Gomez focuses on the U.S.A. in the period before 1830, and, therefore, does not discuss Baquaqua, nonetheless his work also demonstrates the preponderance of males among enslaved Muslims, despite a few examples of Mus-

---

205. Cf. Paul Lovejoy, "Biography as source material: towards a biographical archive of enslaved Africans," in Robin Law, ed., *Source Material for Studying the Slave Trade and the African Diaspora* (Centre of Commonwealth Studies, University of Stirling, 1997): 119–40.

206. For gender and age ratios of the deported slave population in the nineteenth century, see David Eltis and Stanley Engerman, "Fluctuations in Sex and Age Ratios in the Transatlantic Slave Trade, 1663–1864," *Economic History Review* 46 (1993): 308–23; and the updated analysis derived from David Eltis, Stephen D. Behrendt, David Richardson, and Herbert S. Klein, *The Trans-Atlantic Slave Trade: A Database on CD-ROM* (New York, 1999).

207. Curtin, ed., *Africa Remembered*. All ten biographies in this volume are male; half are Muslims, one of whom was free. It should be noted that there is no claim that the collection is representative of the slave trade. However, the collection is representative of the predominance of males in surviving accounts and also of the fact that Muslims are represented in such accounts disproportionately to their actual numbers within the slave population in the Americas.

208. Austin, *African Muslims Sourcebook*.

lim women in North America.[209] Sylviane Diouf, too, has noted that most of the enslaved Africans who came from Muslim areas were males.[210] These studies confirm the conclusion of one of the present editors that the overwhelming majority of enslaved Africans exported to the Americas from the central Sudan, including Borgu, were males, most of whom went to Bahia in the early nineteenth century.[211] Baquaqua's journey varied from this broader pattern in that he went to Pernambuco, not Bahia, and followed a route to the coast that was further west than that followed by most enslaved Muslims from the central Sudan who ended up in Brazil; the more usual route was through the Yoruba kingdom of Oyo to Porto-Novo or Lagos.[212]

As regards his experiences in North America, Baquaqua's story stands out not only by his African birth and his experience of slavery in Brazil rather than the U.S.A., but also by his unique passage from Brazilian slavery via the Underground Railroad to freedom in Haïti, before returning to the U.S.A. for education. His subsequent passage to Canada was also unusual in that he was not, like most of the fugitives from the U.S.A. who settled in Canada West, an escaped slave from the U.S. South, nor a member of the free black community in the U.S. North seeking sanctuary from the risks of re-enslavement which followed the enactment of the Fugitive Slave Act of 1850 that legitimized vigilante justice and the return of suspected fugitives to the South. Here too, however, his work fits into wider patterns of African-American autobiography of the period, notably in linking

209. Michael Gomez, *Exchanging Our Country Marks: The Transformation of African Identities in the Colonial and Antebellum South* (Chapel Hill, 1998), 59–87.

210. Diouf, *Servants of Allah*, 38–41.

211. Paul E. Lovejoy, "Jihad e Escravidão: As Origens dos Escravos Muçulmanos de Bahia," *Topoi: Revista de História* 1 (2000): 11–44, which updates "Background to Rebellion: The Origins of Muslim Slaves in Bahia," in Paul E. Lovejoy and Nicholas Rogers, eds., *Unfree Labour in the Development of the Atlantic World* (London, 1994): 151–82. Also see Ubiratan Castro de Araújo, "1846: Um ano na rota Bahia-Lagos: Negócios, negociantes e outros parceiros," *Afro-Ásia* 21–22 (1998-1999): 83–110; and Pierre Verger, *Flux et reflux de la traite des Nègres entre le Golfe de Bénin et Bahia de Todos os Santos du XVIIe au XIXe siècle* (Paris, 1968).

212. Law and Lovejoy, "Borgu and the Atlantic Slave Trade."

personal self-advancement to spiritual salvation.[213] Further, his individual experiences, both as an activist in abolitionist networks and as one of the first black students at a university college in the U.S.A., throw light on the situation of free blacks in this period more generally. As one who succeeded in publishing his biography under his own copyright, he was manifestly exceptional, but the story of his unique achievement simultaneously serves to document the more general constraints which he overcame.

213. On which, see William L. Andrews, *To Tell a Free Story: The First Century of Afro-American Autobiography* (Urbana, IL, 1986).

AN INTERESTING NARRATIVE.
BIOGRAPHY
OF
MAHOMMAH G. BAQUAQUA

AN INTERESTING NARRATIVE.
BIOGRAPHY
OF
MAHOMMAH G. BAQUAQUA,

A Native of Zoogoo, in the Interior of Africa.
(A Convert to Christianity.)

With a Description of that Part of the World;
Including the

Manners and Customs of the Inhabitants,

Their Religious Notions, Form of Government, Laws, Appearance of the Country, Buildings, Agriculture, Manufactures, Shepherds and Herdsmen, Domestic Animals, Marriage Ceremonies, Funeral Services, Styles of Dress, Trade and Commerce, Modes of Warfare, System of Slavery, &c., &c.

Mahommah's early life, His Education, His Capture and Slavery in Western Africa and Brazil, His Escape to the United States, from thence to Haiti (the City of Port au Prince,) His Reception by the Baptist Missionary there, the Rev. W.L. Judd, His Conversion to Christianity, Baptism, and Return to his country, his Views, Objects and Aim.

Written and Revised from his own Words,
BY SAMUEL MOORE, ESQ.,
Late publisher of the "North of England Shipping Gazette,"
author of several popular works, and editor of sundry reform papers.

MAHOMMAH G. BAQUAQUA

Detroit:
Printed for the Author, Mahommah Gardo Baquaqua,
BY GEO. E. POMEROY & CO., TRIBUNE OFFICE.
1854.

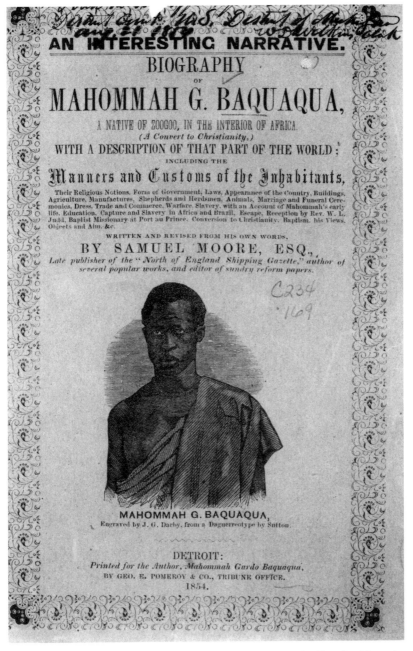

AN INTERESTING NARRATIVE.

BIOGRAPHY
OF
MAHOMMAH G. BAQUAQUA,

A NATIVE OF ZOOGOO, IN THE INTERIOR OF AFRICA.
(A Convert to Christianity,)

WITH A DESCRIPTION OF THAT PART OF THE WORLD:
INCLUDING THE

Manners and Customs of the Inhabitants,

Their Religious Notions, Form of Government, Laws, Appearance of the Country, Buildings, Agriculture, Manufactures, Shepherds and Herdsmen, Animals, Marriage and Funeral Ceremonies, Dress, Trade and Commerce, Warfare, Slavery, with an Account of Mahommah's early life, Education, Capture and Slavery in Africa and Brazil, Escape, Reception by Rev. W. L. Judd, Baptist Missionary at Port au Prince, Conversion to Christianity, Baptism, his Views, Objects and Aim, &c.

WRITTEN AND REVISED FROM HIS OWN WORDS,

BY SAMUEL MOORE, ESQ.,

Late publisher of the "North of England Shipping Gazette," author of several popular works, and editor of sundry reform papers.

MAHOMMAH G. BAQUAQUA,
Engraved by J. G. Darby, from a Daguerreotype by Snitton.

DETROIT:
Printed for the Author, Mahommah Gardo Baquaqua,
BY GEO. E. POMEROY & CO., TRIBUNE OFFICE.
1854.

PLATE 2. Pamphlet cover, Mahommah Gardo Baquaqua, An Interesting Narrative. Biography of Mahommah G. Baquaqua, A Native of Zoogoo, in the Interior of Africa (A Convert to Christianity,) with a Description of That Part of the World; including the Manners and Customs of the Inhabitants (Detroit, 1854) showing copyright date, August 21, 1854 (Burton Historical Collection, Detroit Public Library).

[p. 3] NUMBERS[1]:

Afo [àfó], one.

Ahinka [àhínká], two.

Ahiza [àhínzà], three.

Attoche [àtáátyí], four.

Ahgo [àyìggúú], five.

Aido [àyìíddúú], six.

Aea [àyyéé], seven.

Aeako [àyyààkú], eight.

Aega [àyyìggá], nine.

Away [awéy], ten.

Awaychinefaw, eleven.

Awaychineka, twelve.

Awaychineza, thirteen.

Awaychinetache, fourteen.

Awaychinago, fifteen.

Awaychinedo, sixteen.

Awaychinea, seventeen.

Awaychineako, eighteen.

Awaychinego, nineteen.

Awarranka [àwáránká], twenty.

Awarrankachnefaw, twenty-one.

Awarrankachineka, twenty-two.

Awarrankachnega, twenty-three.

Awarrankachintache, twenty-four.

Awarrankachinego, twenty-five.

Awarrankachinedo, twenty-six.

Awarrankachinea, twenty-seven.

Awarrankachineako, twenty-eight.

Awarrankachinega, twenty-nine.

Awarranza [àwáránzà], thirty.

Awarranzachinefaw, thirty-one.

Awarranzachineka, thirty-two.

Awarranzachineza, thirty-three.

Awarranzachintoche, thirty-four.

Awarranzachinego, thirty-five.

Awarranzachinedo, thirty-six.

Awarranzachinea, thirty-seven.

Awarranzachineako, thirty-eight.

Awarranzachinega, thirty-nine.

Waytoche, forty.

Waytochechinefaw, forty-one.

Waytochechineka, forty-two.

Waytochechineza, forty-three.

Waytochechintoche, forty-four.

Waytochechinego, forty-five.

Waytochechinedo, forty-six.

Waytochechinea, forty-seven.

Waytochechineaka, forty-eight.

---

1. Although this is not explicitly stated, presumably these numbers are in Baquaqua's native language. They are, in fact, in Dendi, the language of the Muslim community of Djougou (Dendi equivalents given in square brackets following the terms as given in the text), as are many of the items of vocabulary given in the main text; identifications of Dendi terms here and in the following footnotes are generally derived from Petr Zima, *Lexique Dendi (Songhay) (Djougou, Bénin)* (Köln, 1994). Austin (*African Muslims Sourcebook*, 594 & 645, n. 5) drew attention to the similarity of these numerals to those given in nineteenth-century sources for the "Timbuktu" language, i.e., Songhai, which is closely related to Dendi.

Waytochechinega, forty-nine.
Waygodada, fifty.
Waygochinefaw, fifty-one.
Waygochineka, fifty-two.
Waygochineza, fifty-three.
Waygochintoche, fifty-four.
Waygochinego, fifty-five.
Waygochinedo, fifty-six.
Waygochinea, fifty-seven.
Waygochineako, fifty-eight.
Waychinaga, fifty-nine.
Waydo, sixty.
Waydochinefaw, sixty-one.
[p. 4] Waydochineka, sixty-two.
Waydochineza, sixty-three.
Waydochintoche, sixty-four.
Waydochinego, sixty-five.
Waydochinedo, sixty-six.
Waydochinea, sixty-seven.
Waydochineako, sixty-eight.
Waydochinega, sixty-nine.
Wayea, seventy.
Wayeachinefaw, seventy-one.
Wayeachineka, seventy-two.
Wayeachineza, seventy-three.
Wayeachintoche, seventy-four.
Wayeachinego, seventy-five.
Wayeachinedo, seventy-six.
Wayeachinea, seventy-seven.
Wayeachineako, seventy-eight.
Wayeachinega, seventy-nine.

Wako, eighty.
Waykochinefaw, eighty-one.
Wakochineka, eighty-two.
Wakochineza, eighty-three.
Wakochintoche, eighty-four.
Wakochinego, eighty-five.
Wakochinedo, eighty-six.
Wakochinea, eighty-seven.
Wakochineako, eighty-eight.
Wakochinega, eighty-nine.
Wayga, ninety.
Waygachinefaw, ninety-one.
Waygachineka, ninety-two.
Waygachineza, ninety-three.
Waygachintoche, ninety-four.
Waygachinego, ninety-five.
Waygachinedo, ninety-six.
Waygachinea, ninety-seven.
Waygachineako, ninety-eight.
Waygachinega, ninety-nine.
Zongfawdaday, one hundred.
Zongeka, two hundred.
Zongeza, three hundred.
Zongtoche, four hundred.
Zonggo, five hundred.
Zongedo, six hundred.
Zongea, seven hundred.
Zongeako, eight hundred.
Zongega, nine hundred.
Zongway, one thousand.

[p. 5]

PREFACE AND
COMPILER'S NOTES.

In compiling the following pages, many difficulties have had naturally to be encountered, in consequence of the imperfect English spoken by Mahommah,[2] but great care has been taken to render the work as readable and clear as possible to the capacities of all classes of readers; the description of the people (their manners and customs) of that country, which is little known to the world at large, will be found highly instructive—the friends of the poor African negro and the colored race generally, will be greatly benefitted by reading the work carefully from beginning to end; they will there see throughout its pages, the horrible sufferings and tortures inflicted upon that portion of God's creatures, merely because "their skin is of a darker hue," notwithstanding their hearts are as soft and flexible as the man of paler cast. The cherished object of Mahommah has been for a long time past, indeed ever since his conversion to christianity whilst at Hayti, to be enabled to return to his native land, to instruct his own people in the ways of the gospel of Christ, and to be the means of their salvation,[3] which it is to be hoped he will be able to accomplish

---

2. An account of Baquaqua's fund-raising lectures for the American Baptist Free Mission Society in 1853 similarly alludes to his "quite broken English": letter of A.L.P [= Post], Montrose, July 1853, in *The American Baptist*, 28 July 1853. Baquaqua himself, in his correspondence with George Whipple of the American Missionary Association, observes that "the English language has been very hard for me to understand and speak," and that to become a missionary in Africa, "I must understand English language more than I dose [sic] now" (McGrawville, 8 October 1853, 20 January 1854); but the letters themselves, although containing many errors of spelling and syntax, are generally readily intelligible. The reference here to "the ... English *spoken by* Mahommah" (cf. also p. 7 below, to the story as being *"from the mouth* of a native") implies that Moore took down the account from Mahommah's dictation, rather than editing a written text.

3. Cf. below, p. 59.

ere long;[4] in the meantime he has become a subject of the Queen of England, and is **[p. 6]** at present living under her benign laws and influence in Canada,[5] stirring up the colored population and agitating for the abolition of slavery all over the world, a cause which ought to occupy the hearts and feelings of every benevolent and charitable man and woman throughout the world; the slaves themselves, it is to be hoped, will be benefitted by every line that is written in their favor, simple as the style may be; as their cause is the cause of suffering humanity, how can any one boasting of the religion of Jesus Christ, for one moment seek to uphold slavery as it is for a single day? No, it cannot be; the system of slavery and the doctrines of Christ are quite opposed to each other; no matter what the defenders of the system may say! Readers, judge for yourselves, and act for yourselves; depend not on the dogmas of any man or class of men, but read, mark, learn and inwardly digest the subject matter of these pages, and compare the treatment of those poor creatures under the yoke of slavery, and the gospel of Christ, and you will soon come to the conclusion, that it will not bear comparison with any one portion of the good book, which says "my yoke is easy and my burden is light"—for the yoke of slavery is *hard* and the burdens are not *light*, but exceedingly heavy.

Too much cannot be said, written or published, on the horrible system of slavery. To bring the brutal subject to an end, the more that is said and done in the way of agitating the subject, the better for all the classes, the better for slave owners, to get rid of the "accursed sin," and the better for the poor slaves to rid them of their yoke; let all whose hearts are not of adamant and whose nerves are not of steel,

---

4. The Rev. William Judd, of the American Baptist Free Mission in Haiti, when Baquaqua joined his household in 1847, expressed the hope that, if converted, he might go as a missionary to Africa: letter of W.L. Judd, Port-au-Prince, 28 October 1847, in *Christian Contributor and Free Missionary*, 22 December 1847. Baquaqua himself, on his conversion in 1848, espoused the same hope (cf. p. 59 below). Baquaqua's letters written in the U.S.A. between August 1853 and January 1854 all relate to his desire to go as a missionary to Africa.
5. Cf. below, p. 64.

advance his [sic] views in every possible way and the slave may soon
become free, and bless the day that made him so, and the hands that
knocked the shackles from his bleeding hands and feet, and snatched
the whip from out the tyrant master's hand, who bound up all the
negro's wounds and **[p. 7]** applied balm to his writhing body. Can the
humane and philanthropic who struggled for the freedom of the
slaves in the West India possessions some years ago, and which cost
the British people, some millions of pounds sterling,—I say can they
forget the pleasurable feelings that event gave to them. The Society of
Friends[6] were the principal agitators in that movement, and the blessings and prayers of the poor liberated slaves ascended the altars of
heaven on that great occasion; can they forget the kindlier feelings of
their nature that was [sic] stirred up within them on that occasion, can
they ever, think you, forget the glorious day which made their fellow
creatures free; can they forget the first day of August of that eventful
year?[7] Oh then, friends of humanity, bestir yourselves again, as did
those good men on that occasion, and persevere until you have
accomplished the work you have set yourselves to do, as those in days
gone by had done.

This little work may have its desired effect wherever it is read, and
no doubt the sufferings of the subject (Mahommah) will bring the tear
to many a pitying eye, and the blush to many a dimpled cheek, in
shame for the cruelty practised upon him by men bearing the image
of their Maker, many a blush will be summoned to the cheeks of inno-
cence whilst this work is in progress of perusal.

The descriptive part of this work cannot but prove highly interesting to the general reader, as such descriptions coming from the mouth
of a native[8] who had passed through all the places described, in the
interior of a country like Africa. Many works descriptive of the coun-

---

6. I.e., Quakers.
7. Referring to the abolition of slavery in British colonies, enacted in 1833 and effective
from 1 August 1834.
8. Cf. n. 2, above.

try have issued from the press from time to time, but none have appeared like the present; it is simply a compilation or narration of events happening in the life of the man himself who narrates them, and given without any figured speech, but in the plainest style possible; all the phrases used are "familiar as household words," consequently it will be easi- **[p. 8]** ly understood by all who read it; it is written so plainly in point of speech, that "he who runs may read." The different customs and ceremonies are very amusing, and may, according to the way in which it is read, prove highly instructive, as well. It is hoped that, at any rate, good may be accomplished by its publication. If it should be the province of Mahommah to go out to Africa as a missionary, according to his heart's desire, it is his intention, if he is permitted to return to this country, to issue this work in a larger form, with the addition of matters that has [sic] either been entirely left out or curtailed for want of space, together with his success amongst his native race, the people of his own clime.

[p. 9]

BIOGRAPHY
of
MAHOMMAH GARDO BAQUAQUA
&c., &c.

CHAPTER I[9]

The subject of this memoir was born in the city of Zoozoo,[10] in Central Africa,[11] whose king was tributary to the king of Berzoo[12] His age is not known to the year exactly, as the Africans have altogether a different mode of dividing time and reckoning age, but supposes he is about 30 years old, from the remembrance of certain events which took place, and from the knowledge he has lately acquired in

---

9. The title page suggests that this chapter was intended to have the subheading, "Their Religious Notions."

10. "Zoogoo" on the title page, and later in the text; this is clearly the correct form, "Zoozoo" being presumably a miscopying of the manuscript. One of Baquaqua's extant letters (McGrawville, 29 January 1854) gives the spelling "Zogoo." For the identification with Djougou, in the north of the modern Republic of Bénin, see Introduction.

11. The term "Central Africa" in this period was commonly used to denote Tropical Africa, rather than according to modern usage; cf. e.g., the book by the U.S. Baptist missionary T.J. Bowen, *Central Africa: Adventures & Missionary Labours* (1857), which is mainly concerned with Liberia and Yorubaland.

12. "Bergoo" later in the text, which is presumably the correct form, 'Berzoo' being here again a miscopying. Austin's suggestion (*African Muslims Sourcebook*, 645, n. 6; *Transatlantic Stories*, 162) that this represents "Borgu" is probably correct; in which case, the reference is probably to Nikki, which was usually accounted the "capital" of Borgu (cf. Dupuis, *Journal of a Residence in Ashantee*, lviii, cv, cxii; Clapperton, *Journal of a Second Expedition into the Interior of Africa*, 83), and whose king was commonly called the "King of Borgoo," as noted by the Landers in 1830: Richard Lander and John Lander, *Journal of an Expedition to Explore the Course & Termination of the River Niger* (London, 1830): i, 370–71 [8 September 1830]. Local tradition confirms that Djougou, although not itself part of Borgu, owed "homage" to the king of Nikki during the nineteenth century: Lombard, *Structures du type "féodal" en Afrique noire*, 112. This identification is also consistent with the later (p. 29) statement that "Bergoo" was east of Zoogoo; Nikki being in fact 170 km. east of Djougou. Philologically and geographically, an alternative identification of "Bergoo" might be the town of Parakou, 120 km. southeast of Djougou (note that "Barragoo" in T.E. Bowdich, *Mission from Cape Coast Castle to Ashantee* [London, 1819]: 208, seems to represent Parakou, rather than "Borgu"); but there is no evidence or likelihood that Parakou ever exercised sovereignty over Djougou.

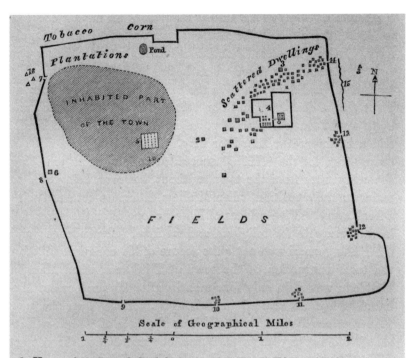

1. House where I was lodged during my first stay in Kátsena in 1851.
2. House belonging to the quarter Dóka, where I was lodged in 1853.

3. The Zénsere.	11. Kofa-n-Káura.
4. Palace of the governor.	12. Kofa-n-Marúsa.
5. Market-place.	13. Kofa-n-Dúrdu.
6. Old mosque.	14. Kofa-n-Samrí.
7. Kofa-n-Gúga.	15. A brook formed by a spring.
8. Kofa-n-Yendúkki.	16. Former place of encampment of salt-
9. Kofa-n-Koya.	caravan.
10. Kofa-n-Gazúbi.	

PLATE 3. Katsina: 'His mother being a native of Kashna...' (Biography, p. 9); sketch of city in 1851, from Heinrich Barth, *Travels and Discoveries in North and Central Africa, being a Journal of an Expedition undertaken under the auspices of H.B.M.'s Government in the Years 1849–1855* (London and New York, 1859), i, 477.

figures.[13] But this not being a very important matter in his history, we here leave it to its own obscurity, not for a moment believing the narration will lose any of its interest from the lack of the particular figure.

He states his parents were of different countries, his father being a native of Berzoo, (of Arabian descent) and not very dark complexioned.[14] His mother being a native of Kashna[15] and of very dark complexion, was entirely black. The manners of his father were grave and silent; his religion, Mahomedanism.[16]

As the interior of Africa is comparatively little known, a brief sketch cannot prove but very interesting to most of our **[p. 10]** readers; accordingly we shall proceed with the details as set forth by Mahommah himself. Their mode of worship is something after the following style:

My father, (says Mahommah) rose every morning at four o'clock

---

13. This would place his birth c.1824, and his age at the time of his sale into transatlantic slavery in 1845 c.21. Earlier sources, however, suggest that he was born somewhat later: e.g., the brief biographical note published in 1850 gives his date of birth as 1830 (Foss & Mathews, *Facts for Baptist Churches*, 392), and this date is accepted by Austin, *Transatlantic Stories*, 159. But this would make his age at enslavement and export only 15, which seems impossible to reconcile with the details of his life as given in his biography: for further discussion, see Introduction.

14. The reference to Arabian descent may refer to *shurfa* (Hausa: pl. *sharifai*) origins (i.e., claim of descent from the Prophet Muhammad), which was common among merchants from North Africa, especially Morocco; see discussion in the Introduction and also Lovejoy, *Caravans of Kola*, 58–59, 68–69, 70–71, 73n. Also see below (p. 21).

15. I.e., Katsina, in Hausaland (modern northern Nigeria). The Baptist Free Mission in Haiti in 1847 understood that Baquaqua himself was "from the city of Kashina, of the tribe Houssa," but this must be a misunderstanding of a statement about his mother's origins: letter of W.L. Judd, 28 October 1847; and for further discussion, see Introduction. Katsina was the most important town in Hausaland in the eighteenth century, but declined as a result of insecurity arising from the *jihad* (1804-48), and much of Katsina's trade shifted to Kano. Nonetheless, the various towns around Birnin Katsina continued to be important in long-distance trade to the Volta basin via Djougou: see Lovejoy, *Caravans of Kola*, 52–60, 64–68, 83–84.

16. Baquaqua later explains (p. 21) that his father had formerly been "a traveling merchant." He evidently belonged to the Muslim (and Dendi-speaking) merchant community of Borgu, known as Wangara: for which, see esp. Brégand, *Commerce caravanier*, for Djougou in particular, see 82–85, and for Nikki, 90–91. Baquaqua's mother probably also belonged to the Muslim community of Djougou, which included families which traced their origins to Katsina, including the Mande family which provided most of the imams of the town: Brégand, *Commerce caravanier*, 111.

for prayers, after which he returned to bed, at sunrise he performed his second devotional exercises, at noon he worshipped again, and again at sunset.[17]

Once a year a great fast is held, which lasts a month, during this time nothing is eaten during the day, but in the evening, after some ceremonies are performed, eating is allowed;[18] after eating, worship is permitted in their own homes, and then assemblies for public worship are held. The place of worship was a large and pleasant yard belonging to my grandfather, my uncle was the officiating priest.[19] The people arrange themselves in rows, the priest standing in front, the oldest people next to him, and so on, arranging themselves in order according to age.

The priest commences the devotions by bowing his head toward the earth and saying the following words: "Allah-hah-koo-bar," the people responding "Allah-hah-koo-bar," signifying "God, hear our prayer, answer our prayer."[20] The priest and people then kneel and press their foreheads to the earth, the priest repeating passages from the Koran, and the people responding as before. After this portion of the ceremony is over, the priest and people sitting on the ground count their beads, the priest occasionally repeating passages from the

17. It is normally held in Islam that prayers should be offered five times a day: Baquaqua appears to omit the afternoon prayer.

18. A reference to Ramadan, the ninth month of the Islamic year, marked by daytime fasting.

19. Austin's comment that this indicates "a pre-mosque community" (*African Muslims Sourcebook*, 646, n. 10; also *Transatlantic Stories*, 162) seems unwarranted. It is improbable that there was no mosque in Djougou at this period (and indeed, Baquaqua himself later [p. 27] alludes to mosques, in connection with Islamic education). The "yard" referred to here as a place of "public" prayer may have been outside a mosque, but the wording suggests that it was in Baquaqua's family's private home, although the worship organized there was evidently open to members of other households. In any case, it does not seem likely that Baquaqua's uncle, mentioned as the "officiating priest" of the ceremonies described here, is the same as the "chief priest" mentioned later (p. 11) as officiating in public worship at the end of Ramadan, i.e., the (chief) imam of the community, although he may well have held a subordinate position within the Muslim hierarchy: Baquaqua himself refers (ibid.) to "four subordinate priests," who attended the "chief priest" on this occasion. It is not clear whether the uncle mentioned here was the same as the one mentioned subsequently (pp. 26–28), who was Baquaqua's mother's brother, and described as "blacksmith."

20. Arabic *Allahu akhbar*, actually meaning "God is Great."

Koran.—They then pray for their king, that Allah would help him to conquer his enemies, and that he would preserve the people from famine, from the devouring locusts, and that he would grant them rain in due season.[21]

At the close of each day's ceremonies, the worshippers of the prophet[22] go to their respective homes, where the best of everything is provided for the evening's repast. This same worship is repeated daily for thirty days, and closes with one immense mass meeting.[23] The king comes to the city on this occasion[24] and great multitudes from the country all round about, who together with the citizens, collect at the place appointed for worship, called Gui-ge-rah, a little out of the city.[25] This place consecra- [p. 11] ted to the worship of the false prophet, is one of "God's first Temples." It consisted of several very large trees, forming an extensive and beautiful shade, the ground sandy and entirely destitute of grass, is kept perfectly clean, many thousands can be comfortably seated beneath those trees, and being upon high ground, the appearance of such a mighty assembly, is

21. Baquaqua goes on (in the following paragraph) to refer to the king attending Muslim prayers at the end of Ramadan. Austin assumes that the king was nevertheless non-Muslim (*African Muslims Sourcebook*, 646, nn. 12–13, 16; *Transatlantic Travels*, 162). This was indeed the common pattern in Borgu proper: cf. Nehemiah Levtzion, *Muslims and Chiefs in West Africa* (Oxford, 1968): 173–78. But it is uncertain whether it in fact applies to Djougou. According to Dupuis in 1820, the king of Djougou ("Zogho") was "a rigid Moslem," though his evidence is admittedly hearsay (based on information heard at Kumasi, the capital of Asante, in modern Ghana, to the west) and perhaps not reliable: *Journal of a Residence in Ashantee* (London, 1824): xlvii. According to Yves Person, "Zugu, ville musulmane" (Fonds Person, Bibliothèque de Centre de Recherches Africaines, Paris), the first king of Djougou to declare himself a Muslim was Atakora II (1899–1921); but already earlier in the 1890s it was reported that "the royal family and a large part of the population [of the city of Djougou] are mahometans," although the surrounding villages were still "essentially pagan": Klose, *Le Togo sous drapeau allemand*, 390.

22. Presumably the phraseology is Moore's rather than Baquaqua's; even if the latter may have internalized the categorization of Muhammad's prophecy (later in this paragraph) as "false," he would surely have known that Muhammad, unlike Jesus, is not "worshipped."

23. The festival of *'id al-fitr* at the end of Ramadan, marked by communal prayers.

24. The wording seems to imply that the king did not reside within the "city"; but Baquaqua later (p. 13) makes clear that the king's palace, although separate from "the principal part of the city," was situated within the city walls.

25. *Dyingire* in Dendi actually refers generically to any place of worship, including mosques: the place of prayer outside the city used for the public ceremonies is called *idi dyingire*.

imposing in the extreme, the seats are merely mats spread out upon the ground. A mound of sand (this sand differs from the sand of the desert, it is a coarse red sand mixed with earth and small stones and can easily be formed into a substantial mound)[26] is raised for the chief priest[27] to stand upon whilst he addresses the people. On these occasions he is dressed in a loose black robe, reaching nearly to the ground, and is attended by four subordinate priests, who kneel around him, holding the bottom of his robe, waving it to and fro.[28] Occasionally the chief priest will "squat like a toad," and when he arises, they resume the operation of waving his robe. These ceremonies concluded the people return home to offer sacrifice, (sarrah)[29] for the dead and living. Thus ends the annual fast.

26. I.e., laterite.

27. I.e., the imam. In Djougou a list of sixteen imams prior to the present incumbent (installed in 1998) is recalled, suggesting that the first listed dates from the early 19th century: list communicated by Zakari Dramani-Issifou; cf. also Brégand, *Commerce caravanier*, 114–15.

28. Compare the description of communal prayers at Kaiama in eastern Borgu by the Landers in 1830, which likewise says that while the "chief mallam" recited prayers "two priests of inferior order knelt beside him to hold the hem of his tobe, and a third, in the same position, held the skirts from behind": *Journal* [2 June 1830]: i, 213.

29. Dendi *sara*, from Arabic *sadaqa,* 'alms,' but used in Dendi as offerings to the dead. See Arifari Bako, "La Question du peuplement dendi dans la partie septentrionale de la République Populaire du Bénin: Le cas du Borgou," 178, 197.

CHAPTER II.

Government in Africa.

In Africa they have no written or printed forms of government, and yet the people are subject to certain laws, rules and regulations. The government is vested in the king as supreme, next to him are chiefs or petty sovereigns, there are also other officers, whose titles and office cannot be explained very well in English.[30]

The king of Zoogoo, as before stated, is tributary or subservient to the king of Bergoo.[31] Theft is considered the greatest crime in some parts of Africa, and the thief frequently re- **[p. 12]** ceives the punishment of death in consequence. When any one is suspected or charged with theft, he is taken before the king, where a sort of trial is given him; if found guilty, he is either sold or put to death; where the latter sentence is carried into effect, any one is allowed to stone or otherwise abuse and maltreat him, when he is finally led to the top of a small hill in the city and either stoned or shot to death.[32] Murder is not considered so great a crime, and a murderer does not receive capital punishment, but is mostly sold as a slave and sent out of the country.

The crime of adultery is severely punished, but the heaviest punishment is inflicted upon the man; a case in point is thus described by Mahommah, he says: "I remember an individual that was severely punished for this crime. The king's brother had several wives, one of whom was suspected of incontinency. Both were brought before the king—I was with him at the time.[33] The king ordered me to get a rope,

30. Presumably the distinction is between the "chiefs" of surrounding villages subordinate to Djougou and "officers" within the town of Djougou itself.

31. I.c., of Nikki, cf. n. 12 above.

32. Contrast Baquaqua's reported statement in Haiti in 1847, that "a person convicted of stealing, has his right arm cut off" (letter of Mrs. N.A.L. Judd, 8 October 1847). Amputation of the hand (rather than the whole arm) is the orthodox Islamic punishment for theft; here Baquaqua presumably reports the indigenous practice, as enforced in the royal court.

33. As noted by Austin, *African Muslims Sourcebook*, 647, n. 18, the reference here would appear to be not to "the king" of Djougou, as the immediate context seems to imply, but rather the king of the neighboring and subordinate town in whose service Baquaqua spent some time, as reported later (p. 31). Such ambiguities in allusions to "the king," "our king" in the text probably reflect problems of communication between Baquaqua and his editor Moore.

which was fastened around the man's arms, behind his back and tied, then a stick was placed in the rope, which had been wetted so as to make it shrink, and then twisted around until the poor creature was forced into a confession of his guilt, when he was released and given away as a slave. The woman received no other punishment than that of witnessing the torture inflicted upon her guilty paramour.["]

The farmers have their crops secured in this way.—The farms not being fenced in, the king makes a law, that every man who owns a horse, donkey, or other animal, must keep them from his neighbors' premises. If any animal strays upon the neighbors' premises, and does the least damage, he is caught and tied up, and the owner obliged to pay a heavy fine before he can recover the animal. This is the style of impounding in Africa.

Debts are sometimes collected in the following manner, viz:—If a person in one town or city, is indebted to a person residing at a distance and refuses or neglects to pay such a debt, the creditor residing in such a distant town or city may seize upon any of his neighbors, whom he may happen to catch in that town, and if he has any money or thing valuable, the creditor is allowed to take it from him, and tell such stranger to get it from **[p. 13]** his fellow townsman when he returns home again; if he has no property about him, he is allowed to seize upon his person and detain him until the debt is paid.[34] Such a law in this country would have very great effect in keeping the citizens pretty much confined to their own homes, as the danger of traveling would be very great; the chances of return to an anxious and affectionate wife, would in most civilized countries be very small

34. This practice of seizing property or persons to enforce payment of debts is well attested to on the West African coast, where it was known as "panyarring" (from Portuguese *penhorar*, "to distrain"): see Robin Law, "On pawning and enslavement for debt on the pre-colonial Slave Coast," in Toyin Falola and Paul E. Lovejoy, eds., *Pawnship in Africa: Debt Bondage in Historical Perspective* (Boulder, Colorado, 1994): 62–63. But no other evidence has been found of the practice in Borgu, or indeed elsewhere in the interior. There is no reference to it in the discussion of debt in Borgu in Djibril Mama Debourou, "Commerçants et chefs dans l'ancien Borgu (des origines à 1936)" (Thèse de Doctorat du 3e cycle, Université de Paris I, 1979): 159–62.

indeed. Supposing the rambler to be destitute of property,[35] and supposing him to be a man of means, there is no doubt of his means being considerably reduced, ere his return to his happy home.[36]

The soldiers are a privileged class, and whatever they need either in town or city, they are allowed to take, and there is no redress, from any complaint made against them.[37] If a slave becomes dissatisfied, he leaves his master and goes to the king, and becomes a soldier, and thereby gains his freedom from his master.[38] No "fugitive slave law" can touch him.[39] These are some of the principal matters which are brought before the king for adjustment, which he disposes of, according to the laws of the land.

35. The syntax here seems incorrect; this clause should be preceded by a comma rather than a period.

36. This seems to be Moore rather than Baquaqua speaking ("this country" being the U.S.A.).

37. This probably alludes to royal bodyguards (*tkiriku*, alternatively, *tyiriku*), whose depredatory activities Baquaqua later describes (pp. 32–33), from his personal experience of service in the palace of a local ruler.

38. This again probably alludes to enrollment as palace bodyguards (*tkiriku*). In Borgu, it is recalled that murderers could escape justice by placing themselves under the protection of chiefs, whose servants (*tkiriku*) they then became, but there is no reference in this context to runaway slaves: Lombard, *Structures de type "féodal,"* 122.

39. The controversial Fugitive Slave Law in the U.S.A. (1850) provided for the return of escaped slaves, even if they succeeded in reaching states where slavery was illegal. Two of Baquaqua's extant letters in 1850–51 refer critically to this legislation: letters written apparently to W. Walker, editor, 28 September 1850, 21 February 1851, in *The American Baptist*, 10 October 1850, 6 March 1851.

CHAPTER III.

Appearance and Situation of the Country.

It is rather difficult to give a very correct account of the geography of that part of Africa, described as the birthplace of Mahommah; but it must be situate[d] somewhere between ten and twenty degrees north latitude, and near the meridian of Greenwich.[40] It is situated in the peninsular [sic] formed by the great bend of the river Niger.

Up to the time that Mahommah was "forced from home and **[p. 14]** all its pleasures," the foot of the white man had not made its first impress upon the soil;[41] therefore the facts, matters, and things hereby related, will be the more interesting to all those whose hearts and souls are turned toward the wants and woes of that portion of the globe.

The city of Zoogoo is in the midst of a most fertile and delightful country; the climate, though exceedingly hot, is quite healthy. There are hills and mountains, plains and valleys, and it is pretty well watered. About a mile from the city there is a stream of water, as white as milk and very cool, and not far from that there is a spring of very cold water, also quite white. The residents often go from the city thence [sic: = there] for water.

It is not in the midst of a wilderness, as some suppose, but there are some quite extensive plains, covered with very tall rank grass,

---

40. Djougou is actually situated at about 9°30 north, 1°40 east.

41. This was true of Baquaqua's birthplace, Djougou, which seems not to have been visited by any European before the German Ludwig Wolf in 1888: see W. Wolf, "Dr Ludwig Wolfs letzte Reise nach Barbar (Bariba oder Borgu)," *Mitteilungen aus den Deutsche Schutzgebieten,* 4 (19891): 1–22. In 1826 a member of a British exploring expedition, Thomas Dickson, did reach Nikki, but died without leaving any account of it: U.K. Parliamentary Papers, Correspondence relating to the Slave Trade 1849–50, Class B, inclosure 9 in no. 9, Journal of Lieutenant Forbes, 18 October 1849. Other members of the same expedition, Hugh Clapperton and Richard Lander, and subsequently (1830) Richard Lander and his brother John traveled through eastern Borgu, visiting Kaiama, Wawa, and Bussa: Clapperton, *Journal of a Second Expedition into the Interior of Africa* (London, 1829); Richard Lander, *Records of Captain Clapperton's Last Expedition to Africa* (London, 1830); Richard & John Lander, *Journal of an Expedition to Explore the Course & Termination of the Niger* (London and New York, 1832).

which is used by the people to cover their houses, after the fashion of thatching. On these plains there are but few trees, but what there are, are of great size. And here also, roams the elephant, the lion, and other wild animals, common to the torrid zone. There are two kinds of elephants, one very large, called Yah-quim-ta-ca-ri, the other small, called Yah-quin-ta-cha-na.[42] The teeth of the elephant lie scattered about in abundance all over the plains, and can be collected in any quantity.[43] The natives use the teeth to make musical instruments, which they call Ka-fa.[44]

The city itself is large, and surrounded by a thick wall, built of red clay and made very smooth on both sides. The outer side of the wall is surrounded by a deep moat or ditch, which in the rainy season is filled with water. Beyond this, the city is further protected by a hedge of thorns, grown so thickly and compactly together that no person could pass through them; it bears a small white blossom, and when in full bloom looks exceedingly beautiful.[45]

The king's palace (if it may be so called) is within the city wall, at some little distance from the principal part of the city,[46] surrounded by (what in some countries would be called) a park, on a most extensive scale, at the back of which is a dense thicket,[47] precluding the neces-

---

42. The first three syllables common to both terms probably represent Dendi *térékúnté*, elephant (the first syllable "Yah" being perhaps miscopied for "Tah"); the suffix "cha-na" in the second term is presumably Dendi *tyéénè*, small, but 'ca-ri' in the first is not identified (Dendi for "large" being *béérì*). The distinction between large and small elephants may allude to the smaller subspecies of the African elephant, loxodonta africana cyclotis, also called the "forest elephant."

43. In eastern Borgu in the 1820s, Clapperton reported that ivory was available "in great plenty," but there was no market for it: *Journal*, 93. However, Baquaqua later (p. 23) refers to trade in ivory.

44. The account of Borgu musical instruments in Jacques Lombard, "Aperçu sur la technologie et l'artisanat bariba," *Etudes dahoméennes*, 18 (1957), 42–44, does not mention either ivory horns, or the term "ka-fa"; cf. however Hausa *kafo*, horn (though not specifically of ivory).

45. Klose in the 1890s described Djougou as surrounded by "a prickly hedge and a wall of banko [i.e., mud brick]": *Le Togo sous drapeau allemand*, 389.

46. Djougou consisted of two distinct parts: the royal quarter, called Kilir (or Killinga) to the southwest, and the Muslim merchants' quarter (here designated as "the principal part of the city"), called Wangara, to the northeast: cf. Klose, *Le Togo sous drapeau allemand*, 389–90.

47. Klose in the 1890s likewise described the palace at Djougou as situated within "a large park with tropical vegetation": *Le Togo sous drapeau allemand*, 389.

PLATE 4. King's Palace, Djougou: 'The king's palace … is within the city, at some distance from the principal part of the city' (see Biography, pp. 14–15); outer and inner entrances, 1999 (photography by Lovejoy).

sity of any protecting wall on that side of **[p. 15]** the royal domain. A broad avenue leads from the city to the king's house, with an extensive market on either side, beautifully shaded with large overhanging trees.[48] The people of America can have no idea of the size and beauty of some of the trees in Africa, particularly in the cities, where they stand a good distance apart, by that means having the best chance of attaining their full growth. There is a tree called Bon-ton,[49] which grows to a very great height, but the branches do not spread so wide as some others; it is very beautiful.

The entrance into the city, is through six gates, which bear the names of their respective keepers, something similar to the city of London and most of the old fortified towns in England, and indeed of most parts of the old country.[50] These gate keepers are chosen for their courage and bravery, and are generally persons of rank. It may perhaps, instruct as well as amuse our young friends, who may read this work, to know their names, and on that account we will give them. 1. U-boo-ma-co-fa. 2. Fo-ro-co-fa. 3. Bah-pa-ra-ha-co-fa. 4. Bah-too-loo-co-fa. 5. Bah-la-mon-co-fa. 6. Ajaggo-co-fa.[51] The word

48. This is still the location of the principal market in Djougou, between the Kilir and Wangara quarters: cf. also Klose, ibid., 389.

49. Dendi *bántàn*, the silk cotton tree.

50. Presumably the comparison with London and England ("the old country") more generally is contributed by the editor Moore, rather than by Baquaqua himself.

51. There may be some confusion on Moore's part here, since at least four and probably five of the six names given here for the "gatekeepers" seem to be rather the names of quarters of the city (or the titles of their chiefs), still recognizable today. "U-boo-ma" thus represents Yobumc (literally, "behind the market"), which is remembered as the former name of the quarter nowadays called Petoni-Poho, in the south of the city (see Person, "Zugu, ville musulmane"); "Foro" is Foro-Magazin ("field of the Magazin"), in the center; "Ba-pa-ra-ha" is probably a corrupt version of Bakparakpei, the head of the resident Muslim traders, whose quarter is on the east of the city; "Bah-too-loo" is Batoulou, the title of the deputy to the Baparapei, whose quarter is to the northeast; and "Bah-la-mon" is Ba-Leman, or imam. There are nowadays two "Ba-Leman" quarters in Djougou, representing two families which have supplied imams, Leman-Mande (the older-established), in the north of the city, and Leman-Bogou, to the west; but it is probable that there was still only one in Baquaqua's time: cf. Brégand, *Commerce caravanier*, 113–15.

cofa means gate,[52] and Bah, means father.[53] Ajagga is the name of a woman whose son was noted for his valor. In times of war, these gates are strongly guarded, hence the necessity of having chosen men of known valor and courage to keep them.

The houses are built of clay, low and without chimneys or windows.

The following description of one of the dwellings will give a pretty accurate idea of the generality of the houses of the city. A dwelling is composed of a number of separate rooms built in a circle, with quite a space between them; within the outer circle is another circle of rooms, according to the size of the family to occupy them. These rooms are all connected by a wall; there is one large or main entrance in front of the others, in which to receive company. Each family is surrounded by their own dwelling, so that when they are in any apartment, they cannot see any other dwelling, or any one passing or repassing. In consequence of this mode of building, the city occupies a very large space of ground.

[p. 16] There is a regularly appointed watch to the city, who are paid by the king, he also acting as chief magistrate over the watch.

52. In Djougou, the term *kofa* is nowadays explained as referring to the bush beyond the limits of the inhabited area of the town, rather than meaning "gate": fieldwork, April 1999. But cf. *kofa*, "gate" in Hausa (also used metaphorically to refer to senior chiefs, who served as intermediaries in approaching the ruler).

53. *Ba* is actually the Baatonu (Bariba) term for "father" (the Dendi word being *bàabá*), but it appears in many titles in Djougou, including that of Bakparakpei.

CHAPTER IV.

Agriculture, Arts, &c.

The agriculture of the country is in but a very rude state; the few implements used are made by the country people, and consist of a large kind of hoe, to dig up the ground, and small ones to plant and dress the corn, or whatever is to be raised.[54] This process of preparing the ground is very laborious and tedious, but the richness of the soil compensates in some degree; for one acre well tilled, will yield an immense crop. Corn[55] is raised, sweet potatoes and Harnee,[56] which very much resembles the American broom corn in appearance, and is very much used as an article of food. Harnebee,[57] which is a very fine grain, grows on a very large stalk, and is unlike anything in this country; it is roasted in the ear, and the grain rubbed out with the hands and eaten as the American people do parched corn; it is very good. Rice is raised in large quantities, and of an excellent quality; it is planted in rows, and one planting will serve two or three years, as it will come up of itself without any attention. It grows very luxuriously. Beans are also cultivated. Fruits grow in great abundance and variety, spontaneously. Yams are cultivated and grow to great perfection. Pine Apples grow spontaneously, but are not eaten, as the natives fear they are of a poisonous quality, but that is only fear, from the want of knowing better. Peanuts are plentiful and of good quality: and there is also a great variety of grain and fruits of other kinds;[58] and supposing they had the means of cultivation, the same as they have in more civilised countries, Africa would be capable of supporting within herself an immense population.

---

54. Various sorts of hoes in use in Borgu are described in Lombard, "Aperçu sur la technologie," 11.

55. I.e., presumably (according to American usage) specifically maize, as distinct from the other species mentioned immediately after.

56. Dendi *hááni*, millet, i.e., probably specifically bulrush millet (*pennisetum*).

57. Dendi *hááni bi* (lit. "black millet"), sorghum.

58. Klose in the 1890s refers to the cultivation of rice, millet, sorghum, yams, groundnuts, and also tobacco: *Le Togo sous drapeau allemand*, 391–92.

The manufactures of Africa are very limited; they consist of **[p. 17]** farming utensils, cotton cloths[59] and silk. Silk is but little manufactured, but might be much more, as silkworms are to be found in abundance, and might be increased to any extent.[60] The cotton tree grows very large, and the cotton is of good quality.

The women do the spinning by a very slow process, having to twist the thread with their fingers; the men do the weaving; they weave the cloth in narrow strips, and then sew it together.[61] Women also grind the corn. The process of grinding is this: They take a large stone and fix it in the ground, they then have a smaller one prepared, so that it can be easily handled; it is pecked on one side after the manner of our mill stones; the women then put the grain or whatever they wish to grind on the large stone and take the other and rub the grain until it is fine; if they wish to make it very fine, they take another stone prepared for the purpose, and by patient labor they succeed in making it as fine as the finest American flour. They grind dried yams by pounding them in a mortar and a fine kind of grain called Har-nee, before named, mixed together; of this mixture they make a kind of stiff pudding, and eat it with gravy made of greens and a variety of vegetables, seasoned with pepper and onions. No kind of food is ever eaten without onions.

The *Shepherds and Herdsmen of Africa*, are a distinct and subordinate class of people, and belong to the government.[62] They have long, straight hair, and are as light complexioned as the inhabitants of

---

59. Klose found local cloth on sale in the Djougou market, and commented that this indicated "a highly developed weaving industry": *Le Togo sous drapeau allemand*, 389. One quarter of Djougou, Kakabounouberi, is traditionally associated with weaving.

60. Presumably a confusion on Moore's part; although silk was used in local weaving, it was certainly not produced locally. Clapperton in the 1820s reported that traders from Borgu purchased unwrought silk at Kulfo, the principal market in western Nupe to the east: *Journal*, 137; cf. also Lovejoy, *Caravans of Kola*, 12, 125, 133 n. 32.

61. This sexual division of labor is confirmed by recent accounts of Borgu: Lombard, "Aperçu sur la technologie," 26–27. Cf. also Clapperton, *Journal*, 94 (for Wawa, in eastern Borgu).

62. Cattle-keeping in Borgu was restricted to the Fulbe (sing. Pullo; whence the usual French term "Peul"), who were subordinate in status, clients of rulers or nobles: Lombard, *Structures de type "féodal,"* 36–37, 130–33.

southern Europe;[63] they are nearly white; they take care of the flocks and herds, supply the city with milk, butter and cheese, (the butter is quite good and hard, which is an evidence of its being cooler in this locality than in most other parts of the torrid zone.) They are Mahomedans in their religion, and strictly adhere to the rites and ceremonies of that class of religionists.[64] They speak the Arabic and Flanne[65] languages, hence it must be inferred that they are of Arabian descent, but of their further history, we are in ignorance.

The Domestic Animals of Africa, are much the same as in this and other countries, consisting of the horse, cow, sheep, goat, donkey, mule and ostrich.[66] Birds are abundant, such as geese, turkeys, peacocks; guinea hens and barn fowls; the lat- **[p. 18]** ter are very large and are in great abundance.[67] They are, together with their eggs, used as the common food for the people in the forests. Besides these, there are abundance of swans in the river,[68] and a variety of wild fowl; there is also a kind of water fowl that is very beautiful, and whose plumage is as white as snow, and about the size of an ordinary dove,[69]—they congregate in large flocks. Parrots are quite common, and singing birds are very numerous.

The rivers abound with the river horse,[70] the crocodile, &c.

63. This comparison seems more likely to derive from Moore than from Baquaqua. A similar observation was made by Clapperton in the 1820s of the Fulbe in eastern Borgu, "they are as fair as the lower class of Portuguese, or Spaniards," *Journal*, 96.

64. Fulbe in the Borgu region were certainly predominantly Muslim. But in eastern Borgu, Clapperton in the 1820s found that some Fulbe were 'not Mahometans, but pagans': *Journal*, 96.

65. I.e. Fulani, which is specifically the Dendi, and also the Hausa, form of the name Fulbe.

66. Klose in the 1890s refers to horses, donkeys, cattle, sheep, goats: *Le Togo sous drapeau allemand*, 392–93. The ostrich is presumably incorrectly classified as a "domestic" animal. In eastern Borgu in the 1820s, Clapperton found ostrich feathers available "in great plenty," although there was no market for them: *Journal*, 93.

67. Klose in the 1890s refers to chickens, guinea fowl, turkeys, peacocks: *Le Togo sous drapeau allemand*, 393.

68. Perhaps referring to the great white egret, an aquatic bird common throughout West Africa.

69. Presumably a form of duck.

70. I.e., hippopotamus.

CHAPTER V.

Manners, Customs, &c.

Great respect is paid to the aged; they never use the prefix mister or mistress, but always some endearing term, such as, when speaking to an aged person, they say Father or Mother, and an equal, they call brother or sister. Children are brought up to be obedient and polite; they are never permitted to contradict or sit in the presence of an aged person, and when they see an elderly person coming, they immediately uncover, and if they have shoes upon their feet they immediately remove them. They bend their knee to the aged, and the aged in turn bend their knee to them, and request them at once to rise; and in every respect a deference is paid to age. The best seat is reserved for them, and in their places of worship, the place next to the priest is reserved for them. Should not these facts put to shame the manners of the children in this country towards the aged? How painful it is to witness the disrespect shown to grown up people by the rising generation of this country, and in many cases the shameful behavior of children towards even their own parents, and that without a single check of censure or rebuke![71]

[p. 19] It is here that the great moral regeneration of our land must commence. Children should be early taught to render obedience and respect to their superiors, and they will then be prepared to render to all, equal rights, when they become men and women, and will in turn be prepared to govern well their own households.

The reader will please pardon this digression; it has been made with a view to draw attention more powerfully to the subject, as it is of vital importance to the well-being of any community, that the young should be properly trained "in the way they should go," so that when they grow up they should "not depart from it." And if this con-

---

71. Clearly this sentence, and the following two paragraphs, represent the voice of Moore (cf. "our land," i.e., America, in the following paragraph), rather than of Baquaqua.

trast in the behavior of the poor African children, with that of those of our own enlightened nation, may be the means of but one step in the march of improvement and reform in this respect, the compiler of these pages will feel amply repaid for the little exertion bestowed upon these few extra lines. This is one good, nay one of the best features of Africa; another is the law of kindness, which everywhere prevails in the mutual intercourse of those of the same ranks; whatever a person has, he freely divides with his neighbor, and no one even enters a house without being invited to eat.

But the same as in more civilized countries, if a person rises to wealth and honor, he is sure to be envied, if not hated; they do not like to see one of their own number rise above them. A person who has always been rich, they esteem more highly.[72] This seems to be pretty well the case all over the world, go where you will, like seems to produce (in cases of this kind) like. We see the very same thing manifest amongst us every day of our lives, here in our very midst, so that it does not appear that we are greatly removed from the benighted African, with all our wisdom and learning, with all our boasted institutions; truly the whole world is a strange compound of "black, white and gray, and the ways of all mankind are turned every way."

Fighting is of very common occurrence, and is by no means considered disgraceful, there is a place in the city where the young men meet together for that purpose; and as elsewhere, there are two parties who never agree; each party occupies dif- **[p. 20]** ferent portions of the city, and they meet for personal combat, which often ends in a general flight, but they never kill each other.[73]

---

72. These two sentences, by contrast, seems to represent Baquaqua's own thoughts, alluding to his explanation of his own enslavement and sale out of the country, as related in detail later in his narrative (p. 34). The comparative observations which follow in the remainder of this paragraph, however, are clearly contributed by Moore ("amongst us" being, again, in America).

73. Tradition suggests that Djougou in this period (c.1820–50) suffered from a "time of troubles," involving "30 years of civil war" (Person, "Zugu, ville musulmane"). The wording, however, suggests ritualized recreational fighting rather than serious combat. Such fights between "quarters of the same village," performed annually, is reported as a feature of Dendi culture: Arifari Bako, "La Question du peuplement dendi," 192.

CHAPTER VI.

Marriage Ceremonies, &c.

When a young man wishes to marry, he selects a choice fruit called Gan-ran,[74] and sends it by his sister or some female friend to the object of his choice; if the fruit is accepted, he understands that he will be favorably received, and remains at home for about a week before he pays her another visit. After some time spent in visiting and receiving visits, arrangements are made for the marriage ceremony. They do not [sic?] have a particular day set, and a wedding at the bride's father's, but she is kept ignorant of the time; the arrangements are made by the bridegroom and her parents.[75] At the time appointed, the bridegroom sends a number of young men to the house of her father at night; they remain out of doors very still and send a child in to tell her some one wishes to speak with her. She goes to the door and is immediately surrounded and carried off by the young men, to a place called Nya-wa-qua-foo,[76] where she is kept six days; during this time she remains veiled and has a number of female friends with her, who spend their time in play and amusements. The bridegroom in the meantime confines himself at home and is attended by his young friends, who also spend their time in feasting and merriment until the seventh day.

Whilst they are thus confined, a general invitation is given to the friends of both parties. The invitation is made in this way: It will be said that My-ach-ee and Ah-dee-za-in-qua-hoo-noo-yo-haw-coo-nah, which signifies that the bride and bridegroom are **[p. 21]** going out

---

74. Dendi *góórò*, kola; also Hausa, *goro*, commonly presented as gifts and in receiving guests at weddings, funerals and other ceremonies in the Muslim areas of the savanna; see Paul E. Lovejoy, "The 'Coffee' of the Sudan: Consumption of kola nuts in the Sokoto Caliphate in the nineteenth century," in Jordan Goodman, Paul E. Lovejoy, and Andrew Sherratt, eds., *Consuming Habits: Drugs in History and Anthropology* (London, 1993): 103–25.

75. The "not" in the first clause seems to be an error, since if there was no "particular day set" it would make no sense to say that the bride was "kept ignorant of the time."

76. Not fully identified, but the last syllable is Dendi *fúù*, 'house.'

today.[77] They all meet at some convenient place named for the purpose. The friends of the bridegroom conduct him there, and the friends of the bride, conduct her also; both bride and groom having their heads covered with white cloths. A mat is prepared for them to be seated; the friends advance and salute the bridegroom, at the same time handing him some money.[78] The money is then placed before the couple, who are thus considered man and wife. Money is likewise scattered for the drum king and his company; also for the children of the populace to pick up. After this, they are conducted to the house of the bridegroom. The ceremonies are thus brought to an end. It ought to have been stated that the favor of the lady's father is obtained by presents.

Polygamy is practised to a great extent, and sanctioned by law. A man's property is sometimes estimated by the number of wives he has. Occasionally a poor man has a number of wives, and then they have to support him. When a rich woman marries a poor man (as is sometimes the case) he never has more than one wife. Mahommah's mother was a woman of rank and wealth.[79] His father had been a wealthy man; he was a traveling merchant; carried his merchandise on donkeys, and had slaves to accompany him; but by some means he lost the greater part of his property, and at the time of his marriage

77. Dendi-speaking informants have suggested that "My-ache-ee" and "Ah-dee-za" here represent personal names, Mahiachi and Adiza, presumably those of the prospective bridegroom and bride. The remainder of the phrase, "in-qua-hoo-noo- yo-haw-coo-nah," cannot be deciphered in its entirety but clearly includes Dendi *hùnú* ("hoo-noo"), "go out", and perhaps *hó?* ("haw"), "today," and hence the phrase appears to be an invitation announcing that Mahiachi and Adiza "are coming out today," i.e., getting married.

78. One of several allusions by Baquaqua to "money"; he nowhere explains what this consisted of, but other evidence shows that the current money in the Borgu area consisted of cowry shells: cf. e.g., Dupuis, *Journal of a Residence in Ashantee*, cxiv.

79. Baquaqua later (p. 31) explains that his mother was "related" to "our king"—in the context, apparently not the king of Djougou itself, but of a neighboring subordinate town (perhaps, as argued later, Soubroukou). Mrs. Judd in Haiti earlier likewise understood that "their [sic] parents, particularly his mother, were related or in some way connected with the prince, or chief of the country where he lived": letter of Mrs. N.A.L. Judd, 24 March 1848, in *Christian Contributor and Free Missionary*, 17 May 1848. Given her foreign origin (from Katsina), the relationship was presumably by marriage.

was comparatively poor; he consequently had but one wife.[80] This is another reason why it is supposed he was of Arabian birth, as many of the Arabs travel in this way to gain property.[81]

The women in Africa are considered very inferior to the men, and are consequently held in the most degrading subjection. The condition of females is very similar to that in all barbarous nations. They never eat at the same table with the men, or rather in their presence, (they having no tables) but in separate apartments.

When a person dies, they wrap the body in a white cloth, and bury it as soon as possible. After the body is laid out facing the east, the priest is sent for, and a religious ceremony performed, which consist of prayers to Allah for the soul of the departed.

[p. 22] The manner of burying is to dig a place in the ground, several feet deep and ten or twelve feet horizontally, in which they deposit the body and close up the entrance with a large flat stone. Other ceremonies are also performed by the priest over the grave.[82]

Great lamentations are made for the dead, by loud and bitter cries and wailings, which continue for six days. The friends of the departed, shut themselves up for that space of time, holding meetings for prayer every night. The seventh day, a great feast is held and the term of mourning ends, when the family appear as usual.[83]

The Africans are a superstitious race of people, and believe in

80. Mrs. Judd in Haiti in 1847 explained that Baquaqua's father was "inclined to intemperance and gambling, by which he spent the most part of his own, and also his wife's estate": letter of Mrs. N.A.L. Judd, 8 October 1847. The allegation of intemperance seems, however, incompatible with statements in the *Biography*, stressing Baquaqua's father's Islamic piety and "grave and silent" character (p. 10) and insisting that Muslims never drink (p. 24). In the *Biography*, it is rather Baquaqua himself who is represented as given to drinking (pp. 34–35), and it may be that Mrs. Judd misunderstood a reference to his own drinking as applying to his father.

81. Cf. above, n. 14.

82. This evidently describes the practice of Muslims, rather than of pagans. At Wawa in eastern Borgu, Clapperton noted that Muslims were interred in their own "burying-ground," but pagans in their own houses: *Journal*, 89.

83. The Landers, in eastern Borgu, also reported lamentations maintained for the space of seven days: *Journal* [16 August 1830]: i, 327,

witchcraft and other supernatural agencies.[84] Bodies of light, something after the manner of *Ignus Fatuas*,[85] or Will o' the Wisp, are often seen on the hills and high places, which move fitfully about. These phenomena are supposed to be evil spirits; they have a strange appearance from a distance, and with less ignorant people than the Africans, might be taken for a very different object. They are much larger in appearance than the Jack-o'-Lanthorn of Europe, and seem to proceed from the extended arms of a human being.

When they suppose any person is bewitched, they consult their astrologer, who consults the stars, and by that means trace out the supposed witch,[86] which generally happens to be some poor decrepit old woman, whom they take and put to death. This practice seems to be very similar to what was formerly practised in the eastern states, in most parts of old England, and indeed generally throughout Europe "in days gone by." Indeed in many parts of England, in small isolated towns and villages, the same thing is done at the present day. Of course all such notions have their origin in the grossest ignorance, hence the necessity of educating the masses of the people in every part of the world.

There is a class of men called medicine men, whom the people suppose nothing can hurt; these men have the office assigned them of putting to death these supposed witches. They are called Unbahs and are scattered all about the country; go in **[p. 23]** a state of nudity; eat swine's flesh, and are considered by the Mahommedans as a very wicked people.[87]

---

84. For belief in witches (*tyerko*) among the Dendi, cf. Arifari Bako, "La Question du peuplement dendi," 143.85. Sic: correctly, *ignis fatuus* (lit. "foolish fire"), referring in Europe to lights caused by the spontaneous combustion of marsh-gas (but popularly attributed to evil spirits), which lured travelers astray.

85. Sic: correctly, *ignis fatuus* (lit. 'foolish fire'), referring in Europe to lights caused by the spontaneous combustion of marsh-gas (but popularly attributed to evil spirits), which lured travelers astray.

86. The practice of consulting diviners (Dendi *góbà*) to determine whether sickness was caused by human agency is described in *Dendi Cine tila Bukatante/Livre du dendi pratique* (n. d.), 20, which was confirmed during fieldwork, April 1999.

87. For "magicians" among the Dendi who combated witchcraft, cf. Arifari Bako, "La Question du peuplement dendi," 143, 183–84; but he gives a different term for them, *gunu*.

It is customary for the Mahommedans to wear a loose kind of trousers, which are made full at the bottom and are fastened round about the hips by a cord. A loose robe is worn over this, cut in a circular form, open at the centre, sufficiently large to put over the head, and allowed to rest on the shoulders, with loose sleeves, the neck and breast being exposed. The women wear a cloth about two yards square, doubled cornerwise, and tied around the waist, the tie being made at the left side.[88] The king's dress is made in a similar style, but of more costly materials. Children do not wear much clothing.

The trade carried on between Zoogoo and other parts of the country,[89] is done by means of horses and donkies.[90] Salt is brought from a place called Sab-ba.[91] They exchange slaves, cows and ivory for salt.

88. Cf. Klose, *Le Togo sous drapeau allemand*, 391, who says that Muslims in Djougou wore "a Hausa jacket, with a turban and a Phrygian cap" (but pagans a leather apron), and women a cloth.

89. Djougou was an important stage on the trade route connecting Asante with Hausaland, as noted, e.g., by Bowdich, *Mission from Cape Coast Castle to Ashantee*, 208; Dupuis, *Journal of a Residence in Ashantee*, civ, cxxv, cxxx. The Landers in 1830 also heard of the commercial importance of Djougou (which they call "Loogoo," probably miscopied for 'Zoogoo'): "they are enriched by the thousands of merchants who trade to Gonja for the goora [kola] nut, &c.": *Journal* [19 August 1830]: i, 335.

90. It is usually asserted that horses were never used as pack animals in Borgu: Lombard, "Aperçu sur la technologie," 40. However, there are references to the use of ponies to carry kola from Gonja to Hausaland: Robin Law, *The Horse in West African History* (London, 1980): 162.

91. The geography of this passage, one of Baquaqua's most concrete references to local trade, is unfortunately obscure. Informants at Djougou, April 1999, suggested the "Sa-ba" mentioned here as a source of salt was in modern Ghana, referring perhaps to Sabari, a place on the route to Yendi in Dagomba. In this case, the salt would presumably have come from Daboya, which was the principal source of salt in northern Ghana: Lovejoy, *Caravans of Kola*, 12, 18, 34, 126, 134 n. However, other accounts based on local tradition suggest different sources of salt. According to Person, "Zugu, ville musulmane," Djougou imported its salt from the coast, from the Little Popo area: along this route, a possible candidate for identification with "Sab-ba" might be the town of Savalou, north of Abomey. But other accounts assert that the main source of salt in the Borgu region was from the valley of the Dallol Fogha, to the north: Brégand, *Commerce caravanier*, 67-69; Debourou, "Commerçants et chefs dans l'ancien Borgu," 127; Arifaro Bako, "La Question du peuplement dendi," 111. Contemporary evidence tends to confirm this last account. For example, W. B. Baikie, stationed on the lower Niger and Benue, reported in 1862 that Dallol Fogha salt "supplies the whole caravan road to Gonja": Baikie to Lord Russell, 22 March 1862, Public Record Office (PRO), FO 97/434, No. 19. Dupuis at Kumasi in 1820 heard that salt sold at the markets of Nikki, Bussa, and Yauri came from a lake two–three days' journey east of Nikki, called "Callio Makaro": *Journal of a Residence in Ashantee*, xcix. Despite the incorrect direction and too short distance from Nikki, this probably also refers to the Dallol Fogha.

This journey occupies about two months generally.[92] Occasionally European goods are brought from Ashantee, but they are very costly.[93] Most of the articles used are of home make. Earthenware is made out of clay, they have a nice red and white clay, but the articles they make are very coarse, as they know very little of that kind of manufacture,[94] indeed hardly of any other.

They have strange notions concerning the white man. Their notions are very vague and dreamy concerning them. They suppose they live in the ocean, and that when the sun goes down, it warms the water, so that the white people cook their food by it.[95] They consider the white people superior to themselves in every respect, and fear to make needles, as they imagine that the white men can look through an instrument and see all that's going on; and they believe the white man is very angry with them for making needles; they fear very much when thus occupied, and would not be seen by the white man at such a time, could they help it, for all the world. When they are busy at needle making, they of course imagine that they are being looked at; of course this arises from the belief that they are wrongfully engaged, and the same as throughout the whole human race, when a *supposed* wrong is being perpetrated, fear **[p. 24]** takes possession of the mind. This is but natural to all mankind; they imagine, for making needles, the whites have the power to put out their eyes. On account of such

92. Wherever "Sab-ba" was located, the distance seems excessive; cf. Baquaqua's own later (p. 30) reference to the journey from Djougou to Daboya (further west than Yendi) as taking only seventeen days. But the reference may be to the duration of a round trip.

93. In the 1890s Nikki in Borgu was reported to be importing from Salaga (the principal market for Asante's trade with the northeastern interior), in addition to kola nuts, some goods of European provenance—beads, red yarn, and "a little rum and powder (apparently very little of the latter)": Margery Perham & Mary Bull, eds., *The Diaries of Lord Lugard* (London, 1963): iv, 189 (11 November 1894). The association of European goods with Asante here is consistent with Baquaqua's later (p. 29) observation of the abundance of European goods in Daboya—by implication, in comparison with Borgu. The implication is that Djougou had relatively weak commercial links with the coast to the south, via Dahomey.

94. For earthenware in Borgu, cf. Lombard, "Aperçu sur la technologie," 17–20.

95. Clapperton in the 1820s likewise found that the king of Bussa "thought, and always have heard, that you [British] live on the water," but did not record the story about the sun heating their cooking water: *Journal*, 102.

notions prevailing, of course needles are not made to any great extent, but still some are found hardy and daring enough to make them notwithstanding.[96] From whence such notions sprang, we cannot very well explain, but the all-seeing instrument, is no doubt our telescope, which at some time or other has been exhibited likely by seamen, who have traveled in some parts of Africa, and the story circulated by the wonder-mongers of the sable tribe.[97]

Wars in Africa are very frequent, the country being divided into so many divisions or petty kingdoms. The kings are continually quarreling, which quarrels lead to war.[98]

When a king dies, there is no regular successor, but a great many rivals for the kingdom spring up, and he who can achieve his object by power and strength, becomes the succeeding king, thus war settles the question.[99]

Slavery is also another fruitful source of war, the prisoners being sold for slaves.[100] The weapons used, are bows and arrows, guns, and a kind of knife or short sword, of home manufacture.[101] This knife or

96. Baquaqua later (p. 27) describes the method of making needles, evidently from his own experience as apprentice to his uncle, a metalsmith. The story about fear of Europeans is difficult to fathom, but presumably Europeans were supposed to disapprove of the local manufacture of needles because it competed with imports which they supplied. It may be noted that Clapperton's mission to eastern Borgu in 1826 is said to have dispensed an "immense ... quantity of needles," and that the subsequent mission of the Landers in 1830 consequently found that they had been devalued in local markets: *Journal*, i, 266 [2 July 1830].

97. This comment (referring to "our" telescope) is clearly Moore's.

98. Local tradition corroborates this picture of conditions in Borgu, where there was reportedly "a state of permanent war": Debourou, "Commerçants et chefs dans l'ancien Borgou," 113. Clapperton in eastern Borgu in the 1820s remarked that "one town will plunder another whenever an opportunity offers": *Journal*, 74.

99. This may be generalized (maybe by Moore) from Baquaqua's observations of Gonja in the 1840s (p. 29). But similar contested successions were common in Borgu itself, for example, "every succession at Nikki gave rise to an armed confrontation": Debourou, "Commerçants et chefs dans l'ancien Borgou," 114.

100. Capture in warfare was the most common source of slaves in Borgu, as elsewhere in Africa: Lombard, *Structures de type "féodal,"* 121-22.

101. Klose in the 1890s lists the weapons used at Djougou as bows and arrows, knives and guns (the last possessed only by "a few of the king's men"): *Togo sous drapeau allemand*, 391. The account of Borgu weapons in Lombard, "Aperçu sur la technologie," 29–34, describes various sorts of daggers and swords, as well as bows and arrows (and also spears and clubs, not mentioned by Baquaqua).

sword is worn in time of peace as side arms, as well as in time of war. The Africans never go unarmed.—Sometimes great numbers are killed in the wars, but never so many as in European and other countries. Their prisoners are treated very cruelly; they flog and otherwise abuse them, until an opportunity occurs of disposing of them as slaves. They drink considerably before going to battle, in order to strengthen them and instil them with courage and daring; (of course this has no reference to those professing Mahommedanism, as they use no kinds of intoxicating drinks on any occasion.)[102] Sometimes whole cities are destroyed and the country round about laid waste, when famine ensues.

This alas is too often the consequence of war, wherever it is practised, not only in Africa, but in all parts where the bloody strife is engaged in. When the Gospel, with its beauteous truths are fully understood and appreciated by the people generally, peace and good will shall reign supreme, and "wars and rumors of wars," shall be no more forever.

[p. 25] How strange that nations boasting of enlightenment and the power of the glorious Gospel of Christ to govern them, should so engage, "hand to hand and foot to foot" in such scenes of carnage and destruction.[103] How can christian nations so engaged ever think to succeed in their mission of converting the heathen, when their practises at home are so much at variance with the blessed truths set forth in the sacred volume. Let the christian spirit and the spirit of war array themselves in everlasting opposition, and the day is not far distant

---

102. In Borgu (as in several other areas of the West African interior) there was a conceptual opposition between the ruling warrior aristocracy and Islam (evidently a matter of ideal types, which was not inconsistent with individual warriors being, at the level of personal belief, Muslims): cf. Lombard, *Structures de type "féodal,"* 224–31. In such circumstances, drinking alcohol (especially in public) served as an affirmation of identity as a member of the non-Muslim warrior class. It may be in this light that Baquaqua's own drinking of alcohol (below, pp. 34–35) should be understood; although from a Muslim family, he had enlisted as a palace bodyguard, by implication in a non-Muslim warrior milieu.

103. At the time of writing, Europe was engaged in the Crimean War (1853–55), which pitted France and Britain against Russia. Evidently, this passage is contributed by Moore rather than by Baquaqua himself.

when the wilderness shall blossom as the rose with flowers, fitted for the garniture of peace and holiness. Christians, and those professing the doctrines of the Gospel, should do all in their power to banish war. Then would their "yoke be easy and their burthen light," and the work of conversion would go rapidly on.

Slavery in Africa.—The greatest source of misery to Africa is her system of slavery, which is carried on to a fearful extent; but domestic slavery in that country is nothing when compared to this;[104] but the trading of slaves is very horrible. Slaves are taken from the interior and hurried to the coast, where they are exchanged for rum and tobacco, or other articles of merchandize.[105] This system of slavery causes much bloodshed and consequent misery. Mahommah was once taken prisoner and sold, but was redeemed by his mother, but more of this in the proper place.[106]

104. Cf. also observations recorded by Mrs. Judd in Haiti earlier, that Baquaqua's own "sufferings and degradation" in slavery in Africa "were comparatively nothing, to what they were after he was taken to the coast, and sold to the white man": letter of Mrs. N.A.L. Judd, 24 March 1848. The comparative mildness of slavery in Africa, relative to America, was a standard observation of contemporaries: cf., e.g., Duncan, *Travels*, i, 159–60 (referring to Dahomey and the Mahi country), who describes slavery in local societies as "easy servitude."

105. This statement seems at odds with the earlier (p. 23) observation that European goods were imported only "occasionally" and through Asante to the west, rather than directly from the coast. Perhaps Moore is generalizing from the case of Baquaqua himself, who was enslaved and taken to the coast via Dahomey, as related later in the *Biography* (pp. 35–41). Other evidence suggests that most of the slaves sold from Borgu went to internal African markets, rather than to the Europeans at the coast. The Landers in eastern Borgu in 1830 reported that "the greatest and most profitable market" for slaves was Timbuktu, where they were sold on into the trans-Saharan trade: *Journal* [24 August 1830]: i, 345–46. See also Law and Lovejoy, "Borgu in the Atlantic Slave Trade."

106. Seemingly a confusion on Moore's part; the subsequent narrative shows that Baquaqua was redeemed (after capture in war in Daboya) by his brother, not by his mother (pp. 30–31); but this brother himself on a distinct and earlier occasion (after capture in war in Borgu) had been redeemed by their mother (p. 29).

CHAPTER VII.

Mahommah's Early Life, &c.

We shall now proceed at once to the more important portion of the work, describing the early history, life, trials, sufferings, and conversion of Mahommah to christianity; his arrival in America; his journey to, and sojourn in Hayti, and return to this country again; his views, objects and aims.

[p. 26] His parents, as before stated, were of different tribes or nations. His father was Mahommedan in religion, but his mother was of no religion at all. He states: "my mother was like a good many christians here, who like to be christians in name, but do not like to worship God much. She liked Mahommedanism very well, but did not care much about the worshipping part of the matter."[107] Mahommedans are much greater worshippers than Christians, and worship with more apparent zeal and devotion.

The family consisted of two sons and three daughters, besides twins that died in infancy. The Africans are very superstitious about twins; they imagine that all twins are more knowing than any other children, and so with respect to the child born next after twins. They are considered to know almost everything, and are held in high esteem. If the twins live, an image of them is made out of a particular wood, one for each of them, and they are taught to feed them, or offer them food whenever they have any; if they die, the one next to

---

107. The description of Baquaqua's mother as "of no religion at all" probably represents an ill-informed gloss by Moore, since it is effectively contradicted by the following statement, directly quoted from Baquaqua, that she "liked Mahommedanism very well," although not participating much in actual worship. It was, in fact, normal in Islam for women to play little role in public worship in the mosque. Note also the contradictory account reported on Baquaqua's arrival in Haiti in 1847, that "His mother was inclined to religion, and was quite strict in her observance of her prayers and the ceremonies of her belief ... he distinctly remembers his mother's teaching him to pray": letter of Mrs. N.A.L. Judd, 8 October 1847; however, in the light of the evidence of the *Biography*, it seems possible that Mrs. Judd here misunderstood a statement by Baquaqua about his father as applying to his mother.

them by birth has an image of them made, and it is his duty to feed them, or offer them food.[108] Mahommah was the next born after twins,[109] and these little duties he faithfully performed. It is supposed the image keeps them from harm and preserves them in war. He was consequently highly esteemed on account of his birth; it was supposed he never said anything wrong, and everything he wished was done for him on the instant. This no doubt was the reason his mother so fondly loved him, and was the cause of his youthful recklessness. They never crossed or controlled him, his mother was the only person who dared even check him; his love for his mother was exceedingly great. His uncle was a very rich man, who was blacksmith to the king,[110] and he wanted Mahommah to learn that trade, but his father destined him for the mosque, intending to bring him up as one of the prophet's faithful followers. For that purpose he was sent to school, but not liking schooling very much, he went to live with his uncle and learned the art of making needles, knives and all such kinds of things. His father afterwards replaced him at school, but he soon ran away; he did not like the restraint that his brother **[p. 27]** (the teacher) put

108. This passage presents a major difficulty. A cult of twins (*ibeji*), including the making of wooden sculptures, was practised among the Yoruba, the southeastern neighbors of Borgu. We have not traced any reference to such a cult in Borgu or Djougou; although there were some Yoruba immigrants in the Djougou area, and also in the Atacora Mountain region, at Bante and Basila in northern Bénin, and at Sokode in Togo (personal communication, Elisée Soumonni, Obare Bagodo, and Mrs. Orou-Yoruba; also see Person, "Zugu, ville musulmane"). It seems improbable that Baquaqua's family would have practiced the cult as described, since the making of "images" of any sort is frowned upon in Islam. Maybe the editor Moore conflated statements by Baquaqua about his status as the next born after twins within his own family and about the cult of twins in neighboring communities which he knew.

109. Baquaqua's middle name, Gado ("Gardo"), is that given to a son born after twins in the Borgu region—and also in Hausaland, his mother's country of origin.

110. As is later made clear (p. 28), this was Baquaqua's mother's brother. From Baquaqua's own account, he was evidently not a blacksmith specifically, but a generic metalsmith, working in gold, silver, and brass as well as iron. One-quarter of the city of Djougou, Zembougouberi, is associated with ironworking. However, the smiths in this quarter are said to have been Tem (Kotokoli) (Person, "Zugu, ville musulmane"), which does not fit Baquaqua's uncle, who (if he is correctly identified as Baquaqua's mother's brother) was of Hausa origin. Smiths enjoyed high status in Borgu, the "chief of smiths" (perhaps the position held by Baquaqua's uncle) enjoying some of the privileges of nobility: Lombard, "Aperçu sur la technologie," 16–17.

upon him.[111] His brother was a staunch Mahommedan and well learned in Arabic.[112]

Mahommah did not progress very well in learning, having a natural dread of it.[113] The manner of teaching is rather different to other countries, the Africans having neither books nor papers, but a board called Wal-la,[114] on which is written a lesson which the pupil is required to learn to read and write before any other is given; when that lesson is learned, the board is cleaned and a new one written.

Scholars are not permitted to be absent without special leave from the teacher; if truant is played, punishment follows. No fees are due until education is completed. School inspection is made in the following manner: A large meeting house, generally a mosque,[115] is selected, whither the pupils repair together with the teachers, who must read twenty chapters of the Koran, and if the pupil reads the whole twenty chapters, without missing a single word, his education is considered finished and the fees of instruction are immediately paid.[116]

111. Cf. the similar account recorded in Haiti in 1847, that "they put him to his books very closely, but loving play, he used to leave home clandestinely": letter of Rev. W.L. Judd, 28 October 1847. Baquaqua was evidently, by his family's standards, only a lax Muslim. In addition to dropping out of Islamic education, he also, as subsequently related (pp. 34–35), indulged in alcoholic drinks.112. Cf. letter of Rev. W.L. Judd, 28 October 1847: "He says his oldest brother was well educated, could read and write Arabic with fluency." Baquaqua subsequently relates (p. 29) that this brother served "the king" (presumably of Djougou) and later also the king of Gonja as an adviser-diviner.

112. Cf. letter of Rev. W. L. Judd, 28 October 1847: "He says his oldest brother was well educated, could read and write Arabic with fluency." Baquaqua subsequently relates (p. 29) that this brother served "the king" (presumably of Djougou) and later also the king of Gonja as an adviser-diviner.

113. Nevertheless, in one of his letters to George Whipple, Baquaqua claimed to understand Arabic, as well as the "Zogoo" language (i.e., Dendi) (McGrawville, 29 January 1854). When he arrived in Haiti in 1847, the Rev. Mr. Judd reported that he could write Arabic "with considerable facility," and even assumed incorrectly that it was his "native language": letter of W.L. Judd, 28 October 1847. But this probably reflects only the limitations of Judd's own knowledge of Arabic. A few years later, at least, Baquaqua's literacy in Arabic was evidently limited, as attested by his incomplete attempt to write the "*bismi'llah*" in another of his letters: to George Whipple, 26 October 1853.

114. Cf. Baatonu *wàrá*; presumably the Dendi term was the same or similar (cf. also Hausa *allo*; all derived from Arabic *allauhu*).

115. Cf. n. 22 above.

116. In fact, students are normally required to memorize the entire text of the Quran, which comprises 114 "chapters" (*sura*), but for instructional purposes is usually divided into sixty sections (*ahzal*). Baquaqua's statement that students learned "twenty chapters" might suggest that he only completed a third of the Quran. See J. Spencer Trimingham, *Islam in West Africa* (Oxford, 1959): 159.

Mahommah's uncle had property in Sal-gar, whither he would repair to buy gold, silver, brass and iron for the purposes of his business.[117] The gold and silver he made into bracelets, for the arms, and ear rings and finger rings, the Africans being very fond of such kinds of ornaments.

The needles in Africa are made by hand, the process is very tedious; in the first place the iron is hardened or converted into something like steel, it is then made into fine wire, by a process of hammering, and cut into suitable lengths as required, when it is again beaten and made sharp at the point by filing, and finally polished by rubbing on a smooth stone with the hand. From this description of needle making, it may be clearly seen how much labor has to be bestowed upon all branches of manufacture, for want of better tools and machinery.

An African bellows deserves some notice. It is said "necessity is the *mother* of invention;" whoever doubted this fact, let him attentively read the following, and if they deny that position, they surely cannot but say that the invention of the bellows in Africa, certainly had a *"father."*

[p. 28] The bellows is composed of a goat skin taken off whole, a stick passes through from the neck to the hinder legs, where it is fastened, and by an ingenious contrivance. The legs are moved up and down by hand, an old gun barrel being used for the pipe.[118]

Whilst his uncle was at Sal-gar on business he died, and left his property to Mahommah's mother.[119] He then worked a short time with

117. Salaga, in eastern Gonja (modern northern Ghana), at this period the principal market for trade between Asante and the countries to the northeast, including especially the kola trade through Borgu to Hausaland: cf. Levtzion, *Muslims and Chiefs in West Africa*, 26–48; Lovejoy, *Caravans of Kola*, 18–23, 29–34, 37–41. The route from Salaga to Djougou (via Bafilo, Alejo, and Yarakeou) is described by Dupuis, *Journal of a Residence in Ashantee*, ciii–civ. The gold purchased here was mined in Asante, but the silver and brass would have been brought from the coast, where it was imported by Europeans. The reference to iron as purchased at Salaga may be a confusion, since this was mined and smelted in the Borgu region itself: see Lombard, "Aperçu sur la technologie."

118. For bellows in Borgu (made of "goat or antilope skin," but there is no reference to a gun barrel), cf. Lombard, "Aperçu sur la technologie," 14.

119. This shows that this "blacksmith" uncle was Baquaqua's mother's brother.

another relative.

It is laborious work, manufacturing farming implements and tools. Machinery is greatly needed in Africa, the want of which is a great drawback to the manufactures of that country. The iron is of first-rate quality, very much superior to the iron of America. Iron, copper and brass are twisted into rings, which are worn as ornaments about the ancles and arms.

There are hundreds and thousands of men in the world who rejoice to do good, and who are seeking means to employ their time and their talents. To such as these who peruse the pages of this work, the hint here thrown out may not be lost. A wide field of usefulness presents itself in that much neglected part of the world, where men are to be found, who only need the teaching to make good citizens, good mechanics, good farmers, good men and good christians. To those who would direct their efforts in the behalf of such a nation, no doubt remains but that God would bless their works; their deeds would praise them, and millions yet unborn would called them blessed. Go then, ye philanthropists, and christian men and women, to these benighted people, offer them the hand of assistance and raise them to the standard of their fellow-men, and give all the countenance you can to their endeavors to usefulness and goodness, never caring for the scoffs and frowns of a cold and callous world; let your works be of such a nature as all good men will speak well of you, and your own consciences approvingly assent.

Africa is rich in every respect (except in knowledge.) The knowledge of the white man is needed, but not his vices. The religion of the white man is needed, but more of it, more of the spirit of the true religion, such as the Bible teaches, "love to **[p. 29]** God and love to man." Who will go to Africa? Who will carry the Bible there? And who will teach the poor benighted African, the arts and sciences? Who will do all this? Let the reply be prompt, let it be full of life and energy! Let the Savior's command be obeyed. "Go ye out into all the world and preach the gospel." Save all those who are perishing for lack of knowledge, for the lack of that knowledge, you have the power to impart. Hesitate no longer, for now is the time, the accepted time, "the night cometh when no man can work," and the day (our day) is fast waning. Oh, christian friends, up and be doing.

Mahommah's brother was a kind of fortune teller, who when the king was about to go to war, was consulted by him, to know whether the issue of the war would be in his favor or not; this was done by signs and figures made in the sand, and all he predicted, was fully believed would come to pass, so that by his own mysterious power he could either cause the king to wage war or bring the matter to an end.[120]

He at one time went to Bergoo, some distance from [sic: = to] the east of us, where he remained two years.[121] A great war was fought during that time and he was taken prisoner, but was released by his mother paying a ransom, when he returned home again.[122] He then went to Da-boy-ya, which was a long way off to the south-west of Zoogoo, beyond a very large river.[123] At that place a great many kinds of articles of European manufacture were to be found, such as glass bottles, glasses, combs, calicos, &c.,[124] but the buildings were mostly the same as those at Zoogoo, but the city was not surrounded by

120. For the provision of religious services, including divination, by Muslim clerics (*alfa*) to rulers in the Borgu area, see Brégand, *Commerce caravanier*, 140–48.

121. Borgu, i.e., probably Nikki (cf. n. 12 above). Although this is not explicitly stated, presumably Baquaqua's brother in Nikki (as in Djougou, and later in Daboya) was serving the local king as a diviner-adviser. Tradition names two "diviners" in the service of Siru Kpera, king of Nikki (d. 1836), Alfa Salifu and Sibuko, of whom the first at least was clearly a Muslim (*alfa* = a Muslim cleric): P. Mercier, "Histoire et légende: la bataille d'Illorin," *Notes africaines*, 47 (1950): 94. But there is no basis for identifying either of these with Baquaqua's brother.

122. Perhaps alluding to the war of c.1834–36, in which Siru Kpera, king of Nikki, and other Borgu rulers went to assist the Yoruba kingdom of Oyo, to the south-east, against attack from the Muslims of Ilorin, who were in allegiance to the Sokoto Caliphate. After early successes the allies were defeated before Ilorin, and several Borgu kings, including Siru Kpera of Nikki, were killed: see Robin Law, *The Oyo Empire c.1600–c.1836* (Oxford, 1977): 292–95. According to Nikki tradition the Borgu captives taken in this war were set free by the ruler of Ilorin at the request of Kpé Lafia, a rival prince of Nikki who had taken refuge in Ilorin (and who later himself became King of Nikki), who conducted them home: Mercier, "Histoire et légende," 94.

123. Daboya, in western Gonja, 350 km. west of Djougou. The river is presumably the White Volta.

124. Cf. n. 93 above.

walls, as at the latter. Here also the king was at war and invited my brother. The cause of this war, was that a king had died, and a dispute having arisen (as is very often the case) between two brothers, which should be the king; they adopted such means to decide who should succeed, and he who could gather the greatest forces was the successor. The unsuccessful candidate placing himself under the protection of a neighboring king, until he could gather up sufficient forces to enable him successfully to push on the war, and thus wrest the kingdom from his brother.[125]

[p. 30] After Mahommah's brother had been sometime with the king, Mahommah himself went thither, with many others to carry grain, as it had become scarce there on account of the war.[126] It was about seventeen days' journey from Zoogoo,[127] the manner of travel being on foot, with the sacks of grain upon their heads;[128] a rather tedious and unpleasant mode of traveling and transporting merchandize, considering the facilities for such purposes, afforded in America and Europe.

They arrived safely on a Saturday, and heard that war would be waging that day, but it was not resumed until the next. The king was

125. Probably alluding to civil wars in Gonja following the death of king Danga in the early 1830s. His initial successor Safo was overthrown by Kali; Safo himself committed suicide, but some of his sons and supporters took refuge in Wa, to the northwest (whose ruler is presumably the "neighbouring king" referred to here). Kali died shortly afterwards, but his successor Saidu Nyantakyi in turn suffered continued opposition from the former partisans of Safo, supported by outside intervention from Wa. After being defeated by his enemies, Nyantakyi abandoned his capital Yagbum, and established his base in Daboya. These troubles eventually provoked intervention by Gonja's overlord Asante in 1841–44, when Asante forces occupied Daboya and hunted down and executed Nyantakyi: see Ivor Wilks, *Wa and the Wala* (Cambridge, 1989): 100; and idem, *Asante in the Nineteenth Century*, 275–79. The king whose service Baquaqua's brother now entered was presumably Nyantakyi, after his removal to Daboya. The rival Gonja leaders were not literally "brothers," but chiefs of the component divisions of the Gonja kingdom, all of whom belonged to the royal dynasty and who in principle succeeded to the paramount kingship in rotation.

126. Given Baquaqua's youth at this point (he would have been only c.17 in 1841), he was presumably employed as a porter, rather than operating as an independent trader.

127. The itineraries in Bowdich, *Mission from Cape Coast Castle to Ashantee* (London, 1819): 177, 179, 208, give a total of nineteen days' journey between Djougou and Daboya: eight days from Daboya to Yendi, eleven days from Yendi to Djougou.

128. The wording seems to imply that grain was transported all the way from Djougou, but this seems improbable; more likely, it was brought from somewhere closer to Gonja.

advised by his counsellor[129] to go out and meet the enemy in the woods, but did not do so. He [= Baquaqua?] then went to the King's house, and after breakfasting next morning, the guns began to boom away, and the war went on in earnest. Guns were used by them on this occasion, much more than bows and arrows. The war was too hot for the king, when he, together with his counsellor, fled for their lives.[130]

My companions (says Mahommah) and myself ran to the river but could not cross it; we hid ourselves in the tall grass, but the enemy came and found us, and made us all prisoners. I was tied up very tightly; they placed a rope around my neck and took me off with them. We traveled through a wood and came to a place I shall never forget, full of mosquitoes! But they were *indeed* mosquitoes, none of your small flys, gnats and such like, that people in North America call mosquitoes, but real big hungry fellows, with stings and suckers enough to drain every drop of blood out of a man's body at one draw. They came whim! whim! about our ears, and bite they did, full of wrathful vengeance. I never wish to be in that place again, or any other like it; it was truly horrible.

Whilst traveling through the wood, we met my brother,[131] but neither of us spoke or seemed to know each other; he turned another way without arousing any suspicion; and then went to a place, and procured a person to purchase me. Had it been known who it was, they would have insisted upon a very great price as my ransom, but it was only a small sum that was required for my release. It should have been mentioned that the city was [p. 31] destroyed, the women and children having been sent away.[132]—When the wars come on sudden-

---

129. Meaning presumably Baquaqua's brother; but see n. 131, below.

130. Probably referring to the flight of Nyantakyi from Daboya, in the face of the Asante intervention against him (cf. n. 125, above); the reference to the use of guns supports the inference that the enemies were Asante, who made much more use of guns than the Gonja themselves.

131. If Baquaqua's brother was the king's "counselor" who had fled with him, it is difficult to see how he could have been around to meet the enemy army (unless he had defected).

132. After the flight of Nyantakyi from Daboya, the local chief of Daboya is said to have blown up his own palace with gunpowder, killing himself and several Asante officers: Wilks, *Asante in the Nineteenth Century*, 277.

ly, the women and children have no means to escape, but are taken prisoners and sold into slavery.

After my purchase and release, my brother sent me home again with some friends, and on my return home, I paid our king a visit.[133] He was related to my mother.[134] In a few days after, whilst at home, the king sent for me and said he wished me to live with him entirely, so, accordingly, I remained in his house, and he appointed me a Che-re-coo, that is a kind of body guard to the king.[135] I stood only third from the king, Ma-ga-zee and Wa-roo, being the two only in rank above me, next to the king himself. Ma-ga-zee was an old man, and Wa-roo, a youth.[136] I remained with the king day and night, ate and drank with him, and was his messenger in and out of the city.

The king did not reside in the city, but a few miles from it.[137] (The Africans have a curious way of reckoning distances, they carry their burdens upon their heads and proceed until tired, which is called Loch-a-fau, and in English, means one mile!)[138] The king (continues Mahommah) kept nothing from me, but sometimes, when he had very important affairs in hand, he would consult the more experienced Ma-ga-zee.

The kings are called Massa-sa-ba, and govern several places, and,

133. From what follows, this was not the king of Djougou, but of a neighboring and subordinate community.

134. Cf. n. 79 above.

135. Dendi and Baatonu, *tkiriku*, royal servants and messengers: cf. Lombard, *Structures de type "féodal,"* 121, 125. Technically, these palace servants were slaves in status, which may account for the statement of Mrs. Judd in 1848 that, "It seems, from what he has informed us lately, that he was several years a slave in Africa": letter of Mrs. N.A.L. Judd, 24 March 1848; cf. also Foss and Mathews, *Facts for Baptist Churches*, 392. For further discussion, see Introduction.

136. *Magazin* (from Hausa *magaji*) is recognized as a senior title in the Djougou area: e.g., in Djougou itself the *magazin* is the head of one of the quarters of the town. "Waroo" may represent the personal name Woru, given in Borgu to first-born sons (and spelled by Baquaqua in a subsequent passage, pp. 40–41, as "Woo-roo," though the reference there is evidently to a different person). Baquaqua may give an exaggerated impression of his standing in the court; the category of *tkiriku* to which he belonged were technically slaves; if, however, he was head of the palace servants he would have been a powerful (if not, strictly, high-status) figure.

137. This makes clear that the king whom Baquaqua served was not that of Djougou, but of some neighboring and subordinate town.

138. Term not identified.

like the Pharaohs of old, all are called Massa-sa-ba. When the king of the city dies, the Massa-sa-bas are called upon to decide who shall succeed him.[139] If war comes upon them, he [= the Massa-sa-ba] is found foremost amongst the brave; his residence is generally in a dense thicket, built after the manner of the country, but garnished on the outside with marble. There are two kinds of marble there, one quite white, and the other red; these marbles are pounded to a fine dust, and whilst the mortar which is used in the building of houses is soft, pieces of the marble are taken and pressed into it, in any fantastic shape and figure they fancy, which makes the wall stronger and gives the building, when finished, a pretty, ornamental appearance.

The mortar in which the women grind yams and Harnee into flour, mentioned in a previous part of this work, requires some **[p. 32]** like notice, as it is very interesting. A number of men go into the forest and select a very large tree of a particular kind which is used for the purpose, cut it down, and cut off a log about four feet long; it is then hollowed out and made very smooth, and when all is ready the king invites a large number of men, who roll it by hand to his house and place it where it is designed to stand. This mortar is generally so large in circumference that ten or fifteen persons may stand around it to work at one time.

Massa-sa-ba was a generous man and given to hospitality, consequently had a great deal of company. They love feasting in Africa as well as in any other part of the world, and when the kings give feasts, everything that the country affords is provided. This makes them very popular with the people.

Mahommah cannot distinctly state how long he lived with the king, but it was a considerable length of time;[140] whilst he was there

139. This implies that "massa-sa-ba" was a generic title for the rulers of towns subordinate to Djougou (which is presumably "the city" here referred to). In Djougou today, however, *masasawa* is explained as the title of one specific town, Soubroukou, about 6 km. southwest of Djougou: fieldwork, April 1999.

140. If Baquaqua had been in Gonja during the Asante campaign of 1841–44 (cf. above, n. 125) and was taken as a slave to Brazil in 1845 (cf. below, p. 59, with n. 219), his period as a palace servant cannot have been more than one or two years.

he became very wicked. But, (says he,) at that time, I scarce knew what wickedness was; the practises of the soldiers and guards, I am now convinced, was [sic] very bad indeed, having full power and authority from the king to commit all kinds of depredations they pleased upon the people without fear of his displeasure or punishment. At all times, when they were bent on mischief, or imagined they needed anything, they would pounce upon the people and take from them whatever they chose, as resistance was quite out of the way, and useless, the king's decree being known to all the country round about. These privileges were allowed the soldiery in lieu of pay, so we plundered for a living.[141]

If the king needed palm wine[142] for a feast, or at any other time, he would send me; and I would take some of his slaves along with me, and knowing by what road the country people laden with wine would come into the city, I would, with the slaves, hide in the long grass, whilst one of our number would climb a high tree, and be on the lookout, for any one coming. As soon as he would espy a woman with a calabash on her head, (women only carry the wine to market,) he would inform us, and we would instantly surround her and secure the wine. If the wine was good, she lost it; if poor, we would return it to her, as the king **[p. 33]** never drank bad wine, but with the caution, that she was to tell no one that the guards were in ambush, otherwise we should not be enabled to fall upon others, so that the king would have to go without his wine. In this way, toll is levied upon all who bear wine into town, whenever the king needs it. If one woman does not carry sufficient wine for the king's use, others are served in the same way until sufficient is obtained; other articles are also seized upon whenever the king needs them.

---

141. This picture of the licence permitted to palace servants is corroborated by Clapperton's observations in eastern Borgu in 1826, where he witnessed royal slaves from Kaiama and Wawa plundering livestock from villages through which they passed: *Journal*, 65, 115–16.

142. Klose in the 1890s noted the presence of wine and oil palms in the Djougou area: *Le Togo sous drapeau allemand*, 389. The area forms an enclave of forest-type vegetation within a generally drier region.

In front of the king's house or palace, was a very large courtyard, beautifully shaded by lofty trees; on one side of this court were three or four trees, under which a rude throne was built of earth thrown into a heap, and covered over with mortar, being joined from tree to tree, which was several feet high, and ascended by steps of the same material. On the throne there was a seat, cushioned, and covered with red leather, made from the skin of the Bah-seh,[143] which was used for no other purpose. On either side, were seats for his two young wives, which was occupied by two of his favorites in their absence. My seat were [sic] at the foot of the throne, on the one side of the steps, and that of Wa-roo on the other; beyond was the seat occupied by Ma-ga-zee.

The king would drink in the presence of his wives, but not eat. Whenever he drank, one of his wives or favorites would kneel before him and place her hands under his chin, so as to prevent any of the drink being spilled upon his person. In their absence, that duty devolved upon me. Whenever the king required me for anything, he would say Gar-do-wa.[144] I would reply Sa-bee (a term used only in speaking to the king,)[145] and immediately run towards him, falling on my face before him, in an attitude of the most respectful attention.[146] He would then state what he needed, when I would go at full speed to obey his commands, walking not being permitted when about the king's business.—When he desired anything of Ma-ga-zee, he would call me, to communicate to him his will. Thus was I kept running

143. Probably Dendi *béésè*, antelope.
144. Presumably this phrase includes Gado, Baquaqua's middle name; *wa* means "come" in Yoruba, which is a language spoken in the Djougou/Borgu area, but it does not seem likely that it would have been the language in use in a local royal court. The comparable word in Dendi is *ka*.
145. Sabi in Dendi (and in Borgu more generally) is a personal name, given to the second-born son, but it seems more likely that the phrase is short for *sabeni*, "majesty" (personal communication, Arifari Bako).
146. Austin, *African Muslims Sourcebook*, 651, n. 69, suggests that Baquaqua omits that persons prostrating also threw dirt over themselves. But cf. Clapperton, *Journal*, 74: "Their manner of salutation to superiors is by prostration at full length on the ground, but without throwing dust on the head or body."

about from morning till night, while his feasts lasted. It was very hard work to attend upon such a king, I can assure you, kind readers.

[p. 34] At the king's feasts, all the principal personages would assemble and dine with him, those most of consequence would be entertained at the house of Ma-ga-zee, and those next at other houses, so that the guests were scattered all round about. It is the duty of the women to prepare the food, &c.

To give more fully a description of the manners and customs of the people, would no doubt be highly interesting to most of our readers, and it would give us great pleasure to do so, would the limits of the present work admit of it; but at present, we must hope they will be contented and pleased, with what has already been written for them, and it is to be hoped, they will profit by its perusal. At some other time, should the public think fit to patronize these few stray sheets, it may be, that a larger and more extensive volume may be issued by the author of the present work, in which will be given more fully everything within his knowledge of Africa and the Africans.

We will now, at once, turn to the more interesting portion of Mahommah's history, which treats of his capture in Africa and subsequent slavery. We will give the matter in nearly his own words.

It has already been stated, that when any person gives evidence of gaining an eminent position in the country, he is immediately envied, and means are taken to put him out of the way; thus when it was seen that my situation was one of trust and confidence with the king, I was of course soon singled out as a fit object of vengeance by an envious class of my countrymen, decoyed away and sold into slavery.[147] I went to the city one day to see my mother,[148] when I was followed by music (the drum) and called to by name, the drum beating to the measure of

147. Note that Baquaqua implies that he was the victim of a conspiracy by personal enemies, rather than random kidnapping.

148. I.e., presumably to Djougou; this reference confirms that the king in whose service Baquaqua now entered was not that of Djougou, but of some neighboring town: perhaps, as noted earlier, Soubroukou.

a song which had been composed apparently in honor of me, on account of, as I supposed, my elevated position with the king. This pleased me mightily, and I felt highly flattered, and was very liberal, and gave the people money and wine, they singing and gesturing the time. About a mile from my mother's house, where a strong drink called Bah-gee,[149] was made out of the grain Har-nee; thither we repaired; and when I had drank plentifully of Bah-gee, I was quite intoxicated, and they persuaded me to **[p. 35]** go with them to Zar-ach-o, about one mile from Zoogoo, to visit a strange king that I had never seen before.[150] When we arrived there, the king made much of us all, and a great feast was prepared, and plenty of drink was given to me, indeed all appeared to drink very freely.

In the morning when I arose, I found that I was a prisoner, and my companions were all gone. Oh, horror! I then discovered that I had been betrayed into the hands of my enemies, and sold for a slave.[151] Never shall I forget my feelings on that occasion; the thoughts of my poor mother harrassed me very much,[152] and the loss of my liberty and honorable position with the king, grieved me very sorely. I lamented bitterly my folly in being so easily deceived, and was led to drown all caution in the bowl.[153] Had it not been that my senses had been taken from me, the chance was that I should have escaped their snares, at

149. Dendi *bádyì*, beer.

150. This name might represent Yarakeou, south-west of Djougou (which appears as "Yarakoo" in Dupuis, *Journal of a Residence in Ashantee*, ciii-civ). This is in fact rather more than 20 km. from Djougou, but cf. Baquaqua's earlier (p. 31) explanation of the local term translated as "mile."

151. Different accounts of Baquaqua's enslavement are given in earlier accounts recorded by the Judds in Haiti. In 1847 he is said to have been "taken captive when a child, while playing at some distance from his mother's door," in one account while playing truant from school: letters of Mrs. N.A.L. Judd, 8 October 1847; Rev. W.L. Judd, 28 October 1847. For discussion of these discrepancies, see Introduction.

152. Here and elsewhere, Baquaqua consistently refers to his feelings for his mother, but does not mention his father. This is probably because, as Baquaqua indicated to Judd in 1847 (though this is never explicitly stated in the *Biography*), his father had died before he left Africa: letter of W.L. Judd, 28 October 1847 (Appendix 2, no. 2).

153. As noted by Austin, *African Muslims Sourcebook*, 652, n. 71, this is probably intended to refer to the circumstances of Baquaqua's enslavement, rather than implying that he responded to this misfortune by further drinking.

least for that time.

The man, in whose company I found myself left by my cruel companions, was one, whose employment was to rid the country of all
such as myself.[154] The way he secured me, was after the following
manner:—He took a limb of a tree that had two prongs, and shaped it
so that it would cross the back of my neck, it was then fastened in
front with an iron bolt; the stick was about six feet long.[155]

Confined thus, I was marched forward towards the coast, to a place
called Ar-oo-zo, which was a large village;[156] there I found some
friends, who felt very much about my position, but had no means of
helping me. We only stayed there one night, as my master wanted to
hurry on, as I had told him I would get away from him and go home.
He then took me to a place called Chir-a-chur-ee,[157] there I also had
friends,[158] but could not see them, as he kept very close watch over
me, and he always stayed at places prepared for the purpose of keeping the slaves in security; there were holes in the walls in which my
feet were placed, (a kind of stocks.)[159] He then took me on to a place
called Cham-mah, (after passing through many strange places, the
names of which I do not recollect) where he sold me.[160] We had then
been about four days from home and had traveled very rapidly.[161]

154. The wording seems to imply something other than a regular slave-trader; probably this
reflects Baquaqua's claim that he was the victim of a conspiracy, rather than merely of a crim-
inal kidnapping.

155. Clapperton in eastern Borgu in the 1820s noted that slaves on the march to the coast
were "fastened night and day by the neck with leather things or a chain": *Journal*, 94.

156. Probably Alejo ("Arjou" in Dupuis, *Journal of a Residence in Ashantee*, civ), about 55
km. southwest of Djougou (around 30 km. beyond Yarakeou), close to the modern Bénin-Togo
border; possibly the original text wrote "Aroogo."

157. Later (p. 36) spelled "Chir-a-chir-ee": i.e., Krikri (also called Adjede), in Kotokoli
(Tem) country, about 15 km. south of Alejo (in modern Togo).

158. There was a Muslim community in Krikri, which probably included families from
Djougou: cf. Levtzion, *Muslims & Chiefs* (Oxford, 1968): 178; and Raymond Delval, *Les
Musulmanes au Togo* (Paris, 1980): 108.

159. Clapperton likewise notes that "refractory" slaves on the march to the coast were "put
into irons, in addition to the other fastening, during the night": *Journal*, 94.

160. Tchamba, a further 15 km. south of Krikri.

161. The four days from "home" presumably include the day spent in traveling from
Djougou to Yarakeou, prior to Baquaqua's actual enslavement. The total distance from Djougou
to Tchamba is about 80 km., which does not in fact seem an especially rapid rate of travel.

I remained only **[p. 36]** one day, when I was again sold to a woman, who took me to E-fau; she had along with her some young men, into whose charge I was given, but she journeyed with us; we were several days going there;[162] I suffered very much traveling through the woods, and never saw a human being all the journey. There was no regular road, but we had to make our passage as well as we could.

The inhabitants about Cham-mah live chiefly by hunting wild animals, which are there very numerous; I saw many during the two days,[163] but do not know their names in English; the people go nearly naked and are of the rudest description.[164] The country through which we passed after leaving Chir-a-chir-ee, was quite hilly, water abundant and of good quality, the trees are very large; we did not suffer anything from heat on the journey, as the weather was quite cool and pleasant;[165] it would be a healthy and delightful country, were it inhabited by civilized people, and cultivated; the flowers are various and beautiful, the trees, full of birds, large and small, some sing very delightfully. We crossed several large streams of water,[166] which it had not been the dry season, [167] would have been very deep, as it was they were easily forded, being no more than three feet of water in some places. There were great quantities of aquatic birds sporting about; we saw swans in abundance, we tried to kill some, but found it very difficult, as their movements are very quick upon the water; they have a most beautiful appearance when on the wing, the necks and wings

162. "E-fau" is presumably Fon, an alternative name for Dahomey, whose capital Abomey Baquaqua seems to have reached three days later (p. 38).

163. In the previous paragraph, Baquaqua speaks of spending only "one day" in Cham-mah; presumably this means he stayed there over only one night.

164. The reference to near-nakedness here seems to be a Muslim stereotype of the non-Muslim people of this region, who generally wore only animal skins.

165. Since Baquaqua makes clear later in this paragraph that he traveled to the coast during the dry season, this should probably be understood as alluding to the effects of the harmattan, which blows from the north during January and February, and which reduces humidity (and hence the discomfort of the heat) during the day and produces cooler temperatures overnight.

166. These would have been affluents of the River Mono, to the west.

167. The dry season in central Togo, through which Baquaqua was now passing, is normally from around November to March. This is consistent with the suggestion (n. 218 below) that Baquaqua was shipped from Africa to Brazil in March 1845.

extended in the air, they are perfectly white, never fly very high nor far away; their flesh is sweet and good, and considered a great dish. After passing through the woods, we came to a small place, where the woman who had purchased me, had some friends; here I was treated very well, indeed, during the day, but at night I was closely confined, as they were afraid I would make my escape; I could not sleep all night, I was so tightly kept.[168]

After remaining there for the space of two days, we started on our journey again, traveling day after day; the country through which we passed continued quite hilly and mountainous; we passed some very high mountains,[169] which I believe were called **[p. 37]** the mountains of Kong.[170] The weather all the time continued cool and pleasant, water was found in great abundance, of very excellent quality, the roads, in some places, where the land was level, was [sic] quite sandy, but only for short distances together—The country was very thinly settled all the way from Cham-mah, the woods along the route are not very extensive, but large tracts of land, covered with a very tall grass. We passed some places where fire had consumed the grass, something after the manner of the prairies of South and South-western North America.

I will here describe the manner of firing grass in Africa. The grass when it has attained a large growth, is a refuge or haunt for the wild animals, abounding in that part of the country, and when it is decid-

168. The itinerary here becomes difficult to follow, but this unnamed stopping place was by implication between Tchamba and "Efau."

169. Perhaps alluding to Mounts Guègère, Igbéré, and Kouda (all around 400 m. high), just inside the modern Togo border.

170. The term "the mountains of Kong" is evidently not a genuine local toponym, but derives from European cartographic tradition, beginning with Mungo Park, who first reported mountains of (or in) Kong in the interior of Senegambia in 1796: Thomas J. Bassett and Philip W. Porter, "'From the best authorities': The Mountains of Kong in the cartography of West Africa," *Journal of African History*, 32 (1991): 367–413. The term had been subsequently applied by European travelers to various regions in the interior of West Africa, including to the Mahi area immediately north of Dahomey by John Duncan in the mid-1840s: *Travels in Western Africa* (London, 1847): i, 272, etc. It seems extremely unlikely that Baquaqua heard this usage locally; more probably he (or more likely, his editor Samuel Moore) took the name from Duncan's account, which had been published a few years earlier.

ed to fire the grass, notice is sent to all people for miles round about, and the hunters come prepared with bows and arrows, who station themselves all around for several miles, and form a large circle; when the fire is applied at one point, it is soon discovered by the party on the opposite, who immediately fires his portions, and so on, all round about until the whole is fired; the fire strikes inward, toward the centre, never spreading outside the circle; the hunters follow up the flames, and being prepared with branches of trees, bearing large leaves, throw them down before them to stand upon, so as to let fly their arrows upon the terrified animals, who flee before the devouring element into the centre of the fire; the hunters of course follow up their game around the outside of the burning mass, slaying all before them as they proceed; they are excellent marksmen, and the poor affrighted creatures have very little chance for their lives, at such times; immense numbers are killed, as well as serpents in great quantities.[171]

But to return:—Whilst passing over those places which had been recently burned, our travel was much quicker, not having much of anything to impede our progress, but where the grass stood as a wall on either side of us, we had to travel very cautiously, fearing the wild animals would spring out and fall upon us. The people of America do not know anything about tall grass, such as in Africa; the tall grass of the American prairies [p. 38] is as a child beside a giant, in comparison with the grass of the torrid zone. It grows generally twelve feet high, but sometimes much higher, and nothing can be seen that is ever so near you, it being so thick and stout; closer even than the small groves of timber in this country.[172] At length we arrived at Efau, where I was again sold; the woman seemed sorry to part with me, and gave

171. Although Baquaqua refers only to hunting, the burning of grass was also part of the preparation for planting crops. This fits Baquaqua's earlier statement (p. 36) that he was taken to the coast during the dry season, since this was normally done late in the dry season.

172. Duncan in 1845, between Savalou and Djalloukou, at least roughly the same district as now traversed by Baquaqua (in fact, probably somewhat to the east of it), also remarked on the tallness of the grass, according to him "nearly six feet": *Travels*, ii, 238.

me a small present on my leaving them. Efau is quite a large place, [173] the houses were of different construction to those in Zoogoo, and had not so good an appearance.[174]

The man to whom I was again sold, was very rich, and had a great number of wives and slaves. I was placed in charge of an old slave; whilst there a great dance was held and I was fearful they were going to kill me, as I had heard they did so in some places, and I fancied the dance was only a preliminary part of the ceremony; at any rate I did not feel at all comfortable about the matter.[175] I was at Efau several weeks and was very well treated during that time; but as I did not like the work assigned me, they saw that I was uneasy, and as they were fearful of losing me, I was locked up every night.[176]

The country around Efau was very mountainous, and from the city the mountains in the distance had a noble appearance.[177]

After leaving Efau, we had no stopping place until we reached Dohama;[178] we remained in the woods[179] by night and traveled during the day, as there were wild beasts in great abundance, and we were compelled to build up large fires at night to keep away the ferocious animals, which otherwise would have fallen upon us and torn us to

173. This place is evidently not the Fon (Dahomian) capital Abomey, which Baquaqua reached only subsequently, after a further three days' journey, but presumably a town to the north or northwest which was subject to Dahomey. According to Duncan, *Travels*, ii, 243–44, the first town in this area which was considered part of Dahomey proper was Djalloukou, about 40 km. northwest of Abomey. Duncan himself took just over three days (21–24 August 1845) from Djalloukou to Abomey: ibid, ii, 253–60.

174. Perhaps alluding to the rectangular buildings characteristic of Dahomey, whereas those in Borgu were circular; see Person, "Zugu, Ville musulmane."

175. This allusion might be interpreted to confirm that Baquaqua had arrived in Dahomian territory, as the Dahomians were notorious for their practice of human sacrifice.

176. The implication seems to be that it was originally intended to keep Baquaqua in slavery at "Efau," and he was only sold on to the coast when he proved refractory. If so, Baquaqua's experience was not untypical, since it appears to have been quite common for slaves to spend some time in servitude locally while in transit to the coast: cf. Herbert Klein, *The Atlantic Slave Trade* (Cambridge, 1999): 155–56.

177. If "E-fau" is Djalloukou (cf. n. 173 above), the mountains visible in the distance would be those of Savalou and Logazohe, some 30–35 km. to the northeast.

178. I.e., Dahomey.

179. Duncan describes the country between Djalloukou and Abomey as "thickly wooded with shea-butter and other trees": *Travels*, ii, 254.

PLATE 5. 'Kong Mountains': 'The country around Efau was very mountainous, and from the city the mountains in the distance had a noble appearance' (Biography, p. 38), sketch of 'The Kong Mountains in the Neighbourhood of Logazohy [1845]', in John Duncan, *Travels in Western Africa in 1845 & 1846: A Journey from Whydah, through the Kingdom of Dahomey, to Adofoodia, in the Interior* (London 1847 [1968]), ii, 218.

pieces, we could hear them howling round about during the night; there was one around in particular, the people most dreaded; it was of the form of a cat with a long body, some were all of a color, others spotted very beautifully; the eyes of which shone like lustrous orbs of fire by night, it is there called the Goo-noo.[180] I presume from the description, it must be what is here known as the Leopard, as from what I understand, the description is about the same.[181]

Dohama is about three days journey from Efau, and is quite a large city;[182] the houses being built differently to any I had pre- **[p. 39]** viously seen. The surrounding country is level and the roads are good; it is more thickly settled than any other part I had passed through, though not so well as Zoogoo, the manners of the people too, were altogether different to anything I had ever before seen.

180. Although Moore understood Baquaqua to say that "goo-noo" was a local (presumably Fon) word, this must be a confusion on his part; it is actually Dendi *gúnnù*, lion.

181. But Baquaqua's own description seems to relate to lions ("all of a color") as well as leopards ("spotted very beautifully").

182. The "city" of Dahomey is presumably Abomey, the capital of the kingdom. In 1850 the size of Abomey was estimated as eight miles in circumference, and its population as "not more than 30,000"; see Forbes, *Dahomey and Dahomans* (London, 1851): i, 14, 68.

I was being conducted through the city, and as we passed along, we were met by a woman, and my keeper who was with me immediately took to his heels and ran back as hard as he could. I stood stock still, not knowing the meaning of it; he saw I did not attempt to follow him, or to move one way or another, and he called me in the Efau language to follow him,[183] which I did, he then told me, after we rested, that the woman we had met was the king's wife, and it is a mark of respect to run whenever she is in sight of any of her subjects.[184] There were gates to this city, and a toll was demanded on passing through.[185] I remained there for but a short time, but I learned that it was a great place for whisky,[186] and the people were very fond of dancing.[187] At this place I saw oranges for the first time in my life.[188] I was told, whilst there, that the king's house was ornamented on the outside with the human skulls, but did not see it.[189] When we arrived here I began to give up all hopes of ever getting back to my home again, but had entertained hopes until this time of being able to make my escape, and by some means or other of once more seeing my native place,[190] but at last, hope gave way; the last ray seemed fading away, and my heart felt sad and weary within me, as I thought of my

183. The implication that Baquaqua had picked up some knowledge of the "Efau" language, presumably during his "several weeks" of residence there, is noteworthy.

184. This requirement to give way and hide at the approach of the king's wives is reported by several European visitors to Dahomey: e.g., Duncan, *Travels*, i, 257–58.

185. Several European visitors to Abomey confirm the existence of gates to the city: e.g., Duncan, *Travels*, i, 276; ii, 260–61.

186. Whisky was not a common European import into Africa, so more likely the reference here is to some other distilled drink, perhaps gin, but more likely *gerebita*, the cheapest *cachaça*, or sugar-cane rum.

187. As Baquaqua passed through Abomey during the dry season, he may have witnessed part of the "Annual Customs," the principal public ceremony of the Dahomian monarchy, which normally began around January.

188. Orange trees were noted at Abomey e.g., by Duncan, *Travels*, i, 218.

189. The ornamentation of the palace walls in Abomey with human skulls was regularly noted by European visitors: e.g., Duncan, *Travels*, i, 219, 241, 245. The wording perhaps suggests that the reference to this practice here reflects prompting by Moore, on the basis of published accounts, rather than information volunteered by Baquaqua.

190. From remarks Baquaqua is reported to have made earlier in Haiti, he seems to have hoped that he might be redeemed by his mother, "whom he was often flattered he should see again, being told she would send money to redeem him": letter of Mrs. N.A.L. Judd, 24 March 1848.

PLATE 6. Abomey: 'There were gates to this city, and a toll was demanded on passing through' (Biography, p. 39); 'Gates of the City of Dahomey', in Frederick E. Forbes, *Dahomey and the Dahomans* (London, 1851 [1966]), I, 69.

home, my mother! whom I loved most tenderly, and the thought of never more beholding her, added very much to my perplexities.[191] I felt sad and lonely, wherever I did roam, and my heart sank within me, when I thought of the "old folks at home." Some persons suppose that the African has none of the finer feelings of humanity within his breast, and that the milk of human kindness runs not through his composition; this is an error, an error of the grossest kind; the feelings which animated the whole human race, lives [sic] within the sable creatures of the torrid zone, as well as the inhabitants of the temperate and frigid; the same impulses drive them to action, the same feeling[s] of love move within their bosom, **[p. 40]** the same maternal and paternal affections are there, the same hopes and fears, griefs and

191. Cf. n. 152 above.

PLATE 7. Ouidah: 'At Gra-fe, I saw the first white man, which you my be sure took my attention very much' (Biography, p. 40); 'The Fetish Man, and the Governor of Whydah', here
depicting the Dahomian governor (the Yovogan), a 'fetish' priest and two Europeans (Forbes
and possibly an agent of a British firm trading there) in Forbes, *Dahomey and the Dahomans*,
i, 103, 112.

joys, indeed all is there as in the rest of mankind; the only difference
is their color, and that has been arranged by him who made the world
and all that therein is, the heavens, and the waters of the mighty deep,
the moon, the sun and stars, the firmament and all that has been made
from the beginning until now, therefore why should any despise the
works of his hands which has been [sic] made and fashioned according to his Almighty power, in the plentitude of his goodness and
mercy.

O ye despisers of his works, look ye to yourselves, and take heed;
let him who thinks he stands, take heed lest he fall. We then proceeded to Gra-fe, about a day and half's journey;[192] the land we passed was

192. "Grafe" represents Glehue, the indigenous name of Ouidah, the principal coastal
"port" of Dahomey, about 100 km. from Abomey. A day and a half was a rapid, although not
impossible, time for this journey: Duncan in 1845 took over two days, staying overnight at
Agrime and Whagbo (*Travels*, ii, 288–94).

PLATE 8. Ouidah: 'The windows in the houses also looked strange, as this was the first time in my life I had ever seen houses having windows' (Biography, p. 40); the French fort, c. 1856: the European factories were the only buildings in Ouidah at this period with windows; after an illustration by Repin in *Le Tour du Monde*, and reproduced in Richard Burton, *A Mission to Gelele: King of Dahome* (London, 1966) 80.

pretty thickly settled and generally well cultivated; but I do not recollect that we passed any streams of water after entering upon this level country.[193] At Gra-fe, I saw the first white man, which you may be sure took my attention very much; the windows in the houses also looked strange, as this was the first time in my life that I had ever seen houses having windows.[194] They took me to a white man's house,[195]

193. In fact, the road from Abomey to Ouidah crosses several watercourses, although they generally have the appearance of swampy ground rather than of clearly defined rivers; and they would have been less noticeable in the dry season (when Baquaqua was traveling), when the water level was lower. Cf. the account of the journey northwards (in December) in Richard Burton, *Mission to Gelele, King of Dahome* (London, 1864): i, 144–91.

194. Baquaqua had earlier (p. 14) noted that the houses in his native Djougou did not have windows.

195. Several European and American traders were resident in Ouidah at this period, including especially slave-traders from Brazil, of whom the most prominent was Francisco Felix de Souza (d. 1849): see Robin Law, "The evolution of the Brazilian community in Ouidah," *Slavery & Abolition*, 22 (2001): 22–41.

where we remained until the morning, when my breakfast was brought in to me, and judge my astonishment to find that the person who brought in my breakfast was an old acquaintance, who came from the same place. He did not exactly know me at first, but when he asked me if my name was Gardo, and I told him it was, the poor fellow was overjoyed and took me by the hands and shook me violently he was so glad to see me; his name was Woo-roo,[196] and had come from Zoogoo, having been enslaved about two years; his friends could never tell what had become of him. He inquired after his friends at Zoogoo, asked me if I had lately come from there, looked at my head and observed that I had the same shave that I had when we were in Zoogoo together; I told him that I had. It may be as well to remark in this place, that in Africa, the nations of the different parts of the country have their different modes of shaving the head and are known from that mark to what part of the country they belong. In Zoogoo, the hair is shaven off each side of the head, and on the top of **[p. 41]** the head from the forehead to the back part, it is left to grow in three round spots, which is allowed to grow quite long; the spaces between being shaven very close; there is no difficulty to a person acquainted with the different shaves, to know what part any man belongs to.[197]

Woo-roo seemed very anxious that I should remain at Gra-fe, but I was destined for other parts; this town is situated on a large river.[198] After breakfast I was taken down to the river and placed on board a boat; the river was very large and branched off in two different directions, previous to emptying itself into the sea.[199] The boat in which the

---

196. Woru is a personal name in Borgu, given to the first-born son.

197. Other evidence suggests that the distinctive haircuts related to social status, rather than different national origins. Palace slaves (*tkiriku*) in Borgu had a distinctive haircut, with one half of the head shaved: Lombard, *Structures de type "féodal,"* 125; cf. also Lander, *Journal*, i, 333–34 [19 August 1830], referring specifically to Nikki. At Djougou itself, Klose in the 1890s also says that slaves (in general, not royal slaves specifically) were distinguished by having half of their heads shaved: *Le Togo sous drapeau allemand*, 392.

198. I.e., the lagoon which runs parallel to the coast, between Ouidah and the seashore.

199. The lagoon does indeed connect with the sea through outlets both to the east of Ouidah (at Lagos) and to the west (at Grand-Popo).

slaves were placed was large and propelled by oars, although it had
sails as well, but the wind not being strong enough, oars were used as
well.[200] We were two nights and one day on this river, when we came
to a very beautiful place; the name of which I do not remember;[201] we
did not remain here very long, but as soon as the slaves were all collected together, and the ship ready to sail, we lost no time in putting
to sea. Whilst at this place, the slaves were all put into a pen, and
placed with our backs to the fire, and ordered not to look about us,
and to insure obedience, a man was placed in front with a whip in his
hand ready to strike the first who should dare to disobey orders;

200. Canoes on the lagoon were normally propelled by poles (cf. Duncan, *Travels*, i, 109,
157), with paddles used in deep water: Francesco Borghero, "Relation sur l'établissement des
missions dans le Vicariat du Dahomé" (1863), in *Journal de Francesco Borghero, premier missionnaire au Dahomey (1861–1865)*, Renzo Mandirola & Yves Morel, eds. (Paris, 1997): 237.
Sails do not seem to have been in common use on the lagoon, but there is some evidence for
their use: Robert Smith, "The canoe in West African history," *Journal of African History*, 11
(1970): 519.

201. It was normal practice at this period for slaves to be taken from Ouidah by canoe along
the lagoon to be embarked elsewhere, as a means of evading the attentions of the British anti-
slaving squadron. In 1849, for example, it was noted that "From the number of slave-merchants
residing at Whydah, that port is strictly watched by the cruizers ... By means of the lagoon the
slaves can be shipped at either Porto Novo, &c. to the eastward, or Popoe [i.e., Little Popo],
&c., to the westward, with much greater safety": PP, Slave Trade 1849–50, Class B, inclosure
10 in no. 9, Lieutenant Forbes, 5 November 1849). Since Baquaqua neglected to state in which
direction he traveled along the lagoon from Ouidah, it is impossible to identify with certainty
the coastal town from which he was ultimately embarked. However, westwards seems more
likely (especially as this was the dry season, when the level of water in the lagoon was lower),
since travelers going eastwards from Ouidah often went on foot overland from Ouidah to
Godomey, on the western shore of Lake Nokué, from where they embarked in canoes for the
journey further east. In 1851, for example, the British Vice-Consul at Ouidah noted that "messengers go from here to Godomey by land, the rest of the route by canoe as far as Lagos": PRO,
FO 886, Journal of Louis Frazer, 30 July 1851. The last recorded batch of slaves exported
through Ouidah, which was embarked from Godomey in October 1863, is explicitly reported to
have walked overland to Godomey: Borghero, *Journal*, 139 (9 October 1863). The major ports
of slave embarkation on the lagoon west of Ouidah were (from east to west) Grand-Popo,
Agoué, and Little Popo (modern Aného). The journey time given by Baquaqua (two nights and
one day) perhaps suggests the most westerly of these; by comparison, Duncan in 1845 took a
day and a night by canoe from Ouidah to Agoué: *Travels*, i, 142. The leading slave trader at
Little Popo in 1845 was Isidoro de Souza (met there by Duncan, ibid., I, 102), who was the
eldest son of Francisco Felix de Souza of Ouidah (cf. above, n. 195). It may be noted that on
18 February 1845, when traveling from Agoué to Ouidah, Duncan met "a large travelling
canoe" going westwards with "several Spanish gentlemen" (with whom he shared a drink and
a smoke) and "about twenty young slaves, male and female": ibid., i, 110–11. Could one of
these have been Baquaqua?

PLATE 9. Ouidah: 'We were chained together, and tied with ropes around our necks' (Biography, p. 41); 'The Slave Chain' observed on 16 March 1850, in Forbes, *Dahomey and the Dahomans*, i, 100, 117.

another man then went round with a hot iron, and branded us the same as they would the heads of barrels or any other inanimate goods or merchandize.[202]

When all were ready to go aboard, we were chained together, and tied with ropes round about our necks, and were thus drawn down to the sea shore.[203] The ship was lying some distance off.[204] I had never seen a ship before, and my idea of it was, that it was some object of worship of the white man. I imagined that we were all to be slaugh-

202. Slaves were branded with their owner's marks prior to embarkation. Duncan explains that, "Each slave-dealer uses his own mark, so that when the vessel arrives at her destination, it is easily ascertained to whom those who died belonged": *Travels*, i, 143.

203. Cf. Duncan, *Travels*, i, 143, 201, who describes slaves as taken for embarkation "perhaps ten or twenty on one chain, which is fastened to the neck of each individual, at a distance of about one yard apart"; "at intervals of a yard are circular links, which open to receive the neck, and are secured by a padlock."

204. Ships trading on the Bight of Benin could not approach close to the shore, owing to dangerous bars and surf, but stood at a distance from the shore, and communicated with it through African canoes. See Law, "Between the sea and the lagoons," 224–29.

PLATE 10. Isidoro de Souza: 'We were two nights and one day on this river, when we came to a beautiful place, the name of which I do not remember [= Little Popo]' (Biography, p. 41); here a portrait of the leading slave trader in the mid-1840s at Little Popo, west of Ouidah, from which Baquaqua may have been embarked; from a painting, c. 1822, in Pierre Verger, *Flux et reflux de la traite des Nègres entre le Golfe de Bénin et Bahia de Todos os Santos du XVIIe au XIXe siècle, Paris* (1968).

tered, and were being led there for that purpose. I felt alarmed for my safety, and despondency had almost taken sole possession of me.

A kind of feast was made ashore that day, and those who rowed the boats were plentifully regaled with whiskey[205], and the slaves were given rice and other good things in abundance. I was not aware that it was to be my last feast in Africa. I did not know my destiny.[206] Happy for me, that I did not. All **[p. 42]** I knew was, that I was a slave, chained by the neck, and that I must readily and willingly submit, come what would, which I considered was as much as I had any right to know.

At length, when we reached the beach, and stood on the sand, oh! how I wished that the sand would open and swallow me up. My wretchedness I cannot describe. It was beyond description. The reader may imagine, but anything like an outline of my feelings would fall very short of the mark, indeed. There were slaves brought hither from all parts of the country, and taken on board the ship. The first boat had reached the vessel in safety, notwithstanding the high wind and rough

205. Very likely *gerebita*, see n. 186.
206. Duncan likewise observes that slaves intended for shipment were "taken out, as if for their usual airing … without any intimation of their fate": *Travels*, i, 142–43.

PLATE 11. Bight of Benin: 'As soon as the slaves were all collected together, and the ship ready to sail, we lost no time in putting to sea .... The next boat that was put to sea, I was placed in' (see Biography, pp. 41–2); loading slaves in c. 1849, Church Missionary Intelligencer, 7:2 (1856) and also Church Missionary Gleaner (1874), 114.

sea; but the last boat that ventured was upset, and all in her but one man were drowned. The number who were lost was about thirty. [207] The man that was saved was very stout, and stood at the head of the boat with a chain in his hand, which he grasped very tightly in order to steady the boat; and when the boat turned over, he was thrown with the rest into the sea, but on rising, by some means under the boat, managed to turn it over, and thus saved himself by springing into her, when she was righted. This required great strength, and being a powerful man, gave him the advantage over the rest. The next boat that was put to sea, I was placed in; but God saw fit to spare me, perhaps for some good purpose. I was then placed in that most horrible of all places,

THE SLAVE SHIP.

207. Embarking (and landing) through the surf along the Bight of Benin was notoriously dangerous, with frequent fatalities. Duncan reported that a ship which embarked slaves from Agoué on 4 March 1845 (certainly not Baquaqua's ship, since it was taken by the British navy shortly after departure) lost two slaves by drowning: Travels, i, 142.

Its horrors, ah! who can describe? None can so truly depict its horrors as the poor unfortunate, miserable wretch that has been confined within its portals. Oh! friends of humanity, pity the poor African, who has been trepanned[208] and sold away from friends and home, and consigned to the hold of a slave ship, to await even more horrors and miseries in a distant land, amongst the religious and benevolent. Yes, even in their very midst; but to the ship! We were thrust into the hold of the vessel in a state of nudity,[209] the males being crammed on one side and the females on the other; [210] the hold was so low that we could not stand up, but were obliged to crouch upon the floor or sit down;[211] day and night were the same to us, sleep being denied **[p. 43]** us from the confined position of our bodies, and we became desperate through suffering and fatigue.

Oh! the loathsomeness and filth of that horrible place will never be effaced from my memory; nay, as long as memory holds her seat in this distracted brain, will I remember that. My heart even at this day, sickens at the thought of it.[212] Let those *humane individuals,* who are in favor of slavery, only allow themselves to take the slave's position in the noisome hold of a slave ship, just for one trip from Africa to America, and without going into the horrors of slavery further than

208. I.e., "entrapped."

209. Slaves were commonly stripped of their clothes prior to embarkation: Duncan, *Travels,* i, 143. Another slave who passed through Ouidah, Cudjo Lewis in 1859 (interviewed in Alabama, USA, in the 1920s), likewise recalled that "the Dahomians avariciously tore their garments from them, men and women alike were left entirely nude," which he remembered as "a great humiliation": Zora Neale Hurston, "Cudjo's own story of the last African slaver," *Journal of Negro History*, 12:4 (1927): 657.

210. Segregation of the sexes was normal practice on slave ships throughout the history of the transatlantic trade: Klein, *The Atlantic Slave Trade*, 130; and for the illegal slave trade in the nineteenth century, cf. F.E. Forbes, *Six Months' Service in the African Blockade, from April to October, 1848* (London, 1849): 95.

211. Frederick Forbes, an officer of the British navy's anti-slaving squadron later in the 1840s, says that the height of slave decks for adults ranged from 3 to 4 feet (though they might be lower for children): *Six Months' Service in the African Blockade*, 87. Cudjo Lewis, exported from Ouidah in 1859, was more fortunate than Baquaqua, recalling that "the hold ... was deep enough to permit the men of lesser stature to stand erect": Hurston, "Cudjo's Own Story," 657.

212. The reference to the sickening stench of the slaves' quarters on the Middle Passage is standard in accounts by both ex-slaves and by European slavers: cf. James Walvin, *Black Ivory: A History of British Slavery* (London, 1993): 48–50.

this, if they do not come out thorough-going abolitionists, then I have no more to say in favor of abolition. But I think their views and feelings regarding slavery will be changed in some degree, however; if not, let them continue in the course of slavery, and work out their term in a cotton or rice field, or other plantation, and then if they do not say hold, enough! I think they must be of iron frames, possessing neither hearts nor souls. I imagine there can be but one place more horrible in all creation than the hold of a slave ship, and that place is where slaveholders and their myrmidons are the most likely to find themselves some day, when alas, 'twill be late, too late, alas!

The only food we had during the voyage was corn soaked and boiled.[213] I cannot tell how long we were thus confined, but it seemed a very long while.[214] We suffered very much for want of water, but was [sic] denied all we needed. A pint a day was all that was allowed, and no more;[215] and a great many slaves died upon the passage. There was one poor fellow became so very desperate for want of water, that he attempted to snatch a knife from the white man who brought in the water, when he was taken up on deck and I never knew what became of him. I supposed he was thrown overboard.[216]

When any one of us became refractory, his flesh was cut with a

213. If this means that this was all slaves were fed on Baquaqua's ship, they were worse fed than was normal. Other evidence shows that a basic diet of boiled corn (or rice, yams, beans, cassava) was normally supplemented by small amounts of meat or fish and seasoning such as pepper and palm oil: Klein, *The Atlantic Slave Trade*, 93–94; Forbes, *Six Months' Service in the African Blockade*, 98.

214. The average sailing time for slave ships between West Africa and Brazil was one month: Klein, *The Atlantic Slave Trade*, 130. For the specific period of Baquaqua's voyage, the average sailing time for ships sailing from the Bights of Benin and Biafra to Brazil in the early 1840s was thirty-two days: David Eltis, *Economic Growth and the Ending of the Transatlantic Trade* (Oxford, 1987): 133. This figure relates to Bahia rather than to Pernambuco, where Baquaqua was taken, but presumably sailing times to the latter were similar. An individual voyage might of course be considerably longer, depending on weather conditions and (in the illegal trade) the need to evade British naval patrols. Also see Carvalho, *Rotinas e Rupturas do Escravismo*, 117–42.

215. According to the British naval officer Forbes, "the fullest allowance [of water] ... is one quart each, daily, though seldom more than a pint is given": *Six Months' Service in the African Blockade*, 99.

216. This episode is also reported in the letter of Mrs. N.A.L. Judd, 8 October 1847; though there the throwing of this man overboard is stated as a fact, rather than a speculation.

PLATE 12. Pernambuco: 'We landed a few miles from the city [i.e., Recife]' (Biography, p. 44); Recife waterfront in 1859; in Ferrez, *Photography in Brazil*, 160.

knife, and pepper or vinegar was rubbed in to make him peace-able(!)[217] I suffered, and so did the rest of us, very much from sea sickness at first, but that did not cause our brutal owners any trouble. Our sufferings were our own, we had no one to share our troubles, none to care for us, or even to speak **[p. 44]** a word of comfort to us. Some were thrown overboard before breath was out of their bodies; when it was thought any would not live, they were got rid of in that way. Only twice during the voyage were we allowed to go on deck to wash ourselves—once whilst at sea, and again just before going into port.[218]

We arrived at Pernambuco, South America,[219] early in the morning, and the vessel played about during the day, without coming to anchor. All that day we neither ate or drank anything, and we were given to

217. In the letter of Mrs. N.A.L. Judd, the rubbing of pepper into wounds is related with respect to the individual slave just mentioned, rather than as here in general terms.

218. This was not normal practice, slaves being more usually brought up to deck daily for feeding and exercise, and to enable their quarters to be cleaned: Klein, *The Atlantic Slave Trade*, 95. However, bad weather and fears of rebellion (and, in the nineteenth century, pursuit by the British navy) might lead to slaves being kept below for longer periods.

219. Since Baquaqua is said to have spent two years in slavery in Brazil (letter of Rev. W.L. Judd, 21 July 1848; Foss and Mathews, *Facts for Baptist Churches*, 392; cited in p. 59 below), before arriving in New York in June 1847 (cf. n. 246 below), his arrival in Brazil can be dated to 1845; but see n. 287 below for further discussion.

understand that we were to remain perfectly silent, and not make any out-cry, otherwise our lives were in danger. But when "night threw her sable mantle on the earth and sea," the anchor dropped, and we were permitted to go on deck to be viewed and handled by our future masters, who had come aboard from the city. We landed a few miles from the city, at a farmer's house, which was used as a kind of slave market.[220] The farmer had a great many slaves, and I had not been there very long before I saw him use the lash pretty freely on a boy, which made a deep impression on my mind, as of course I imagined that would be my fate ere long, and oh! too soon, alas! were my fears realized.

When I reached the shore, I felt thankful to Providence that I was once more permitted to breathe pure air, the thought of which almost absorbed every other. I cared but little then that I was a slave, having escaped the ship was all I thought about. Some of the slaves on board could talk Portuguese. They had been living on the coast with Portuguese families, and they used to interpret to us.[221] They were not

220. The "city" is presumably Recife, capital of Pernambuco. It was normal practice at this time for slaves to be delivered outside the city, in order to evade the attentions of the British navy, the usual landing points being Una to the south and Catuama to the north: PP, Slave Trade 1845, Class B, no. 361, Mr. Goring to Earl of Aberdeen, Pernambuco, 16 May 1846. The ship on which Baquaqua arrived may have been an unnamed Brazilian schooner, bringing slaves from an unspecified African location, which, having overshot its intended landfall at Catuama, put in at Macaro, near the Island of Itamaraca, further north, on 31 March 1845. (Other ships which delivered slaves to Pernambuco during this period are all specified to have brought their cargoes from Angola; see Introduction.) Baquaqua's statement that he was taken to a farm is consistent with reports about this ship, which state that, since it had arrived unexpectedly, most of the slaves in its cargo were initially "disposed of, and secreted in the adjacent Engenhos [sugar estates]," though many of them were later taken into the city: PP, Slave Trade 1846, Class B, no. 173, Consul Cowper to Earl of Aberdeen, Pernambuco, 2 March 1846, with enclosure 1, List of arrival of vessels suspected of being employed in the Slave Trade from the Coast of Africa to the Province of Pernambuco, during the Year ending December 31, 1845. It should be noted that Austin's comment that in Brazil at this time "the slave trade was not yet illegal but was apparently frowned upon" (*Transatlantic Stories*, 164) is misconceived; rather, it was technically illegal, but in practice often connived at by the authorities.

221. An interesting (and rare) allusion to the mechanics of communication between slavers and slaves on the Middle Passage. Evidently, in this instance, interpretation was from Portuguese into an African language, presumably that of the coastal communities where these slaves had been residing, which would have been Fon. Baquaqua himself, as noted earlier (p. 39), had picked up some knowledge of Fon during his passage to the coast, and later (p. 45) remarks that he picked up some Portuguese during the transatlantic passage from these Portuguese-speaking fellow-slaves.

PLATE 13. Pernambuco: 'I was again sold to … a baker, and resided not a great distance from Pernambuco [i.e., Recife]' (Biography, p. 44), perhaps Olinda, pictured here in 1860, with Recife in the distance, in Gilberto Ferrez, *Photography in Brazil* (trans., Stella de Sá Rego, Alburquerque, N.M., 1984), 164.

placed in the hold with the rest of us, but come [sic] down occasionally to tell us something or other.[222]

These slaves never knew they were to be sent away, until they were placed on board the ship.[223] I remained in this slave market but a day or two, before I was again sold to a slave dealer in the city, who again sold me to a man in the country, who was a baker, and resided not a great distance from Pernambuco.[224]

222. Austin suggests (*Transatlantic Stories*, 164) that these slaves were crew members; but Baquaqua's wording implies that they were being sold into export ("sent away," in the following sentence).

223. Probably these people had expected to be protected by the normal African convention, that domestic slaves should not be sold into export (except in punishment for some specific and serious offense). Some years later, when the slave trade at Ouidah revived, after a period of inactivity, in 1857-58, many slaves ran away from there to Lagos, to avoid being sold to slave-ships, including "a large number of … domestic slaves, who had lived several years with their masters, and now speak the Portuguese language": PP, Slave Trade 1857–58, Class B, no. 10, Consul Campbell, Lagos, 27 March 1858.

224. Baquaqua subsequently (pp. 45–46) indicates that the baker who bought him lived in a "town," which was situated on the tidal estuary of a river. These details point to Olinda, at the mouth of the Rio Beberibe, 10 km. north of Recife, or one of the parishes (*povoados*) near Recife, either Várzea, Poço da Panela, or Monteiro, located on the Capibaribe River, which flows into the ocean in Recife's harbor. Olinda was the capital of Pernambuco in the Dutch period; see Carvalho, *Rotinas e Rupturas do Escravismo*, 21–22.

When a slaver comes in, the news spreads like wild-fire, and down come all those that are interested in the arrival of the vessel with its cargo of living merchandize, who select from the **[p. 45]** stock those most suited to their different purposes, and purchase the slaves precisely in the same way that oxen or horses would be purchased in a market; but if there are not the kind of slaves in the one cargo, suited to the wants and wishes of the slave buyers, an order is given to the Captain for the particular sorts required, which are furnished to order the next time the ship comes into port. Great numbers make quite a business of this buying and selling human flesh, and do nothing else for a living, depending entirely upon this kind of traffic.

I had contrived whilst on my passage in the slave ship, to gather up a little knowledge of the Portuguese language, from the men before spoken of,[225] and as my master was a Portuguese I could comprehend what he wanted very well, and gave him to understand that I would do all he needed as well as I was able, upon which he appeared quite satisfied.

His family consisted of himself, wife, two children and a woman who was related to them. He had four other slaves as well as myself. He was a Roman Catholic, and had family worship regularly twice a day, which was something after the following: He had a large clock standing in the entry of the house in which were some images made of clay, which were used in worship. We all had to kneel before them; the family in front, and the slaves behind. We were taught to chant some words which we did not know the meaning of. We also had to make the sign of the cross several times. Whilst worshipping, my master held a whip in his hand, and those who showed signs of inattention or drowsiness, were immediately brought to consciousness by a smart application of the whip. This mostly fell to the lot of the female slave, who would often fall asleep in spite of the images,

225. Cf. above, p. 44.

crossings, and other like pieces of amusement.[226]

I was soon placed at hard labor, such as none but slaves and horses are put to. At the time of this man's purchasing me, he was building a house, and had to fetch building stone from across the river,[227] a considerable distance, and I was compelled to carry them that were so heavy it took three men to raise them upon my head, which burden I was obliged to bear for a quarter of a mile at least, down to where the boat lay. Sometimes the stone **[p. 46]** would press so hard upon my head that I was obliged to throw it down upon the ground, and then my master would be very angry indeed, and would say the cassoori (dog)[228] had thrown down the stone, when I thought in my heart that he was the worst dog; but it was only a thought, as I dared not give utterance in words.

I soon improved in my knowledge of the Portuguese language whilst here, and was able very shortly to count a hundred.[229] I was then sent out to sell bread for my master,[230] first going round through the town,[231] and then out into the country, and in the evening, after coming home again, sold in the market till nine at night. Being pretty honest and persevering, I generally sold out, but sometimes was not quite so successful, and then the lash was my portion.

My companions in slavery were not quite so steady as I was, being

---

226. It is noteworthy that Baquaqua makes no reference to being baptized. In the colonial period, Brazilian law had theoretically required the baptism of slaves brought from Africa, but after independence this was no longer rigorously enforced, and by the 1840s Christian instruction of slaves was being left to the discretion of owners. See Carvalho, "Esclavage et liberté à Recife," 7, 14–17. Christian instruction was also "superficial" in Rio de Janeiro; see Karasch, *Slave Life in Rio de Janeiro* (Princeton, 1987): 255–61.

227. I.e., Rio Beberibe, on which the town of Olinda is situated, or Rio Capibaribe, the location of the *povoados* of Várzea, Poço da Panela, and Monteiro: cf. n. 224 above.

228. Portuguese *cachorro*, "dog," commonly applied as an abusive term to blacks and hence considered an extreme insult. (We would like to thank João Reis for this information.)

229. The rapidity with which newly introduced African slaves learned Portuguese was partly a function of the proportion of slaves of African origin in the total population, which by the 1840s in Pernambuco was very low; see Carvalho, *Rotinas e Rupturas do Escravismo*, 82–91.

230. Slaves in urban Brazil were commonly employed in petty trade on their owner's behalf: for Pernambuco, see Carvalho, *Rotinas e Rupturas do Escravismo*, 21–22, 26–40, 51–54; for Rio de Janeiro, see Karasch, *Slave Life in Rio de Janeiro*, 206–207.

231. I.e., Olinda or one of the parishes on Rio Capibaribe: cf. n. 224 above.

much given to drink, so that they were not so profitable to my master. I took advantage of this, to raise myself in his opinion, by being very attentive and obedient; but it was all the same, do what I would, I found I had a tyrant to serve, nothing seemed to satisfy him, so I took to drinking likewise, then we were all of a sort, bad master, bad slaves.

Things went on worse and worse, and I was very anxious to change masters, so I tried running away, but was soon caught, tied and carried back.[232] I next tried what it would do for me by being unfaithful and indolent; so one day when I was sent out to sell bread as usual, I only sold a small quantity, and the money I took and spent for whiskey,[233] which I drank pretty freely, and went home well drunk, when my master went to count the days, [sic = day's] taking in my basket and discovering the state of things, I was beaten very severely. I told him he must not whip me any more, and got quite angry, for the thought came into my head that I would kill him, and afterwards destroy myself. I at last made up my mind to drown myself; I would rather die than live to be a slave. I then ran down to the river and threw myself in, but being seen by some persons who were in a boat, I was rescued from drowning. The tide was low at the time,[234] or their efforts would most likely have been unavailing, and notwithstand-
[p. 47] ing my predetermination, I thanked God that my life had been

232. Fugitive slaves were a particularly serious problem in Pernambuco in the mid-1840s. Slaves were often "stolen," and many forced a change in masters in a manner suggested here. For a description of the conditions, specifically in the mid-1840s, in Pernambuco, but without reference to Baquaqua's evidence, see Carvalho, *Rotinas e Rupturas do Escravismo*, 202–11. A search of *Diário do Pernambuco* for 1845 and 1846 has failed to identify Baquaqua as a fugitive. Numerous slaves named José, which we assume was his name, as it was in Rio de Janeiro, were identified, but none of the descriptions fit Baquaqua, either because the region of origin was listed as Angola and not West Africa, or because of physical descriptions that rule out Baquaqua. Several fugitives named José worked for bakers, but the location or other details also preclude a positive identification. (We wish to thank Maciel Henrique Carneiro, Rogério Ribau Ferandes, Clarice Sales de Albuquerque, and Otto Cabral Mendes Filho for searching *Diário do Pernambuco* for 1845 and José Cairus for searching *Diário do Pernambuco* for 1846.)
233. Probably *gerebita*; cf. n. 186 above.
234. Hence the town in question was on the tidal estuary of a river, corresponding to an identification with Olinda or one of the parishes on the Rio Capibaribe; see n. 224 above.

preserved, and that so wicked a deed had not been consummated. It led me seriously to reflect that "God moves in a mysterious way," and that all his acts are acts of kindness and mercy.[235]

I was then but a poor heathen, almost as ignorant as a Hottentot, and had not learned the true God, nor any of his divine command-ments.[236] Yet ignorant and slave as I was, slavery I loathed, principal-ly as I suppose, because I was its victim. After this sad attempt upon my life, I was taken to my master's house, who tied my hands behind me, and placed my feet together and whipped me most unmercifully, and beat me about the head and face with a heavy stick, then shook me by the neck, and struck my head against the door posts, which cut and bruised me about the temples, the scars from which savage treat-ment are visible at this time, and will remain so as long as I live.

After all this cruelty he took me to the city,[237] and sold me to a deal-er, where he had taken me once before, but his friends advised him then not to part with me, as they considered it more to his advantage to keep me as I was a profitable slave. I have not related a tithe of the cruel suffering which I endured whilst in the service of his wretch in human form. The limits of the present work will not allow more than a hasty glance at the different scenes which took place in my brief career. I could tell more than would be pleasant for "ears polite," and could not possibly do any good. I could relate occurrences which would "freeze thy young blood, harrow up thy soul, and make each particular hair to stand on end like quills upon the fretful porcupine;" and yet it would be but a repetition of the thousand and one oft told tales of the horrors of the cruel system of slavery.

The man to whom I was again sold was very cruel indeed. He

235. This attempt at suicide by drowning is also recalled in the letter of Mrs. N.A.L. Judd, 8 October 1847.

236. In fact, of course, as a Muslim Baquaqua already acknowledged "the true [i.e., Christian] God." The use of this language, in a first-person statement attributed directly to Baquaqua, may indicate the degree to which he had internalized the anti-Islamic prejudices of the Christian Church; but alternatively, it may reflect the perceptions of the editor Moore, rather than of Baquaqua himself.

237. I.e., Recife.

PLATE 14. Rio de Janeiro: 'After a few weeks he [the Recife slave dealer] shipped me off to Rio Janeiro' (Biography, p.47), as taken in 1850 by F. Pustkov.

bought two females at the time he bought me; one of them was a very beautiful girl, and he treated her with shocking barbarity.

After a few weeks he shipped me off to Rio Janeiro, where I remained two weeks previous to being again sold. There was a colored man there who wanted to buy me, but for some reason or **[p. 48]** other he did not complete the purchase.[238] I merely mention this fact to illustrate that slaveholding is generated in power, and any one having the means of buying his fellow creature with the paltry dross, can become a slave owner, no matter his color, his creed or country, and that the colored man would as soon enslave his fellow man as the white man, had he the power.[239]

238. For the ownership of slaves by ex-slaves (and by other slaves) in Rio, see Karasch, *Slave Life in Rio de Janeiro*, 207.

239. Austin (*African Muslims Sourcebook*, 653, n. 86) attributes these observations to the editor Moore (representing "white man's self-exculpation"); but it seems entirely plausible that Baquaqua himself, from his experience in Africa as well as in Brazil, could have perceived the non-racial dimension of the slavery issue.

I was at length sold to a Captain of a vessel who was what may be termed "a hard case."[240] He invited me to go and see his Senora, (wife.) I made my best bow to her, and was soon installed into my new office, that of scouring the brass work about the ship, cleaning the knives and forks, and doing other little matters necessary to be done about the cabin.[241] I did not at first like my situation; but as I got acquainted with the crew and the rest of the slaves, I got along pretty well. In a short time I was promoted to the office of under-steward. The steward provided for the table, and I carried the provisions to the cook and waited at table; being pretty smart, they gave me plenty to do. A short time after, the captain and steward disagreed, and he gave up his stewardship, when the keys of his office were entrusted to me. I did all in my power to please my master, the captain, and he in return placed confidence in me. The captain's lady was anything but a good woman; she had a most wretched temper. The captain had carried her off from St. Catharine's,[242] just as she was on the point of getting married, and I believe was never married to her. She often got me into disgrace with my master, and then a whipping was sure to follow. She would at one time do all she could to get me a flogging, and at other times she would interfere and prevent it, just as she was in the humor. She was a strange compound of humanity and brutality. She always went to sea with the captain.

Our first voyage was to Rio Grande;[243] the voyage itself was pleasant enough had I not suffered with sea sickness. The harbor at Rio Grande is rather shallow, and on entering we struck the ground, as it

240. I.e., Clemente José da Costa, master and part-owner of the ship *Lembrança*. As a result of passing into this man's ownership, Baquaqua now acquired the Portuguese name José da Costa, by which he is referred to in the New York newspaper reports of 1847: see esp. the affidavit of Clemente José da Costa, New York, [12] July 1847, in *National Anti-Slavery Standard*, 2 September 1847. Since slaves did not usually change their personal names, he was probably known in Pernambuco as José as well.

241. For the employment of slaves on sea-going ships in Rio de Janeiro, see Karasch, *Slave Life in Rio de Janeiro*, 194 (citing Baquaqua as a case).

242. The island of Santa Catarina, off the coast of southern Brazil.

243. Rio Grande do Sul, the southernmost port of Brazil, an important center for trade in dried meat and for whaling.

happened at low water, and we had great difficulty in getting her to float again. We finally succeeded, and exchanged our cargo for dried meat. We then **[p. 49]** went to Rio Janeiro and soon succeeded in disposing of the cargo. We then steered for St. Catharines to obtain Farina, a kind of breadstuff used mostly by the slaves.[244] From thence, returned again to Rio Grande and exchanged our cargo for whale oil and put out again to sea, and stood for Rio Janeiro. The vessel being very heavily laden, we had a very bad time of it; we all expected that we should be lost, but by lightening the ship of part of her cargo, which we did by throwing overboard a quantity, the ship and all hands were once more saved from the devouring jaws of the destructive element. Head winds were prevalent, and although within sight of port for several days, we could not make the harbor, do all we could.

Whilst in the doubtful position of whether we should be lost or not, it occurred to me that death would be but a release from my slavery, and on that account rather welcome than otherwise. Indeed I hardly dared to care either way. I was but a slave, and I felt myself to be one without hope or prospects of freedom, without friends or liberty. I had no hopes in this world and knew nothing of the next; all was gloom, all was fear. The present and the future were as one, no dividing mark, all Toil! Toil!! Cruelty! Cruelty!! No end but death to all my woes. I was not a Christian then;[245] I knew not of a Savior's love, I knew nothing of his saving grace, of his love for poor lost sinners, of his mission of peace and good will to all men, nor had I heard of that good

244. *Farinha* in Portuguese means "flour" generically; but the reference here is probably specifically to cassava flour (popularly called *farinha de pão*, "wood meal," i.e., sawdust, from its appearance), which was commonly used as food for slaves.

245. Baquaqua had, in fact, received some rudimentary Christian instruction while in slavery in Pernambuco, before being sold on to Rio de Janeiro (see p. 45). When he attempted to escape from slavery in New York in 1847, he and his fellow slave José da Rocha were reported to have "some knowledge of the Catholic religion," and were consequently considered competent to swear an oath in court: see note by W.H. Bunn, Commissioner of Deeds, to the affidavit of José da Costa (Baquaqua) and José da Rocha, 21 July 1847. Baquaqua's acquaintance with Christianity in Brazil may well have been superficial; but it is also likely that after his subsequent conversion into the Baptist Church, he internalized the view that Roman Catholicism did not represent "true" Christianity.

PLATE 15. Rio de Janeiro: passengers seeking 'excelentes comodos' in traveling to New York were invited to the office of the *Lembrança*, 93 Rua Direita, as advertised in *Jornal do Commercio* (Rio de Janeiro), 17 April 1847.

land so beautifully spoken of by the poet, "a land of pure delight where saints immortal dwell," and to which land of promise the Christian is daily shortening the journey. No! These "tidings of great joy" had not then been imparted to my gloomy mind, and all was black with despair. But when I heard the Savior's words "come unto me all ye that are heavy laden and I will give you rest." I sought and found him, which came as a balm to my wounds, as consolation to my afflicted soul. When [I] think of all this and consider the past, I am content to struggle on in this world to fulfil my mission here and to do the work that is given me to do. Oh! Christianity thou soother of man's sufferings, thou guide to the blind, and strength to the weak, go thou on thy mission, speak the peaceful tidings of salvation all around and make glad the heart of man, **[p. 50]** "then shall the wilderness be glad and blossom as the rose." Then will slavery with all its horrors ultimately come to an end, for none possessing thy power and under thy influence can perpetuate a calling so utterly at variance with, and repugnant to all thy doctrines.

After great labor and toil we were landed in perfect safety. During this voyage I endured more corporeal punishment than ever I did my life. The mate, a perfect brute of a fellow, ordered me one day to wash down the vessel, and after I had finished, he pointed to a place where he said was a spot, and with an oath ordered me to scrub it over again, and I did so, but not being in the best of humor he required it to be done a third time, and so on again.

When finding it was only out of caprice and there being no spot to clean, I in the end refused to scrub any more, when he took a broom stick to me, having a scrubbing brush in my hand I lifted it to him. The master saw all that was going on, and was very angry at me for attempting to strike the mate.—He ordered one of the hands to cut a piece of rope for him; he told me I was to be whipped, and I answered "very well," but kept on with my work with an eye continually turned towards him, watching his movements. When I had set the breakfast ready, he came behind me before I could get out of his way, and struck me with the rope over my shoulders, and being rather long, the end of it swung down and struck my stomach very violently, which caused me some pain and sickness; the force with which the blow was struck completely knocked me down and afterwards he beat me whilst on deck in a most brutal manner.—My mistress interfered at this time and saved me from further violence.

We remained at Rio Janeiro nearly a month. Whilst there an incident occurred, which I will relate in illustration of the slave system.

One day it was necessary for me to go ashore with my master as one of the oarsmen, and whilst there I drank pretty freely of wine, and seeing my master about returning to the boat I made for where it lay, and being rather confused with drink as **[p. 51]** well as flurried at seeing my master, I fell into the water, but it being only shallow, I suffered nothing further than a good ducking for my drunkenness. I was easily got out. Whilst rowing my master, my head swam very much from the effects of the liquor I had drank, and consequently did not pull very steadily, when my master seeing the plight I was in asked me what was the matter, I said "nothing sir;" he said again, "have you been drinking?" I answered no sir! So that by being ill used I learned to drink, and from that I learned to tell lies, and no doubt should have gone on step by step from bad to worse, until nothing would have been wicked enough for me to have done, and all this through the grace of God, I was led to abandon my evil ways.

When the cargo was landed, an English merchant having a quantity of coffee for shipment to New York, my master was engaged for the purpose,[246] and it was arranged, after some time that I should accompany him, together with several others to serve on ship board.[247]

We all had learned, that at New York there was no slavery; that it was a free country and that if we at once got there we had nothing to dread from our cruel slave masters, and we were all most anxious to get there.[248]

Previous to the time of the ship's sailing, we were informed that we were going to a land of freedom. I said then you will never see me any more after I once get there. I was overjoyed at the idea of going to a free country, and a ray of hope dawned upon me, that the day was not far distant when I should be a free man. Indeed I felt myself already *free!* How beautifully the sun shone on that eventful morning, the morning of our departure for that land of freedom we had heard so much about. The winds too were favorable, and soon the canvass spread before the exhilerating [sic] breeze, and our ship stood for that happy land. The duties of office, on that voyage, appeared light to me indeed, in anticipation of seeing the goodly land, and nothing at all

246. The *Lembrança* carried a shipment of coffee for J.L. Phipps & Co. of New York: *New York Daily Tribune*, 28 June 1847.

247. The *Lembrança* arrived in New York on 27 June 1845 (cf. n. 252, below), after a voyage of sixty days (*New York Daily Tribune*, 28 June 1847), so it left Rio de Janeiro around 23 April 1847.

248. Slavery had been abolished in the State of New York in 1827, and a supplementary statute of 1840 provided that, "All slaves hereafter brought into this State shall be free" (*New York Tribune*, 14 July 1847), which was the basis for Baquaqua's claim to freedom after his arrival in New York: cf. n. 263 below.

PLATE 16. New York City Hall: 'We were afterwards taken…to a very handsome building with a splendid portico in front, the entrance to which was ascended by a flight of marble steps' (Biography, p. 55), where Baquaqua appeared in Court, from an illustration of 1838, I.N. Pheleps Stokes Collection, N.Y. Public Library, also in Lockwood, *Manhattan Moves Uptown*, 2.

appeared a trouble to me. I obeyed all orders cheerfully and with alacrity.

[**p. 52**] That was the happiest time in my life, even now my heart thrills with joyous delight when I think of that voyage, and believe that the God of all mercies ordered all for my good; how thankful was I.

The winds held favorable for a speedy passage several days together, after which we experienced very rough, tempestuous weather, which somewhat retarded our progress, and put us in some danger of being sent "to that bourne from whence no traveler returns," as fears were entertained for our safety. One night during the voyage, it blew a perfect hurricane the whole night, and just previous to day-break, the lamps in the binnacle[249] went out with the heavy rolling of the ship. I was ordered to light it, but on account of the high wind, after

---

249. The case in which the ship's compass is kept.

several attempts I entirely failed. Aha, says the captain, my boy you can't light the binnacle, can't you?

The man at the helm said it was light enough, he could do without it, he could see the compass well enough; but as orders were given, whether the light was wanted or not, they must be obeyed; so three other hands were called and a blanket was placed around the binnacle to keep off the wind, when they succeeded at length in lighting it, but I not understanding how to do it, could not light it; I had tried over and over again. After this the captain got out of his berth, dressed himself and ordered me to light his lamp; when I went to him he took a large stick for the purpose of striking me, and aiming a blow at my head, I raised my arm to prevent my head being struck, he told me to keep my hand down. I did so, but when the blow was falling I again raised my hand and succeeded in saving my skull from being cracked; he did not want to strike my hand as that would prevent me from doing my work, but whether my head was broke or not, I should have had to do my usual work. He then told me to turn round so that he might be able to strike my back. I told him to strike me all that he wanted. He was very angry and struck me at random over my head and body, just where it might happen. I defied him to do his worst, to do what he could and wreak his vengeance fully upon a miserable being like myself. He then called to three of the hands and ordered them to **[p. 53]** tie me to the cannon. I had thoughts of springing into the water, but was not quite satisfied to go alone; if I could have had the pleasure of taking him along with me I should have willingly done so. The three men fastened hold upon me and placed me upon the cannon, face downwards; they were then ordered to whip me, which they did pretty smartly; he then required me to make submission and beg for mercy, but that I would not do. I told him to kill me if he pleased, but for mercy at his hands I would not cry! I also told him that when they untied me from the cannon, he must take care of himself that day, as when I looked upon my lacerated bleeding body, I reflected that though it was bruised and torn, my heart was not subdued.[250]

As soon as I was loosened I made towards the captain, who gave orders to the men to place me securely in the bow of the vessel and not allow me to go near him again. I was so sore from my bruises and cuts that I could not do anything for several days.

The captain during my sickness would send me good victuals from his own table, no doubt to conciliate me after the cruel wrongs he had inflicted on me, but that was in vain. I was not in any great hurry to get to work again, as he frequently, previous to this, caused me to be flogged for not doing what it would have taken any three men to have done, so that I now felt inclined that he should do without any further services altogether.

Slavery is bad, slavery is wrong. This captain did a great many cruel things which would be horrible to relate; he treated the female slaves with very great cruelty and barbarity; he had it all his own way, there were none to take their part; he was for the time "monarch of all he surveyed;" "king of the floating house," none dared to gainsay his power to control his will. But the day is coming when his power will be vested in another, and of his stewardship he must render an account; alas what account can he render of the crimes committed upon the writhing bodies of the poor pitiless wretches he had under his charge, when his kingship shall cease and the great account is called for; how shall he answer? And what will be his doom?—That will only be known when the great book is opened. May **[p. 54]** God pardon him (in his infinite mercy) for the tortures inflicted upon his fellow creatures, although of a different complexion.[251]

The first words [sic] of English that my two companions and

---

250. Cf. also *New York Daily Tribune*, 16 July 1847, referring to Baquaqua (under the name José da Costa) and his fellow slave José da Rocha: "They declare that they have been cruelly treated during the voyage, having been frequently flogged by the captain; and once stretched at full length upon a gun with hands and feet secured to receive the punishment. In some cases Rocha has been compelled to inflict the blows upon his fellow slave."

251. When Baquaqua was moving towards conversion in Haiti in 1848, Mrs. Judd regarded his forgiving of Captain Costa as "the test question" of the genuineness of his faith: letter of Mrs. N.A.L. Judd, 24 March 1848.

myself[252] ever learned was F-r-e-e; we were taught it by an English-
man on board, and oh! how many times did I repeat it, over and over
again. This same man told me a great deal about New York City, (he
could speak Portuguese). He told me how the colored people in New
York were all free, and it made me feel very happy, and I longed for
the day to come when I should be there. The day at length came, but
it was not an easy matter for two boys and a girl, who could only
speak one word of English, to make their escape, having, as we supposed, no friends to aid us. But God was our friend, as it proved in
the end, and raised up for us many friends in a strange land.[253]

The pilot who came aboard of our vessel treated us very kindly,—
he appeared different to any person I had ever seen before, and we
took courage from that little circumstance. The next day a great many
colored-persons came aboard the vessel, who inquired whether we
were free.[254] The captain had previously told us not to say that we
were slaves, but we heeded not his wish, and he, seeing so many persons coming aboard, began to entertain fears that his property would
take in their heads to lift their heels and run away, so he very pru-
dently informed us that New York was no place for us to go about
in—that it was a very bad place, and as sure as the people caught us
they would kill us. But when we were alone we concluded that we
would take the first opportunity and the chance, how we would fare
in a *free* country.

One day when I had helped myself rather freely to wine, I was

252. Identified later in this paragraph as "two boys and a girl"; evidently referring to the two
fellow slaves who later attempted to claim their freedom in New York with Baquaqua, named
as José da Rocha and Maria da Costa. Maria da Costa, like Baquaqua, was owned by the ship's
master Clemente José da Costa, while José da Rocha belonged to Antonio José da Rocha
Pereira, co-owner with Costa of the *Lembrança*: see affidavit of Clemente José da Costa, New
York, [12] July 1847, in *National Anti-Slavery Standard*, 2 September 1847.

253. The *Lembrança* arrived in New York on 27 June 1847: affidavit of Clemente José da
Costa, New York, [12] July 1847, in *National Anti-Slavery Standard*, 2 September 1847; cf. also
the announcement of the ship's arrival in *New York Daily Tribune*, 28 June 1847.

254. Austin (*African Muslims Sourcebook*, 653, n. 91; *Transatlantic Stories*, 165), identifies
those who came on board as members of the New York Vigilance Society, a little-known group
with "mostly black" membership.

PLATE 17. New York City: 'The next day a great many colored-persons came aboard the vessel, who inquired whether we were free' (Biography, 540); view of the East River in 1852, in *The Renascence of City of Hall; Commemorative Presentation Rededication of City Hall, The City of New York, July 12, 1956* (New York, 1956), 84. The Lembrança docked at the foot of Roosevelt Street, opposite Brooklyn Heights.

imprudent enough to say I would not stay aboard any longer; that I would be free. The captain hearing it, called me down below, and he and three others endeavored to confine me, but could not do so; but they ultimately succeeded in confining me in a room in the bow of the vessel. I was there in confinement several days. The man who brought my food would knock at the door, and if I told him to come in he would do so, otherwise he would pass along, and I got no food.[255] I told him **[p. 55]** on one occasion that I would not remain confined there another day with my life; that out I would get; and there being some pieces of iron in the room, towards night I took hold of one of

255. This incident is recalled in the affidavit of Baquaqua (submitted under his Portuguese name José da Costa) and his fellow slave José da Rocha, 21 July 1847, which states that after the former had asked the Captain to go on shore, they had both been beaten and then confined to a "store-room" on the ship for four days, three of them without food. Cf. also *New York Daily Tribune*, 16 July 1847, which, however, states that Baquaqua and his fellow slave had merely asked "to go ashore for a short time on Sunday to see the town," rather than (as claimed here) explicitly claiming their freedom.

them—it was a bar, about two feet long—with that I broke open the door, and walked out. The men were all busy at work, and the captain's wife was standing on the deck when I ascended from my prison. I heard them asking one another who had let me out; but no one could tell. I bowed to the captain's wife, and passed on to the side of the ship. There was a plank from the ship to the shore. I walked across it and ran as if for my life, of course not knowing whither I was going. I was observed during my flight by a watchman who was rather lame, and he undertook to stop me, but I shook him off, and passed on until I got to a store, at the door of which I halted a moment to take breath. They inquired of me what was the matter, but I could not tell them, as I knew nothing of English but the word F-r-e-e. Soon after, the lame watchman and another came up to me. One of them drew a bright star from his pocket and shewed it to me, but I could make nothing of it.[256] I was then taken to the watch-house and locked up all night, when the captain called the next morning, paid expenses, and took me back again to the ship along with him. The officers told me I should be a free man, if I chose, but I did not know how to act; so after a little persuasion, the captain induced me to go back with him, as I need not be afraid.[257] This was on a Saturday, and on the following Monday afternoon three carriages drove up and stopped near the vessel.[258] Some gentlemen came aboard from them, and walked about the deck, talking to the captain, telling him that all on board were free, and requesting him to hoist the flag. He blushed a good deal, and said he would not do so; he put himself in a great rage and stormed somewhat considerably. We were afterwards taken in

---

256. Evidently, an official's or policeman's badge of office.

257. This second attempt at escape is not reported in the contemporary newspaper accounts.

258. Baquaqua's recollection of the days of the week seems to be confused. According to the *New York Herald* (12 July 1847), "On Saturday last the fact [that there were three slaves on board the *Lembrança*] leaked out, and in a few moments quite a collection of negroes and abolitionists assembled at the foot of Roosevelt street, where the vessel was lying." According to the *New York Daily Tribune* (12 July 1847), "a crowd of coloured persons" gathered on the wharf during Friday 9 July, and the ship was boarded and the slaves removed and taken to court on the following day, Saturday 10 July.

PLATE 18. New York City: 'We all had learned, that at New York there was no slavery' (Biography, p. 51); view of lower Manhattan, c. 1842–5, New York Historical Society, New York City, in Charles Lockwood, *Manhattan Moves Uptown: An Illustrated History* (Boston, 1976), 4.

their carriages, accompanied by the captain, to a very handsome building with a splendid portico in front, the entrance to which was ascended by a flight of marble steps, and was surrounded by a neat iron railing having gates at different points, the enclosure being ornamented with trees and shrubs of various kinds; it appeared to me a most beautiful place, as I had never seen anything like it before. I afterwards **[p. 56]** learned that this building was the City Hall of New York.[259] When we arrived in the large room of the building it was crowded to excess by all kinds of people, and great numbers stood about the doors and steps, and all about the court-yard—some in conversation, others merely idling away the time walking to and fro.[260]

259. The hearing was in the Court of Common Pleas in the City Hall.
260. Cf. the report of the *New York Daily Tribune*, 13 July 1847 (referring to the hearing on Monday, 12 July): "There was quite an excitement around the Hall, a large number of colored persons and others assembling in view of the proceedings." According to the *New York Herald* (13 July 1847), "a crowd of colored people of both sexes collected on the steps of the City Hall and in the vestibule, and continued to increase until 12 o'clock, when all ingress and egress to and from the chamber was blocked up. Two extra officers were then appointed to open passage and keep the crowd from forcing into the chamber."

The Brazilian Consul was there,[261] and when we were called upon I was asked if we wished to remain there or go back to Brazil. I answered for my companion[262] and myself that we did not wish to return; but the female slave who was with us said she would return. I have no doubt she would have preferred staying behind, but seeing the captain there, she was intimidated and afraid to speak her mind,[263] and so also, was the man but I spoke boldly out that I would rather die than return into slavery!! After a great many questions had been asked us, and answered, we were taken to prison, as I supposed it was, and there locked up.[264] A few days afterwards we were taken

261. The contemporary newspaper reports confirm that Captain Costa "sent for the Brazilian Consul as his counsel" in the initial hearing on Saturday, 10 July, but say that he did not arrive in time, causing the postponement of the hearing till Monday, 12 July. Probably the Consul attended on 12 July, although this is not explicitly reported, and on the following day, Tuesday 13 July, Costa submitted to the court a letter of protest signed by the Consul: *New York Daily Tribune*, 12 and 14 July 1847. The Brazilian Consul was Luiz Henrique Ferreira d'Aguiar (we wish to thank Alberto da Costa e Silva for this information).

262. From the following sentence, this evidently refers to the other male slave, José da Rocha.

263. The contemporary newspaper reports confirm Maria da Costa's disassociation from her fellow-slaves at this point. At the initial hearing on 10 July, while the two male slaves were placed in a local jail, she opted to return to the ship, on the understanding that the Captain would bring her to court for a hearing; and by the time of the judgment on 17 July, counsel for both parties agreed that she wished to remain in the service of her mistress, and that her status was, therefore, no longer at issue: *New York Daily Tribune*, 12, 16 and 17 July 1847.

264. Baquaqua's account gives a telescoped impression of the proceedings, which were in fact spread over several days. A writ of *habeas corpus* was issued by Judge Daly, of the Court of Common Pleas, on Saturday, 10 July, instructing Captain Da Costa to deliver the slaves José da Costa (i.e., Baquaqua), José da Rocha, and Maria da Costa, but the hearing was then adjourned until the following Monday, 12 July, and Daly's judgment delivered only on Saturday, 17 July. The slaves were initially represented by John and Isaac T. Hopper, but in the final hearing on 17 July by John Jay and Joseph White, apparently retained by the American Anti-Slavery Society; while a Mr. Purroy appeared for Captain da Costa: see *New York Daily Tribune*, 11 August 184. Counsel for the slaves appealed to a New York State law of 1840, by which slaves brought into the state became free; while Purroy cited a U.S.A.-Brazilian treaty of 1829, providing for the return of absconding members of ships' crews. Judge Daly ruled that the two male slaves should be returned to the ship, on the grounds that they were crew members, rather than of their status as slaves: see *New York Daily Tribune*, 13, 14, 15, 16, 17 and 19 July 1847; with text of Daly's judgment in *National Anti-Slavery Standard*, 12 August 1847. The prison (a "private establishment") where Baquaqua and his companion were lodged was on Eldridge Street; see *New York Daily Tribune*, 21 July and 12 August 1847, and affidavit of José da Costa and José da Rocha, 21 July 1847, in *National Anti-Slavery Standard*, 2 September 1847.

again to the City Hall, and asked many more questions.[265] We were then taken back to our old quarters the prison-house, I supposed preparatory to being shipped off again to Brazil, but of that I am not sure, as I could not understand all the ceremonies of locking us up and unlocking us, taking us to the court-house to ask questions and exhibit us before the audience there assembled—all this was new to me; I, therefore, could not fully understand the meaning of all this,[266] but I feared greatly that we were about to be returned to slavery— I trembled at the thought![267] Whilst we were again locked up, some friends who had interested themselves very much in our behalf, contrived a means by which the prison-doors were opened whilst the keeper slept, and we found do [sic: = no] difficulty in passing him, and gaining once more "the pure air of heaven,"[268] and by the assis-

265. Again, Baquaqua's account is somewhat truncated. Following Daly's judgment on 17 July, Baquaqua and his fellow slaves were initially restored to Captain Costa on board his ship, where they were detained in irons, but on Monday, 19 July, a second writ of *habeas corpus* was issued by Judge J.W. Edmonds, of the Supreme Court of New York, and they were returned to Eldridge Street jail pending the outcome. Jay and White again appeared for the slaves, and Purroy for the Captain. Jay and White argued that, since no interpreter had been provided, the two slaves had not been able to understand the proceedings or instruct their counsel; and also disputed their status as crew members, on the grounds that they had received no pay, and counter-charged the Captain with assault and false imprisonment of them. After various adjournments, judgment was finally given, by a different Judge, Henry P. Edwards, on Thursday, 5 August, again in favor of Captain Costa: *New York Daily Tribune*, 19, 20, 21, 22 and 27 July, 2 August 1847; with speeches of Jay and White, and affidavits of Clemente José da Costa, 20 July 1847, and of José da Costa (Baquaqua) and José da Rocha, 21 July 1847, in *National Anti-Slavery Standard*, 12 August and September 1847.

266. These difficulties of understanding, in relation to the earlier hearings before Judge Daly (10–17 July) are alluded to in the joint affidavit of José da Costa (Baquaqua) and José da Rocha, 21 July 1847: "they do not understand the English language, and did not, and could not, comprehend what was said and done."

267. In fact, the case was still unresolved. After the decision of Judge Edwards on 5 August, a third writ of *habeas corpus* was issued by Judge Oakley of the New York Supreme Court, and eventually scheduled for hearing on Monday, 9 August, the two slaves being meanwhile returned to the Eldridge Street jail, rather than to the ship. Negotiations were also initiated with Captain Costa about the possibility of his willingness to accept payment for the redemption of the two men from slavery: see *National Anti-Slavery Standard*, 12 August 1847.

268. The escape occurred on the night of Saturday, 9 August. According to the *New York Daily Tribune* (10 August 1847), "The Keeper of Eldridge St. Jail, in whose custody the two slaves of the L'Emperance [sic] were left, reported, this morning, that they were in the jail last night when he went to bed, but on rising this morning he found that they were gone. He knows nothing about the manner in which they got off." Also see *National Anti-Slavery Standard*, 12 August 1847, which reported that the jailer "fell asleep leaving the keys to the cell" on his desk. The jail was apparently a private establishment; see *New York Daily Tribune*, 12 August 1847.

tance of those dear friends, whom I shall never forget, I was enabled to reach the city of Boston, in Massachusetts,[269] and remained there under their protection about four weeks, when it was arranged that I should either be sent to England or Hayti, and I was consulted on the subject to know which I would prefer, and after considering for some time, I thought Hayti would be more like the climate of my own country and would agree better with my health and **[p. 57]** feelings. I did not know exactly what sort of a place England was or perhaps might have preferred to have gone there, more particularly as I have since learned that nearly all the English are friends to the colored man and his race, and that they have done so much for my people in the way of their welfare and advancement, and continue to this day to agitate anti-slavery and every other good cause. As it was, I determined to go to Hayti; accordingly, a free passage was procured for us,[270] and considerable provisions were collected for my use during the voyage.

There was on board a colored man of the name of Jones, who could speak Spanish very well.[271] During the voyage he took great pains to instruct me, and to give me correct ideas of things which I had formed the most absurd notion of. For instance, a person walking in the sun will see his shadow; this shadow I been led to believe was the soul of man that I had heard much of, and that when the body died the soul went to heaven (that is the shadow), and the body went to earth. His explanation of this shadow puzzled me very much, but the

269. They reached Boston via Springfield: see report from the *Springfield Gazette*, quoted in *New York Daily Tribune*, 23 August 1847.

270. As noted later (p. 58), Baquaqua was accompanied to Haiti by another ex-slave from Brazil. Although this is not specified in the *Biography*, this was the same man who had escaped from the *Lembrança* together with Baquaqua, called in the New York reports José da Rocha (although known to the Baptist Free Mission in Haïti as David): see letters of W.L. Judd, 28 October 1847; Mrs. N.A.L. Judd, 24 March 1848.

271. This Mr. Jones was evidently connected with the American Free Baptist Mission; in fact, although the *Biography* does not mention this, it was he who subsequently introduced Baquaqua to the head of the mission, the Rev. William Judd: letter of Mrs. N.A.L. Judd, 8 October 1847. Another member of the mission was, in fact, the Rev. William L. Jones, but this seems to be a different man; in fact, the Rev. Jones was currently on sick leave in the U.S.A., and did not return to Haiti until November 1848; letter of Rev. W.L. Judd, 19 November 1848, in *Christian Contributor and Free Missionary*, 13 December 1848.

PLATE 19. Haiti: 'When I arrived in Hayti I felt myself free' (Biography, p. 57), panorama of Port-au-Prince in 1870; in Samuel Hazard, *Santo Domingo Past and Present with a Glance at Hayti* (London, 1873).

solution of the mystery pleased me, and I began to feel proud of my learning.[272]

I worked occasionally for the captain on our passage to Hayti.[273] When I arrived at Hayti I felt myself free, as indeed I was. No slavery exists there, yet all are people of color who dwell there.[274] I did not know a word of their language, which was Creole;[275] neither did I know where to go or what to do! We, however, went to the Emperor's

272. A similar account of Baquaqua's conversation with Jones is given in a letter of Mrs. N.A.L. Judd, 8 October 1847.

273. Baquaqua landed at Port-au-Prince, the Haitian capital, probably in mid-September 1847.

274. Slavery had been abolished in Haïti (then the French colony of Saint-Domingue) by the French authorities in 1793 (this being a recognition that the institution had already been effectively destroyed by the rebellion of slaves which began in 1791); a subsequent attempt to re-institute slavery merely had the effect of provoking the independence of Haiti, effective 1 January 1804. The white population of the island had largely been eliminated by massacre and emigration during the course of the Revolution.

275. I.e., Creolized French. Other evidence confirms that, on his arrival in Haiti, Baquaqua spoke "neither French nor English," except for a very little "broken English" which had picked up on the voyage out: letter of Mrs. N.A.L. Judd, 8 October 1847.

PLATE 20. Rev. William L. Judd, with Baquaqua: 'a better man or Christian Mr. Judd, in my opinion, cannot be found' (Biography, p. 58), from the frontispiece, A.T. Foss and Edward Mathews, *Facts for Baptist Churches* (Utica, 1850).

house first.[276] He was very kind to us. One of the Emperor's Generals, De Pe by name,[277] and a mulatto, gave me plenty to eat and drink, and at night allowed me to lay down with his horses in the stables, and the musquitoes [sic] tormented me very much—they teazed me awfully. He often gave me whiskey and brandy to drink, and was every way very kind to me; these favors were (though only trifling in themselves under other circumstances) to me great indeed, considering what my

276. The "Emperor's house" was presumably the Palais National in Port-au-Prince. The reference is to Faustin Soulouque, who had become President of Haiti earlier in 1847. Soulouque did not, in fact, declare himself Emperor ("Faustin I") until August 1849, so that Baquaqua uses the title anachronistically in this context. Emperor Faustin was overthrown in 1859: see Leyburn, *Haitian People* (Westport, CT, 1966): 91–93; and *New York Daily Tribune*, 1 June 1847.

277. To be identified with General Dupuy, appointed Minister of War under President Soulouque: *New York Daily Tribune*, 1 June 1847.

position was.[278] I went about from house to house "a stranger in a strange land," and without being able to speak one word of the language of the people, and what was worse than that, not a copper in my possession to buy even a loaf to satisfy the cravings [p. 58] of my stomach. At length a colored man from America got me to work for him as cook about his house, but he was a very bad man and I did not stay with him very long. At night he took me up stairs and pointed to the floor where I was to sleep, although there was a bed in one corner of the room, but as soon as his back was turned I got into the bed and slept soundly till morning. When he discovered I had slept in the bed he beat me and knocked me about and turned me out of doors. So I became again an outcast and wanderer. I slept in the streets for several nights and became sick, so that when I walked about I was thought to be drunk, as my head was dizzy from the weakness of my system. In this way I went from house to house, and the people could not understand, but thought I was drunk. After this when General De Pe had taken notice of me, as before stated, my fellow in misfortune went to the Baptist Missionary, the Rev. Mr. Judd,[279] and told him our circumstances, stating that we were two slaves from Brazil,[280] and asked him if he could not do something for us, when he agreed to take me into his service, upon which I entered with the most cheerful

278. The wording seems to imply that General Dupuy befriended Baquaqua at the beginning of his stay in Haiti; but the reference to Dupuy later in this same paragraph makes clear that this occurred only later, after Baquaqua had spent "several" days as "an outcast and wanderer."

279. Rev. William L. Judd, of the Baptist Mission at Port-au-Prince. Judd had been baptised into the Baptist Church at age 16 in Stephentown, New York, and licensed to preach at 21, being ordained in 1834 in Michigan. In 1840–47 he was pastor of the Baptist Church in Meredith, New York, where he apparently met his wife, Nancy A. Lake, who came from nearby Milford. Judd, his wife, their young son, and Mrs. Judd's sister, Electa C. Lake, arrived in Port-au-Prince on 15 January 1847: see Foss and Matthews, *Facts for Baptist Churches*, 391–92. Judd remained in charge of the Haiti mission until 1855, when he resigned following criticism of "repeated acts of immorality" on his part; but he remained there as "an independent missionary," retaining the allegiance of the Mission church in Port-au-Prince: ABFMS, Thirteenth Annual Meeting, Norristown, Pennsylvania, 21–22 May 1856.

280. The reference is to José da Rocha, who became known as David in Haiti; see n. 269 above.

alacrity.[281]

I remained with him upwards of two years,[282] and a better man or christian than Mr. Judd, in my opinion, cannot be found. He treated me with every kindness; color to him being no cause of ill treatment. Neither shall I ever forget the kindness of his good lady; she behaved to me all the time of my servitude even as a christian should behave. I loved her for her goodness, although at all times I did not behave even to them as they deserved. I must confess, I sometimes treated them rather badly. I had not much gratitude then. I would often get very drunk and be abusive to them, but they overlooked my bad behavior always, and when Mrs. Judd would try to coax me to go home and behave myself, I would fight her and tell her I would not.[283]

After my conversion to christianity I gave up drinking and all other kinds of vices.[284] At the end of that time a stir was made in Hayti to enrol the militia;[285] and being opposed to the spirit of **[p. 59]** war as well as was [sic] my master and mistress, it was agreed that I should leave Hayti on that account, and they provided for me a passage on board a vessel bound to New York, in order to educate me preparatory to going to my own people in Africa, to preach the Gospel of glad

281. Baquaqua had entered the Judds' service by early October 1847: letter of Mrs. N.A.L. Judd, 8 October 1849. They employed him as a cook: letter of Mrs. N.A.L. Judd, Port-au-Prince, 24 March 1848. It may be noted that the Judds' accounts make no reference to Baquaqua's spending any time in other employment or in destitution prior to joining their household, and imply that he came straight from New York into the mission's service, whereas Baquaqua's account implies that he had initially intended to live independently and only joined the mission when he failed to find a living. In this and other respects, the Baptist Mission sources seem to present an idealized account of Baquaqua's progress towards conversion.

282. October 1847 to October 1849.

283. Cf. the letter of the Rev. W.L. Judd, 21 July 1848, which claims that prior to Baquaqua's baptism, "our hopes ... have been nearly blasted several times, as there were so many to lead him in the downward road to which his own natural heart was too much inclined." This contrasts with the claim in Mrs. Judd's letter of 24 March 1848, that Baquaqua "rarely needs a chiding word"; but his lapses into drunkenness may have occurred subsequently to the writing of the latter letter.

284. Baquaqua's "conversion" was reported in March 1848, and his baptism in July: letters of Mrs. N.A.L. Judd, 24 March & 21 July 1848 and Rev. W.L. Judd, 21 July 1848.

285. Presumably in connection with the war which Emperor Faustin Souluque was currently waging against Spain, for possession of its colony in the eastern half of the island (modern Dominican Republic).

tidings of great joy to the ignorant and benighted of my fellow country-men who are now believers in the false prophet Mahomed.[286]

A book published at Utica, in the State of New York, and entitled
"Facts for Baptist Churches," by Mr. A.T. Foss, of New Hampshire,
and E. Mathews, of Wisconsin, thus speaks of Mahommah:[287]

"After enduring the yoke for two years in Brazil,[288] he escaped and
sought a refuge in this land which boasts of its freedom and philan-
thropy, but that refuge he sought here in vain. Flying, therefore, from
our shores, through a kind Providence, he was conducted to the city
of Port au Prince, in Hayti, and to the christian hospitalities of Wm.
L. Judd. Our missionary received him gladly, and while he provided
him a home and temporal comforts, he failed not to instruct him in
the religion of the Gospel. The instruction was to him as life from the

286. Baquaqua's mentors in Haiti expressed considerable fear that Baquaqua might be
pressed into military service; see letter of Mrs. N.A.L. Judd, 4 December 1849, Westville, New
York, in *Christian Contributor and Free Missionary*, 3 January 1850, and the wording of the
Biography here seems to imply that Baquaqua was sent out of Haïti to avoid conscription.
Nonetheless, it is clear that for some time the intention was to send him to the United States for
education, preparatory to mission work in Africa; the threat of conscription presumably merely accelerated his departure.

287. Foss and Mathews, *Facts for Baptist Churches*, 392–93, which includes the quotation
from the *Christian Contributor and Free Missionary*, presumably an insertion by the editor
Moore. In fact, the quotation in the *Biography* omits the first two sentences in the passage from
Foss and Mathews, which summarizes information from the letters of the Rev. Mr. & Mrs. Judd
published in the *Christian Contributor and Free Missionary* in 1847–48: "Born in 1830, of a
respectable family in Central Africa, he was at an early age, clandestinely seized upon, and
reduced to slavery. For some time he was held in this condition in Western Africa, and then was
transported to Brazil." This passage was evidently omitted because it contradicts statements in
the *Biography* about Baquaqua's age and the circumstances of his enslavement; for further discussion, see Introduction.

288. This information is derived from the letter of the Rev. W.L. Judd, 21 July 1848. Since
he left Brazil in April 1847, to arrive in New York in late June of that year, this indicates that
he was brought as a slave to Brazil in 1845. Other accounts, however, suggest discrepant dates.
A New York newspaper report in 1847, referring collectively to Baquaqua (under his Portuguese name of José da Costa) and the two other slaves who sought freedom with him, José da
Rocha, and Maria da Costa, stated that they had spent "about six years" in Brazil, implying
arrival there c.1841, but this may relate to the time spent there by one or both of the others,
rather than by Baquaqua himself: *New York Daily Tribune*, 13 July 1847. Another account, in
1853, states that Baquaqua had been taken from his home "more than ten years ago," implying
a date of c.1843, but this may be meant to refer to his original enslavement within Africa rather
than his subsequent export to Brazil: AFBMS, Tenth Annual Meeting, 1–2 June 1853, Utica,
New York.

dead, and his heart felt its power. He saw and acknowledged its adapt-
edness to his case as a sinner. He bowed to its authority. He rejoiced
in its truth, and became a disciple of its Divine Author."[289]

The baptismal scene, when Mahommah publicly put his trust in
Christ, is thus described by Mr. Judd. It is taken from the "Christian
Contributor."[290]

"His experience before the Church was very affecting. Several persons present, not professors of religion, wept on hearing it. He is
endowed by nature with a soul so noble that he grasps the whole
world at a stroke, in the movements of his benevolent feelings, and
the expression of such noble feelings in a style so simple and broken
as his, is truly affecting. He now seems filled with the most ardent
desire to labor for the salvation of souls—talks much of Africa, and
prays ardently that her people may receive the Gospel—dreams often
of visiting Kaskua,[291] accompanied by 'a good white man,' as he calls
a Missionary, and being kindly received by his mother.[292] He had been
asking **[p. 60]** for baptism a considerable time, when I felt that I could
not refuse him any longer. We repaired to the sea side very early in
the morning, accompanied by a mixed congregation. After singing
and praying in French, I delivered a discourse of perhaps twenty minutes, mostly extemporaneous, upon (*Les usages pratiques, de l'or-
dannance* [sic] *du Bapteme*) the practical usages of baptism, founded
on Romans vi: 1–4. After this, I prayed in English for the especial
benefit of Mahommah.

"In passing down the gentle de[s]cent to reach a sufficient depth of
water, I asked him if he wished now to devote himself entirely to God
and to the good of the world. He replied, 'O yes, Mr. Judd, *I want to
do all for God, all for good.*' In the water[s] of the great deep, which

---

289. Apart from the first clause relating to Baquaqua's time in Brazil, this paragraph is taken
verbatim from ABFMS, Sixth Annual Report, Charlestown, Massachusetts, 2 May 1849.

290. Letter of Rev. W. L. Judd, 21 July 1848, printed in the *Christian Contributor and Free
Missionary*, 23 August 1848, the full text of which is given in Appendix 2, no. 4.

291. Sic; but "Kachna [= Katsina]" in the original.

292. Cf. n. 152 above.

in their eternal freedom rolling, bathe Africa as well as Hayti[,]
I buried him with Christ in baptism, hoping that he may yet be borne
upon its surface, as a messenger of mercy to the dark land of his
birth."

I will give a slight glance at the voyage from Port au Prince to New
York, and relate the incidents connected with it as briefly as possible.[293] We had a most miserable passage, head winds nearly all the
way; indeed, they continued from our leaving Hayti until reaching a
southern port in the United States of America, into which we were
compelled to run on account of the weather. The wife of Mr. Judd
accompanied me on my voyage, she being on a visit to the States,
where her parents resided.[294]

When the vessel put into port a slave owner came aboard, and seeing me, asked if I was for sale, remarking I was a likely nigger, and
would look well skinned, as my hide was a little too dark.[295] We
encountered at sea very heavy weather, the ship rocking and pitching
most fearfully. We had prayers aboard, but we did not fear the raging
of the sea, as our trust was in Him "who resteth the sea, and stilleth
the tempest." My mistress was very fond of me, and said she did not
feel at all uneasy as long as Mahommah was near her. She had great
confidence in me, not that I could have saved her in case of wreck,
but I suppose she felt more at rest knowing me, and that I had been
about her so long, and served her faithfully.

The weather, however, soon moderated, and we once more set
[p. 61] sail again with a fair wind, and was soon on our way to the
city of New York again, where we arrived on a Saturday.[296] On the following day, one of the seamen who had professed great friendship for
me during the voyage, took it into his head to turn ugly with me. As

---

293. Baquaqua left Port-au-Prince for New York, on the *Desdemona*, 17 October 1849: letter of Mrs. N.A.L. Judd, Westville New York, 4 December 1849, in *Christian Contributor and
Free Missionary*, 3 January 1850.

294. They were also accompanied by Mrs. Judd's sister, Electa C. Lake: ibid.

295. Slavery was, of course, still legal in the Southern states of the U.S.A.

296. The voyage took twenty days (letter of Mrs. N.A.L. Judd, 4 December 1849), so they
arrived in New York around 15 November 1849.

he was about going ashore, I merely said to him, "give my respects to your wife," as he had been so kind to me. What I said was intended merely as a little civility, when as (I found afterwards) he had been drinking. He took it completely amiss, called me a "nigger," and swore he would give me a thrashing. At night, when he returned again on board, he was very drunk and behaved with great violence, swearing that he would break my head with a stick which he flourished about over my head. I had placed chairs round the table for supper as usual, when he remarked, that he did not intend to sit down with a "nigger." He afterwards got more calm, and sat down and ate like a christian, but this was not till I had let him see a little of my own ugliness, and had threatened to beat him, that he became quieted; when he saw I was no longer to be played with, he gave in, and became a good man, only because he was obliged to.

I followed out the Scripture injunction, to be as "wise as serpents, and harmless as doves," not at all intending to beat him, merely to quiet him. My wisdom I displayed in the first place, not needing to display any other spirit than an harmless one; in the second, I found my "wisdom" sufficient for the case at that time.

We safely reached the shore at New York, and were soon on our way steaming it to Albany, at which place we took the cars to within a short distance of Mrs. Judd's mother's house, which was a little way from a village called Milford in the State of New York. We arrived at Milford early in the following morning, and I was sent on to the house, whilst Mrs. Judd stood at the tavern to fetch a conveyance to take her on.[297] When I reached her mother's house, I had a mind to impress them with the belief that I was a fugitive; but questions being put to me of a positive nature, I could not but give positive answers. I told her I was from Hayti, and she immediately conjectured who I was, as ac- **[p. 62]** counts were often sent to her from her daughter in

297. This journey from New York via Albany to Milford is described in a letter of Mrs. N.A.L. Judd, Westville, 28 March 1850, in *Christian Contributor and Free Missionary*, 18 April 1850. Mrs. Judd refers to Baquaqua's presence with her and to the collection of donations for support of his education.

PLATE 21. New York Central College: 'I remained nearly three years in the college' (Biography, p. 62), N.Y. Central College Collection, Cortland County Historical Society, Cortland, N.Y.

papers printed there,[298] and she asked me if I was Mahommah; I said I was. She wanted to know how I had got to America, who had brought me here. I at once told her, when orders were immediately given for horses, and I returned for my mistress, who was soon once more in the embraces of a kind, good mother. Mother and child had once again met after seas had separated them so great a distance.

I remained there about four weeks, then went to Meredith, in Delaware county, amongst the Free Missions, to see whether they would undertake the task of educating me, when they agreed at once to do so.[299] A gentleman by the name of Dalton was exceedingly kind

298. Referring presumably to the various letters of Mrs. N.A.L. Judd printed in the *Christian Contributor and Free Missionary*, between 1847–50.

299. Probably referring to a meeting of the Board of the American Baptist Free Mission Society, which was attended by Baquaqua together with Mrs. Judd and her sister. His education and intention to return as a missionary to Africa were discussed there: ABFMS, Seventh Annual Meeting, Bristol, New York, 5–7 June 1850.

PLATE 22. Cyrus P. Grosvenor: 'at the time C.P.Grosvenor was the President of the College [1849–50]' (Biography, p. 63) and also editor, Christian Contributor and Free Missionary (1845–50); from a photograph at the Lamont Memorial Free Library, McGraw, N.Y.

to me, and undertook my case with the friends of the missions.[300] They then sent me on to McGrawville, at the time C.P. Grosvenor was the President of the College,[301] who was very kind to me, and made much of me, treating me in every way as an equal and a gentleman.

I remained nearly three years in the college, and during that time made very great progress in learning before leaving the college.[302] My teacher, Miss K. King,[303] composed the following lines,

300. Presumably Dalton was associated with the "Free Missions," which the report of the ABFMS, Seventh Annual Meeting, indicates was the Franklin Free Mission Society, which was thanked for looking after Baquaqua after his arrival in the United States.

301. I.e., New York Central College, McGrawville, where Baquaqua now enrolled as a student in the Primary Department. He was introduced at the College by Mrs. Judd and her sister Electa Lake on 16 January 1850: letter of E.C. Lake, Westville, New York, 18 February 1850, in *Christian Contributor and Free Missionary*, 7 March 1850. The College had opened in 1849 and was linked to the American Baptist Free Mission Society, which also sponsored the mission in Haiti with Baquaqua had previously been associated. Cyrus P. Grosvenor, its first President (1849–50) and also Professor of Philosophy there until his retirement in 1853, was a leading abolitionist, initially influenced by William Lloyd Garrison, and was a founding member of the ABFMS. He served as editor of the *Christian Contributor and Free Missionary* until 1850, and, as discussed in the Introduction, he published two of Baquaqua's letters from Haiti and otherwise had taken a personal interest in Baquaqua: see letters of Mrs. N.A.L. Judd, 24 March 1848 (Appendix 2, no. 3); Baquaqua to Grosvenor, 14 November 1848 (Appendix 3, no. 2). Also see Hanchett, "New York Central College, C.P. Grosvenor, and Gerrit Smith."

302. As Baquaqua entered the College in January 1850 (cf. previous note), this indicates that he left it around the end of 1852 or beginning of 1853.

303. Kezia King, teacher in the Primary Department of New York Central College. Austin (*African Muslims Sourcebook*, 654, n. 99; *Transatlantic Stories*, 167) confuses this woman with Mary E. King, a white student at the College, who eloped with Professor William G. Allen, the College's second black professor, in 1853.

PLATE 23. McGrawville: 'If you write to me sent [= send] to McGrawville, Cortland, Co., N.Y.' (letter to George Whipple, Brooklyn, 10 August 1853); downtown McGrawville, as seen in the early 1860s, as photographed by G.L. Holden, dentist and photographer, Lamont Memorial Free Library, McGraw, N.Y.

which were spoken by me, before the primary department of the college.

LINES SPOKEN BY MAHOMMAH.

You can't expect one of my race,
With woolly hair and sable face,
And scarce a ray of knowledge
To interest his friends at college.
But, I will do the best I can,
To prove I mean to be a man.
'Tis truc, my limbs have fetters worn,
'Tis true my back the scourge has borne,
But 'tis *not* true that tyrant's power
E'er made my heart within me cower.
No! that was free as when I played,
Beneath my native palm trees' shade.

Oh! Africa, my native land,
When shall I see thee, meekly stand,
Beneath the banner of my God,
And governed by His Holy word?

[p. 63]

When shall I see the oppressor's rod
Plucked from his hand, my gracious God?
Oh! when shall I my brethren see,
Enjoy the sweets of LIBERTY?

Friends of the crushed and bleeding slave,
Ask God to pity! God to save!!
For all the help of man is vain,
Since man for man has forged the chain.
Oh Righteous Father, thou art just,
To thee I look, to thee I trust;
Oh may thy gracious spirit bear
The Afric's groan, the Afric's prayer,
Up to thy spotless throne above,
Where all is joy and peace and love,
For Jesus' sake, Oh! save the oppressed,
And let their souls in heaven find rest.

Whilst at college, some of the young gentleman there who did not
altogether like my color, played considerable many practical jokes
upon me, and tried to make me some mischief with the principals.
They played all sorts of tricks upon me; they would, when I was out
of the way, scatter my books and papers all over the room, and pile
up my books in a heap; they would also choke up my stove pipe with
shavings, so that when I attempted to make a fire, the room would
become filled with smoke; but of these matters, I had only to com-
plain in the right quarter, and all would be settled. But I did not like

to be continually complaining of them, so I endured a great deal of their vexatious tricks in silence. I could not tell why they plagued me thus, excepting they did not like my color, and that they thought I was a good subject upon which to expend their frolicksome [sic] humor.

After I left the college, I went to the Free Missions, with whom I remained a short time, and received more learning from that source. I went to school at Freetown Corner, under the direction of the missions.[304] I lived with my teacher, working occasionally for my board, during my stay here. I had a room to myself, and being cold weather, I always needed a fire, but being no place for the stove pipe to go into a chimney, a lady suggested that I should take a pane of glass from the window **[p. 64]** and put the pipe through the aperture, which I did, and it answered the purpose very well indeed, until a very windy day came, when the wind blowing down the pipe, caused my room to be filled with smoke; how to remedy the evil, I could not exactly tell, but an ingenious thought struck me. I went to the closet and procured a large fat candle-stick, which I took outside and placed shank downwards. This answered the purpose well enough so far as keeping the wind out, but at dark my room was filled with the choking smoke as bad as ever; the remedy was as bad as the disease. I had imagined that the wind getting into the pipe prevented the smoke getting out, consequently my plan was to adopt some method to keep the wind out, which I did most effectually. The sequel is known. Thus a man may acquire knowledge, piece by piece, and in some things become very clever, but notwithstanding may become entangled in his ideas with the simplest thing imaginable. Cleverer and wiser men than Mahommah, have done even more foolish things than this.

---

304. His additional schooling at Freetown Corners was presumably under the direction of the American Baptist Free Mission, but no record of this further schooling (evidently, during the first half of 1853) has been found in Free Mission Society records. Freetown Corners was a few miles south of McGrawville. Baquaqua's letter to George Whipple of 26 October 1853 (Appendix 3, no. 11), although written after his return to McGrawville, says that he was a member of the Baptist Church at Freetown Corners.

After this I returned to McGrawville for a short time,[305] when, having a desire to see the manners and customs of the people living under
the Government of Queen Victoria, of whom I had heard so much,
induced me to go to Canada, where I remained a short time,[306] and
being so well pleased with the reception I there met with, I at once
determined to become a subject of her Majesty, for which purpose I
attended at the proper office, gave the oath of allegiance, and procured my papers of naturalization without any difficulty.[307]

I was kindly treated by all classes wherever I went, and must say
in my heart I never expected to receive in a nation so distant from my
native home, so much kindness, attention and humanity. I am thankful to God that I enjoy the blessings of liberty, in peace and tranquil-
ity, and that I am now in a land where "none dare make me afraid,"
where every man can or may "sit down under his own vine, and under
his own fig tree:" where every man acting as a man, no matter what
his color, is regarded as a brother, and where all are equally free to do
and to say.

[p. 65] Being thus surrounded by friends, and enabled to enjoy the
blessing of peaceful freedom, I came to the conclusion that the time

305. Baquaqua's extant letters show that he was resident at McGrawville between August-
October 1853 (although he visited Brooklyn, Syracuse, and New Berlin in August-September).
Austin (*Transatlantic Stories*, 168) assumes that Baquaqua returned to McGrawville in order to
resume study at Central College, but this seems unlikely. The *Biography* here, curiously, omits
any mention of the fund-raising activities on behalf of the American Baptist Free Mission
Society undertaken by Baquaqua, to support their proposed African mission in which he was
intended to serve, from June 1853 onwards: letter of A.L. Post, on "Mahommah and the African
Mission," in *The American Baptist*, 28 July 1853; ABFMS, Eleventh Annual Meeting, Albany,
New York, 7–8 June 1854; see also the Introduction, for a fuller discussion. It also fails to men-
tion his attempt to obtain alternative sponsorship for his return to Africa from the American
Missionary Society, from August 1853 onwards, documented in his correspondence with
George Whipple, its Secretary (see Appendix 3).

306. Baquaqua reported his intention to go to Canada in letters written from McGrawville,
8 and 26 October 1853. Although his departure was deferred, presumably he went to Canada
soon afterwards.

307. Baquaqua was at McGrawville in January 1854, presumably after returning from his
first, brief visit to Canada (see his letters written from there to George Whipple, 6 and 22
January1854); but presumably returned to Canada West soon afterwards, settling at Chatham:
see his letters written to Gerrit Smith, 25 May 1854 and 4 July 1854 (Appendix 3, nos. 14
& 15).

had arrived when I might with propriety commit to paper all that has been recounted in this work, and whenever the day may come that a way may be opened to me of being useful in the regeneration of my own loved country, I shall be ready to say "I come," and may God in his infinite wisdom hasten that day, is the constant and fervent prayer of the subscriber, whose sufferings and tortures it is to be hoped have still further opened the ears and hearts of sensibility.

Should a call be given him to return once more to the land of his birth, he will cheerfully respond, and is sure friends will not be wanting to aid him in his benevolent purpose.

MAHOMMAH GARDO BAQUAQUA.

[p. 66]

PRAYER OF THE OPPRESSED.[308]
Oh great Jehovah! God of love,
Thou monarch of the earth and sky,
Canst thou from thy great throne above
Look down with an unpitying eye?

See Afric's sons and daughters toil,
Day after day, year after year,
Upon this blood-bemoistened soil,
And to their cries turn a deaf ear?

Canst thou the white oppressor bless
With verdant hills and fruitful plains,
Regardless of the slave's distress,
Unmindful of the black man's chains.

How long, oh Lord! ere thou wilt speak
In thy Almighty thundering voice,
To bid the oppressor's fetters break,
And Ethiopia's sons rejoice.

---

308. The poem is by James M. Whitfield (1822–71), published in his *America, and Other Poems* (Buffalo, 1853).

How long shall Slavery's iron grip,
And Prejudice's guilty hand,
Send forth like blood-hounds from the slip,
Foul persecutions o'er the land?

How long shall puny mortals dare
To violate thy just decree,
And force their fellow-men to wear
The galling chain on land and sea?

Hasten, oh Lord! the glorious time
When everywhere beneath the skies,
From every land and every clime,
Peans to Liberty shall rise!

When the bright sun of liberty
Shall shine o'er each despotic land,
And all mankind from bondage free,
Adore the wonders of thy hand.

APPENDIX 1

Affidavits of Captain Clemente José da Costa, and the slaves José da Costa and José da Rocha, New York, 1847[1]

1.

To the Honourable Charles P. Daly, one of the Judges of the Court of Common Pleas, in and for the City and County of New-York.[2]

I, the undersigned, master of the Brazilian barque Lembranca, do return to the annexed writ of habeas corpus directed to me: That a negro woman called Maria, and two negro men, one called José Da Rocha, and the other José Da Costa, being the persons produced by me, were under my restraint at the time of the service of said writ; that said Maria is still under my restraint, and the aforesaid two negro men are at present, as I have been informed, and believe, in the custody of the Sheriff of the city and county of New-York, to whose custody they were remanded by an order of the Honourable Charles P. Daly, after they were produced by me, in obedience to the said writ before said Judge.

That no other negro woman than the aforesaid Maria, was at the time of the service of said writ, or now is under my custody, power, or restraint.

And I do further return, that the authority and true cause of the restraint of said three persons, are as follows, viz: The said negro woman Maria, and the said José Da Costa, are slaves, and my prop-

1. Printed in *National Anti-Slavery Standard*, 2 September 1847, under the title, "The Brazilian Slave Case."

2. Captain Costa's return to the first writ of *habeas corpus* against him, issued by Judge C. P. Daly on Saturday, 10 August 1847; although undated, it was presumably submitted at the initial (deferred) hearing of the case on Monday, 12 August Judgment was eventually given by Judge Daly, in Captain Costa's favor, on Saturday, 17 July.

erty, lawfully acquired in Brazil, under the laws thereof, by me,[3] I and the said Maria and José Da Costa being at the time, and now being, inhabitants of, and residents in Brazil, within the dominions and jurisdiction of his Majesty, the Emperor of Brazil, and his subjects. The said José Da Rocha is also a slave, the property of one Antonio José Da Rocha Perrira, of Rio Janiero, in Brazil, lawfully acquired in Brazil aforesaid, under the laws thereof, by said Perrira—the said Perrira and the said José Da Rocha, being at the same time, and now being, inhabitants of, and residents in Brazil, within the dominions and jurisdiction of his Majesty, the Emperor of Brazil, and his subjects. That by the laws and institutions of the empire of Brazil, which is an independent and sovereign nation, and as such recognized by the United States of America, Slavery is recognized and permitted, and the acquisition, possession, and transfer of persons as property and slaves, is allowed, recognized, and protected by law in the same manner as other property.[4]

That the said Maria and José Da Costa so being slaves, and my lawful property, as aforesaid, and the said José Da Rocha being a slave, and the lawful property of the said Perrira, as aforesaid, I set sail from Rio Janiero, in Brazil, as master of and on board of the Brazilian barque Lembranca, of which I am part owner, bound to the port of New-York, and having on board the said Maria, José Da Costa, and José Da Rocha, and arrived in the said port of New-York on the 27th day of June, 1847, having on board said three slaves, with the intention of transacting such lawful business as had brought me to

---

3. Since Baquaqua says that he was purchased and owned by the captain of the ship on which he came to New York (*Biography*, p. 48), it is clearly he who is to be identified with José da Costa.

4. In fact, Baquaqua certainly and probably also his two fellow slaves were strictly not slaves under Brazilian law, having been illegally imported there from Africa; the Brazilian anti-slave trade law of 1831 provided that any Africans introduced into the country after that date were legally free. It is odd that their counsel did not use this argument, since the illegality of their original importation from Africa (in this case, to Cuba) had been central to the earlier (1839) case of the slaves involved in the mutiny on the *Amistad*, also in New York State: see Howard Jones, *The Mutiny on the Amistad: The Saga of the Slave Revolt and its Impact on American Abolition, Law and Diplomacy* (revised ed., Oxford, 1988).

said port, and of immediately thereafter returning to Brazil—my stay in said port of New-York being necessarily of short duration, and in the character of a traveller. That the above named Perrira is also a part owner of the said barque Lembranca, and on the departure of the said barque on the voyage aforesaid, committed to my charge, custody, and care, as his agent, the aforesaid José Da Rocha, his slave, and property, to be by me returned to him on my arrival at the port of departure, and I am now the agent of said Perrira in relation to his said slave or property.

That the said José Da Costa, and José Da Rocha were shipped on board the said barque, on the voyage aforesaid, as part of the crew of said barque, on the voyage aforesaid, and as such, I am required by the laws of Brazil to take them back to Brazil.

That the said Maria has come on the voyage aforesaid, as servant and nurse to my wife and family, in whose service she now is.

That the said slaves were brought to this country under the firm faith and assurance that the rights of property of foreign subjects are held sacred in the United States, and protected and upheld as much as the rights of the citizens of those States of the Union where Slavery exists, and is recognized by law; and also under the solemn faith of the treaty between Brazil and the United States,[5] which stipulates in Article 12th, as follows, viz: "Both the contracting parties promise and engage, formally, to give their special protection to the persons and property of the citizens and subjects of each other, Of all classes, who may be in their territories, subject to the jurisdiction of the one or the other, transient or dwelling therein," &c.[6]

CLEMENTE JOSÉ DA COSTA

5. As specified in no. 3 below, this was a treaty of cooperation signed in 1829.

6. In the subsequent hearings, however, Captain Costa's attorney shifted his ground, citing instead article 31 of the same treaty, which provided for the return of members of ships' crews who deserted; and Judge Daly's decision on 17 July was based on the status of José da Costa and José da Rocha as members of the crew of the *Lembrança*, rather than their status as slaves: see text of Daly's judgment, printed in *National Anti-Slavery Standard*, 12 August 1847.

The facts on this return are hereby all admitted, except the existence of the treaty,[7] and the law applicable to it.

J. HOPPER[8]

2.

*To the Honourable Henry P. Edwards,
one of the Justices of the Supreme Court.*[9]

I, the undersigned, master of the Brazilian barque Lembranca, do respectfully return to the annexed writ of habeas corpus directed to me: That before the issuing and service of the annexed writ of habeas corpus, to wit, on the 10th day of July, instant a writ of habeas corpus was duly allowed and issued by the Honourable Charles P. Daly, one of the Associate Judges of the Court of Common Pleas, in and for the city and county of New-York, and of the degree of Counsellor of the Supreme Court, directed to me, for the purpose, and with the subject of producing before the said Judge, the persons named in the annexed writ, and a negro woman called Maria, for the purpose of inquiring into the cause of their detention or imprisonment by me. That in obedience to the said writ, so issued, by Judge Daly, I produced before him the persons of the two negro men, called Jose Da Costa and Jose Da Rocha, in the annexed writ, allowed by your Honour named, and the person of the said Maria, and made the return, signed by me, con-

---

7. As explained in no. 3 below, it was argued that the 1829 treaty was no longer in force, since it had a fixed term of only twelve years.

8. John Hopper acted as attorney for the slaves in the initial days of the hearing, although (according to their later claim) without their active consent or understanding; they subsequently repudiated this admission which he made on their behalf (in no. 3 below).

9. Captain Costa's return to the second writ of *habeas corpus* against him, issued on Monday, 19 July. The writ was issued by Judge J. W. Edmonds, who is named at the end of the text of Captain Costa's return as receiving it on 20 July; but the case was later transferred to a different judge, H.P. Edwards, who is named in this heading, and who delivered the eventual judgment (again in favor of Captain Costa) on 5 August.

tained in the annexed record of the proceedings had before said Judge Daly, upon the said writ of habeas corpus issued by him. That upon said writ, so issued, by said Judge Daly, and upon the return thereto, proceedings were duly had before the said Judge Daly, who after mature deliberation, and after hearing the allegations and arguments of counsel on both side, decided and adjudged, on or about the 16th day of July, instant,[10] that the said Jose Da Costa and Jose Da Rocha, were legally under my restraint, and that they should be remanded to my custody: Which said decision and judgement of said Judge Daly are still in force, unreversed, not set aside, nor made void. That in pursuance of said decision and adjudication, the persons of the said Da Costa and Da Rocha were recommitted to my custody. That the original record of said proceedings, had before said Judge Daly, is hereto annexed, and now by me produced before your Honour.

And I further return and allege, that no new state of facts has arisen, subsequent to the aforesaid decision and adjudication of the Honourable Judge Daly in relation to the said Da Costa and Da Rocha, between me and the said Da Costa and Da Rocha, but on the contrary thereof, there is at the present time a continuance of these facts upon which the decision and adjudication aforesaid of the Honourable Judge Daly were founded. And I do respectfully insist the that such proceedings and adjudication are a bar to any farther proceedings on this writ of habeas corpus hereto annexed, and allowed by your Honour, and that the matter should be adjudged as res adjudicata,[11] and the annexed writ of habeas corpus allowed by your Honour dismissed.

But if, notwithstanding my foregoing objection, your Honour should deem it proper further to proceed and under the annexed writ of habeas corpus allowed by your Honour, I had Jose Da Costa and Jose Da Rocha in the annexed writ allowed by your Honour named, under my restraint, and that in return of that said last mentioned writ,

10. Actually, on 17 July, as stated in no. 3 below.
11. I.e., a case already judged.

I produced the persons before your Honour, and that they were thereupon remanded by your Honour to the custody of the Sheriff of the
city and county of New-York, where they now are. And I further
return that now have the said Da Rocha and Da Costa under my
restraint, but in the custody of the said Sheriff, under the remanding
of your Honour, as aforesaid. That the authority and true cause of
such restraint are truly and correctly set forth in my return to the said
habeas corpus, issued by Judge Daly and which return, signed by me,
is hereto annexed, and I pray may be taken as part of this, my present
return; and further, the facts and circumstances herein before set
forth.
     CLEMENTE JOSE DA COSTA

Sworn before me this 20th July, 1847.
J. W. EDMONDS

3.
In the matter of the writ of Habeas Corpus
directed to Clemente Jose da Costa, to produce the bodies
of José da Costa, and José da Rocha.[12]

City and county of New-York, ss. José Da Costa, and José Da
Rocha, in answer to the foregoing return of Clemente José Da Costa,
master of the Brazilian barque Lembranca, to the writ of habeas corpus to the said master directed, requiring him to produce the bodies
of these defendants, by him imprisoned, and detained, as it was said,
before the Honourable John W. Edmonds, together with the time and
causes of such imprisonment, and detention, being duly and severally sworn, do depose, and say—That the writ of habeas corpus in the
said return referred to as having been duly allowed and issued, on the

---

12. Response of José da Costa and José da Rocha to no. 2 above, submitted on 21 July 1847.

tenth day of July, instant, by the Hon. Charles P. Daly, one of the Associate Judges of the Court of Common Pleas, in and for the city and county of New-York, directed to the said master, for the purpose of producing these deponents, and a negro woman named Maria, before the said Judge, and for the purpose of inquiring into the cause of their detention and imprisonment, was allowed, and issued, without the request, assent, knowledge, or priority of these deponents, and that John Inverness, upon whose petition the said writ was allowed, was to them, at the said time, and for some time thereafter, an utter stranger.

That after the issuing of the said writ, these deponents were placed by order of the said Judge, as they are informed and believe, in a place called the Eldridge street prison, and were on several occasions taken from thence, and conveyed to the Chambers of the said Judge, as they are informed, and believe, where certain proceedings were had in reference to the said writ of habeas corpus, but what such proceedings were these deponents are ignorant, for these deponents say that they are native Africans, and were many years since kidnapped, and carried to Brazil,[13] and have ever since been held in slavery, and that they do not speak nor understand the English language, and did not, and could not comprehend what was said and done, by, and before the said Judge Daly in the said matter, and that they had no interpreter near them during the said proceedings to interpret and explain the same.[14] And these deponents further say that they did not, and each for himself saith that he did not employ, authorize, or empower any attorney or counsel to appear for, or represent them in the said matter, until the appointment of John Jay, Esquire, as their attorney, by a proper instrument for that purpose, as hereinafter stated.[15] And these depo-

13. Baquaqua himself later stated that he had been brought from Africa only two years earlier, but José da Rocha had probably been in Brazil longer: see *Biography*, p. 59, with discussion in n. 287.

14. Cf. *Biography*, p. 56: "I could not understand all the ceremonies of locking us up and unlocking us, taking us to the court-house to ask questions ... all this was new to me; I, therefore, could not fully understand the meaning of all this."

15. As later specified, this was on 15 July, before Judge Daly's judgement was given on 17 July.

nents further say that they did not, and each for himself saith, that he did not authorize any admission to be made on their behalf, or on behalf of either of them touching the averments, assertions, and declarations, contained and set forth in the return of the said master, Da Costa, to the said first writ of habeas corpus, and that they were utterly and entirely ignorant that any such admissions had been made in the said proceedings by any person acting or professing to act as counsel in their behalf, until after they had been remanded by the said Judge Daly, into the custody of the said master, and had been again brought up, and confined in the said Eldridge street prison upon the second writ of habeas corpus, when the fact of admission having been made, which appears upon the record annexed to the return of the said master, in the words, following, to wit: "The facts in this return, are hereby admitted, except the existence of the treaty and the law applicable to it," was first communicated to these deponents by their counsel, Mr. John Jay. And these deponents say, that they do not admit the facts stated in the said return, as in said admission specified, but on the contrary, utterly and altogether deny several averments in the said return, to wit:

First. They deny that these deponents were shipped on board of the Brazilian barque, Lembranca, as part of the crew of said barque, on the voyage therein referred to, from Brazil to the port of New-York.

Secondly. They deny that as such part of the crew, the said master is required by the laws of Brazil to take these deponents back to Brazil, and they say that if any law exists in Brazil, requiring masters of vessels to return the crews thereof from a foreign port of departure, such law is for the benefit of the crew who may desire so to return, and does not compel the master to return those who may wish to stay in such foreign port.

And the deponents further say, that they do not admit that any such treaty as that referred to in the said return to the writ of habeas corpus, with a particular mention of the twelfth Article, and cited in a memorandum of authorities appended to the said record as "Treaty between the United States Government and Brazil, 17th March,

1829," is now in force—for these deponents are informed, and believe, that the same having been originally entered into to continue for twelve years from the date thereof, has expired by its own limitation, and has never been renewed. And these deponents say, that the fact that the counsel by whom the admissions aforesaid were endorsed upon said return, was not authorized by these deponents to make such admissions, together with other facts relating to the said proceedings, do further appear by the affidavit of John Hopper, Esquire, hereunto appended. And these deponents further say, that they are informed, and believe, that it appears by the opinion of the said Judge Daly attached to the return of the said master, as forming part thereof, that it was under and by virtue of the said admissions, or some of them, and especially of the admission above referred, that these deponents were shipped as part of the crew of the vessel, that the said Judge Daly decided that these deponents should be remanded to the custody, and restraint of the said Captain.

And these deponents further say, and each for himself saith; that they did not, nor did either of them ship on board the said vessel as part of the crew thereof—that they did not, nor did either of them enter into any agreement with the said Captain Da Costa, nor with any other person, to serve on board of the said vessel, nor assent to any such agreement made on their behalf by any other person or persons—that they have not at any time while on board of the said vessel, received any wages or money in return for their services, nor have they been treated by the said Captain as part of the crew thereof. And they do further say, and each for himself saith, that he went on board of the said vessel in Brazil, against his own will and inclination, and because he was forced to do so, and that they have only remained in the said vessel for the reason that they were unable to escape therefrom.

And these deponents further shew, that while the writ of habeas corpus issued by the said Judge Daly was pending, and undecided, to wit on the fifteenth day of July, instant, these deponents, by an instrument duly executed and acknowledged under their hands and seals, for such purpose appointed John Jay, Esquire, of the city of New-York, their sole, true, and lawful attorney for them, and in their name, place, and stead, to maintain before the Court of Common Pleas, and before any and all other Courts, in which their right to liberty should or might be called in question, their right to be discharged from the custody of the said Captain Da Costa, of the Brazilian barque Lem-branca, now lying at the port of New-York, and from all other custody and restraint whatsoever.

And these deponents shew, that as they are informed and believe, immediately thereafter, and before the decision of the said Judge Daly was pronounced in the said matter, the said John Jay appeared before the said Judge Daly, at his Chambers, and asked leave as such attorney, to be heard on behalf of the deponents in answer to the return of the Captain to the said write of habeas corpus, stating in support of such application, that he was the attorney of record, by whom the said writ had been issued, and that he had been detained by illness in the country—that the counsel who had appeared for these deponents during his absence, had so appeared from friendly motives, in consequence of the refusal of said Judge to adjourn the hearing of the said case until the recovery of said Jay, but without any authority from these deponents, and that one of the said counsel had endorsed on the return of the said Captain, an admission of certain facts which these deponents did not admit, which admission was calculated great-ly to prejudice their rights, that these deponents were entitled to a fair hearing, by counsel of their own appointment, and upon proper proofs, and that it would be a denial of justice, and a gross violation of the rights of these deponents, to refuse leave of their said attorney to be heard on their behalf.

That the said Judge Daly thereupon reserved his decision upon the said motion until the next morning, (to wit: Saturday, the 17th July, instant,) and on the said Saturday, as soon as the said Judge took his seat in the Chambers of the Common Pleas, and was ready to proceed with the said cause, the said John Jay asked the said judge if he had decided to grant the said motion, to which the said Judge replied that he denied the motion—whereupon, the said Jay, as the attorney of record by whom the said writ of habeas corpus was issued, and as attorney also for these deponents, dismissed the said writ, and all proceedings thereupon, so that there was no proceeding pending before the said Judge, nor any conflicting claims to require or justify a decision from him upon the questions involved in the return to the said writ, and affecting the life and liberty of these deponents—but that notwithstanding the said dismissal of the writ, the said Judge insisted on rendering the opinion set forth in the record attached to said return, and made an order remanding these deponents to the custody of the said Captain against which their said attorney solemnly protested as a violation of right and justice towards these deponents.

And these deponents do not admit that the said proceeding before Judge Daly is a bar to any further proceedings on this second writ of habeas corpus, or that the matter should be adjudged as *res adjudicata,* and the second writ of habeas corpus dismissed—but they do respectfully insist that under the facts herein set forth, the relator in the said first matter being to them a stranger, and the counsel herein being by them unauthorized, and these deponents not being privy to the proceedings thereto and not being allowed a hearing by their counsel, the said matter was *res inter alios acta*[16], and in no way binding upon these deponents—and further that the said decision was irregular, and inoperative to decide the question involved therein after the formal dismissal of the writ of habeas corpus.

And these deponents further say that they deny the allegation in the said return of the said Captain Da Costa, that no new state of facts has arisen subsequent to the aforesaid decision and adjudication of the Honourable Judge Daly in relation to these deponents and the said Captain Da Costa, but that on the contrary thereof there is at present time a continuance of the same fact upon which the decision and adjudication aforesaid were founded.

And in further denial of the said allegation, these deponents say,

16. That is, "matter transacted between other persons."

that on Saturday last, the 17th July, instant after the rendering of the said order as aforesaid, by the said Judge Daly, these deponents were taken on board of said barque Lembranca, by two police officers of this city, who were employed as these deponents are informed, and believe, by the Captain or Consul-General of Brazil[17] for the said purpose, and that after they had been taken on board, a person on board of said vessel, whom these deponents are informed, and believe, was the Consul-General of Brazil, advised the said Captain to put these deponents in irons—that the said Captain thereupon ordered the steward of the said barque to bring the irons, which he did, and the said Consul-General then directed the said two police officers to put the irons on these deponents, and the said police officers, in obedience to the said order, put handcuffs on these deponents, chaining the right hand of one of the these deponents to the left hand of the other, and these deponents were then forced into a store room in the forward part of the said vessel, and there confined: And these deponents further say that after they had been so ironed and confined, and after the said police officers had removed from the said store-room, the said Captain came up to these deponents, and said to them, that he would let them alone while they were in the port of New-York, but that when he once got them to sea he would beat them until they would only be fit to be thrown over-board—that this deponent, Da Costa, would never see Rio again, and that although he, the said Captain, did not own this deponent, Da Rocha, said deponent would not fare any better.

And these deponents say that from the violence hitherto displayed towards them by the said Captain, as well at the sea, as since they have been in this port, and from his recent threats, they have good reason to believe, and do believe, that their personal safety and their lives would be in danger if they should ever again come into his power.

And these deponents further say, that the writ of habeas corpus

17. The Brazilian Consul-General in New York (Luiz Henrique Ferreira d'Aguiar) supported Captain Costa in his case, as noted in the *Biography*, p. 56.

returnable before the Honourable Judge Edmonds, was sued out by their said attorney, John Jay, by virtue of the authority given to him by them, and in accordance with their wishes, and that the said proceeding is the first and only proceeding instituted by these deponents to secure their freedom.

And these deponents do severally admit the allegations contained in the return of the said Captain to the first writ of habeas corpus, and which is made part of his return to the second writ, to wit: that the authority and true cause of the restraint in which these deponents have been held by the said Captain is, that these deponents were slaves in Brazil, within the dominions and jurisdiction of His Majesty, the Emperor of Brazil. And these deponents insisting that being brought on board of the said barque within the jurisdiction of the State of New-York, they have become free, and entitled to all the rights and privileges of freemen, do further say that they believe and know that it is the intention of the said Captain, unless prevented by the judicial authority of the State, to kidnap these deponents under the pretence that they are part of his crew, and reduce them again to Slavery. And these deponents further say that they are confirmed in the said belief by the conduct of said Captain towards these deponents since their arrival in this port, to wit: during the present month of July—for these deponents say that after their said arrival, and while the said vessel was lying at the wharf in this city, this deponent, Jose Da Costa, in the presence of this deponent Jose Da Rocha, asked the said Captain to allow him to go on shore, and that thereupon, and without other or further provocation of any kind whatsoever, the said Captain took up a stick of wood and struck this deponent Da Costa in the stomach, so that the said deponent fell upon the deck, and after the said deponent had also fallen and was lying upon the said deck, the Captain continued to strike and bruise the said deponent with the said stick, on the face and neck, and other parts of his body, so that the said deponent was badly bruised by said beating. And these deponents further say that the said Captain did, thereupon, strike this deponent Da Rocha several times, with a rope's end, and did then

confine these deponents together, in a store-room on board the said
barque, for four days, and during three days of the said time, gave to
these deponents no food to eat, and threatened to punish these deponents if they attempted to leave the said vessel.[18] And these deponents
further say, that they believe that the said Captain intended to conceal
the fact of these deponents being on board said vessel, from the public and judicial authorities of this city, in order that he might kidnap
the deponents more readily.

In the presence of us,

his
JOSE DA X COSTA
mark

his
JOSE DA X ROCHA
mark

Before me, at the Eldridge street prison, in the city of New-York,
on the 21st day of July, 1847, came the above named Jose Da Costa
and Jose Da Rocha, to me known personally, and also William
Ringold, residing at No. 3, Catherine Lane, in the said city, to me also
personally known, and the said Ringold having been duly sworn
faithfully to interpret the aforesaid affidavit to the said Da Rocha, and
Da Costa, did interpret the same to them in my presence, and the said
Da Rocha and Da Costa having been by me duly examined through
the said interpreter, previously sworn for such purposes, touching the
obligations of an oath, and having satisfied me by their replies to my
questions, that they had some knowledge of the Catholic religion,[19]
and sufficiently understood such obligations, did severally swear that
the said affidavit had been prepared in accordance with information

---

18. Cf. *Biography*, p. 54 (though this mentions only Baquaqua himself as being confined).
19. Cf. *Biography*, p. 45, for Baquaqua's experience of Christian instruction in Pernambuco.

previously given by them to John Jay, Esq. their Attorney, and that the facts stated therein, as of their own knowledge, were true, and that as to such matters as were stated therein on their information and belief, that they believe them to be true.

WM. H. BUNN,
Com. of Deeds

APPENDIX 2

Letters of the Rev. Mr. & Mrs. Judd
concerning Baquaqua, Haiti, 1847–48

1.
Mrs. N.A.L. Judd to Cyrus P. Grosvenor,
Port au Prince, Haiti, 8 October 1847[1]

... [I will] give you a brief account of a fugitive slave that has come to us for protection, within a few days; and as you know the direction in God's word is—"he shall dwell with thee, where it liketh him best," (Deut. 23:16) we have not felt at liberty to turn him away.

He was formerly from a tribe in the interior of Africa; was taken captive when a child, while playing at some distance from his mother's door;[2] and, after travelling several weeks, arrived at the coast, where he was put on board a vessel with a great many others of all ages and classes, and after the usual amount of suffering occasioned by a sea voyage across the ocean, in a crowded slave ship, he was landed on the coast of South America, where he was sold, and after changing hands several times, he was purchased, together with another of his countrymen,[3] by a Brazilian sea captain, and arrived finally in New York. I presume you are much better acquainted with the circumstances of a Brazilian captain being arrested for flogging his

---

1. Printed in the *Christian Contributor and Free Missionary* (of which Grosvenor was editor) 19 January 1848, under the title, "Letter from Sister Judd."

2. Cf. no. 2 below. This is contradicted by the account of Baquaqua's enslavement in the later *Biography*, pp. 34-35; for discussion, see Introduction.

3. No such statement is made in the *Biography*; probably a confusion on Mrs. Judd's part, unless by "one of his countrymen" is meant simply someone also born in Africa. The reference may be to Baquaqua's fellow slave José da Rocha (known to the mission in Haiti as "David"), who was from Africa but not from the same place as Baquaqua (as the Rev. Mr. Judd notes in no. 2 below); although he was not in fact owned in Rio de Janeiro by the same person as Baquaqua (cf. Appendix 1, no. 1).

slaves at New York,[4] and of the final escape of both of them to Boston, and from there to Port au Prince, than we are. There has been evidently in the recent train of events, so clearly the hand of Providence which has led him to us, that we feel strongly inclined to keep him in our family, at present. We trust the Lord that has led him here, will also provide for his temporal wants and grant him the salvation of his soul. The gentleman (Mr. Jones) who accompanied him here, and introduced him to us, says he is, as near as we can ascertain, about sixteen years of age.[5] He can speak neither English or French, except a very few sentences in broken English, which he learned on his passage out here. He conversed with him considerably on his way out in regard to his ideas of God, of the soul, of heaven, &c, and also concerning the customs, productions, &c, of his own country. As Mr. J. could speak but little Portuguese (the only language he understood except his native tongue), he could not, of course, learn so much as he could have done, had he been able to have conversed with him more freely. He succeeded, however, in obtaining the following particulars.

His father and mother were of different tribes,[6] and of quite different characters; the former inclined to intemperance and gambling, by which he spent the most of his own, and also his wife's estate.[7] His mother was inclined to religion, and was quite strict in her observance of her prayers and the ceremonies of her belief,[8] which we judge to have been principally Mahommedanism, from his name, which is

4. Not quite accurate. Baquaqua's owner Captain Costa was not arrested, but served with a writ of *habeas corpus* requiring him to surrender his slaves, although allegations that he had flogged them were made during the course of the subsequent hearings: see Appendix 1, no. 3.

5. Cf. no. 2 below; but in no. 4, written nine months later, his age is estimated as 18. Contradicted by the statement in the *Biography*, p. 9, that Baquaqua was aged about 30 in 1854, which would have made him about 23 in 1847; for discussion, see Introduction.

6. Cf. *Biography*, p. 9.

7. The *Biography*, p. 21, also says that his father was once wealthy, but "by some means he lost the greater part of his property." But the allegation of "intemperance and gambling" seems incompatible with the *Biography*'s emphasis on his father's Islamic piety and "grave and silent" character (pp. 9–10).

8. Contradicted by the *Biography*, p. 26, which says that his mother, although a Muslim, "did not care much about the worshipping part of the matter."

Mahomah, or Mahomed. His name for God is Allah, which, you know, is the Arabic name for the Supreme Being. A book he calls Alcoran, &c. His memory appears to be remarkably good, as he distinctly remembers his mother's teaching him to pray, and he can still repeat those prayers in his native tongue.[9] He seems not only to remember his native language, but also the productions and manner of cultivating them. He also remembers some of the laws of his country, one of which was, that a person convicted of stealing, had his right arm cut off.[10] ... In endeavoring to ascertain his ideas of the soul, and of a future state, Mr. Jones asked him what became of a person after death? when he told him that the earth consumed the body—as he expressed it—"eat up the flesh and bones." Mr. J. then asked him if that was the end of him? He then endeavored to make him understand that there was a principle that still existed. He tried in various ways to express it. At length he stood up, and as the moon shone brightly, he waved his body several times in the light, and directed his attention to the shadow, and pointing upward, told him *that* was the part that went to Allah.[11] But I have not time to mention half the interesting circumstances of this poor youth:—One or two things more, and I must close.—

While coming up here, they crossed the parade ground, which is a large, level plain, nearly a mile square, and is of a fine rich soil. Said he, look here, Mr. Jones, what a beautiful country, all lying waste; and then, directing his attention to the soldiers, he expressed a strong detestation of war and soldiers, saying, if it was not for war, all these men might be employed in cultivating the land, raising bananas, &c. He also expressed his opinion concerning the effects of war on the morals of a country. Said he—"these men have little to do at present. They very soon spend what little money they have—then they take to

9. The prayers would have been in Arabic, rather than in Baquaqua's "native tongue," i.e., Dendi; but the Judds wrongly assumed that Arabic was his native language (as explicitly stated in no. 2 below).

10. Contrast the *Biography*, p. 11–12, which states that thieves were executed.

11. Cf. *Biography*, p. 57.

stealing, and then what are they? They are gone." He is also, strongly opposed to intemperance. When Mr. J. explained to him the object
of our Temperance Pledge, he expressed himself very ready to have
his name attached to it.[12] ... He expresses a very strong desire to
obtain an education—says he had a brother older than himself in
Africa, who could both read and write.[13] He very eagerly embraces
every opportunity to read; and among us all, he manages to get several lessons into [a] day, generally. We have strong hopes that the
Lord will bless him, and yet make him a blessing to his countrymen.

But I must hasten to close this imperfect scrawl, as it is time that
this is sent off, in order to meet the vessel before she sails, so that I
have a moment's time for corrections, but I leave it to you to do what
you please with it....

2.
Rev. W. L. Judd to C. P. Grosvenor,
Port au Prince, Haiti, 28 October, 1847[14]

... PS. I notice by the papers from New York that the case of the
two Brazilian slaves has made some excitement in that ancient city of
sober Dutchmen. I suppose that both their friends and enemies would
like to know their whereabouts. For the satisfaction of all and especially for Capt. Climente,[15] you are at liberty to say that they are both
safe in Port au Prince. One of them is now living in the family of your
missionary. He is the younger of the two, and I think by far the most

---

12. Contrast the admission in the *Biography*, p. 58, that, after entering the Judd household,
until his conversion, he "would often get very drunk."

13. Cf. no. 2; and *Biography*, p. 27.

14. Printed in *Christian Contributor and Free Missionary*, December 22, 1847, under the
title, "Letter from Br. Judd."

15. Clemente José da Costa, Baquaqua's owner in slavery in Brazil, from whom he escaped
in New York.

intelligent. He is, as we suppose, about 16 years of age.[16] It appears that the two Africans are not from the same tribe[17]—The one who is with us is so far advanced in English that I have been able to learn from him precisely his former residence in Africa. He is from the city of Kashina, of the tribe Houssa,[18] in the northern or central part of Soudan. He is acquainted with all the cities between there and the coast, in a southerly direction. His native language is theArabic,[19] which he yet remembers and can even write with considerable facility. I suppose his intercourse with other slaves from the same country,[20] has done much to retain it in his memory, which appears also to be remarkably strong. He remembers well the Yaoors, the next nation west of the Houssas.[21] He says he is acquainted with the city of Kano,[22] and appears to be familiar with the term Soudan, the general name of the country,[23] including some five or six states in the very centre of Africa. He says that in all these States the Arabic language is spoken and cultivated in books. I should think that probably his family is one of considerable importance in the Houssa nation. From his account they must have been rich. His father died before he left.[24] He says his oldest brother was well educated, could read and write the Arabic with fluency.[25] He says they put him to his books very close-

16. Cf. n. 5 above.

17. Perhaps correcting the earlier statement of Mrs. Judd, in no. 1 above; cf. n. 3 above.

18. I.e., Katsina, in Hausaland. Contrast the *Biography*, p. 9, which states that Baquaqua himself was born in Djougou, although his mother was from Katsina. For discussion of this contradiction, see Introduction.

19. Contrast the *Biography*, in which the numerals (pp. 3–4) and most of the vocabulary in the text are in Dendi, the language of the Muslim community in Djougou, which was by implication his native language; his knowledge of Arabic was evidently derived from attending an Islamic school (pp. 26–27).

20. I.e., evidently, while he was a slave in Brazil.

21. I.e., Yauri, on the River Niger.

22. The *Biography* refers to no visit by Baquaqua to Yauri or Kano, implying that he can only have known of these places by hearsay.

23. Sudan in Arabic means "[land of] the blacks," and designated sub-Saharan Africa generally; although it was also sometimes used in a more restricted sense, to mean the countries immediately south of the Sahara, including Hausaland: see Robin Law, "Central and eastern Wangara."

24. Not explicitly confirmed in the *Biography*, but consistent with statements there (pp. 35, 39, 59) which refer to missing his mother, but do not mention his father.

25. Cf. *Biography*, p. 10.

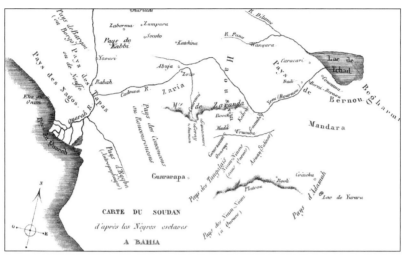

PLATE 24. Sudan map: 'He says he is acquainted with the city of Kano, and appears to be familiar with the term Soudan, the general name of the country, including some five or six states in the very center of Africa' (Letter of Rev. W.L. Judd, 28 October 1847; Appendix 2); contemporary map based on information gathered in c. 1849 from Muslims in Brazil; see 'Carte du Soudan d'après les Négres esclaves a Bahia' [c. 1843], Francis de Castelnau, Renseignements sur l'Afrique Centrale et sur une nation d'hommes a queue qui s'y trouverait, d'après le rapport des Négres du Soudan, esclaves a Bahia (Paris, 1851).

ly, but loving play, he used to leave home clandestinely,[26] and it was in one such affray as this that he was taken by some of the tribes nearer the coast,[27] and sold [to] the Portuguese of South America.

His African name is Mahommah (the first and last sounded like a in man, and the o like a in what). I presume it is the same name which we call Mahomet. All the Arabic words I can pronounce he at once recognizes, and all the Arabic characters that I have been able to show him from my books, he at once reads and explains as well as he can in broken English, their meaning. So that I am entirely satisfied that he knows the Arabic language. If any friend could send me some Arabic books, it would be of great importance, especially the Bible in Arabic. For I have the most sanguine hopes that the Lord will convert

26. Cf. *Biography*, p. 26.
27. Cf. n. 2 above.

his soul before long, and that he will yet become a missionary to his native land. The circumstances of his escape and final arrival in Port-au-Prince, and his entrance into my family, are so clearly providential that I can not doubt but God has some very glorious object to accomplish through him in this connection. To narrate these would require a long letter, and I have no doubt would be very interesting to others as well as to us. But in writing what I have, I have been obliged to trespass upon the time which seemed almost absolutely demanded for other purposes, and have only done so because duty appeared to call loudest in this direction.

But where is the man, to accompany this young lad to his native land, to bear the gospel of Jesus Christ among the millions of that vast country? Who has faith enough to undertake with the false prophet? I have no doubt but some one will be needed, and whoever goes ought to be a man of extraordinary knowledge of the world and able to endure hardships. I think however, that if a person could reach the spot, he would probably find a healthy place, as the city of Kashina is very probably upon the head waters of the Niger.

I hope that while Mahommah is undergoing the necessary preparation, our friends in the States will be upon the qui vive[28] for a man properly qualified to accompany him. A study of the Hebrew and Arabic, would undoubtedly be an essential qualification,[29] while Mahommah could give him the vernacular style.

He says that the people of Dahomey and Ashantee do not speak the Arabic.[30] But I must close as I have spent too long a time already upon this; and other duties are pressing.

Pray for us all, and especially for the early conversion of Mahommah.

28. I.e., on the alert.
29. It is not clear why Judd thought that Hebrew, as well as Arabic, would be required for work in Hausaland.
30. In contrast to Djougou and Hausaland, the Muslim communities in Asante and Dahomey were small, and consisted entirely of foreigners from further north: see, for Asante, Levtzion, *Muslims and Chiefs in West Africa*, 181–87; and for Dahomey, Robin Law, "Islam in Dahomey: the introduction and influence of Islam in a peripheral area of West Africa," *Scottish Journal of Religious Studies*, 7/2 (1986): 95–122.

Appendix to above letter, dated November 5

... I will add that I have received a visit from Br Webley of Jacmel,[31] who spent last Sabbath with us....

By the way, Br. Webley has taken a lively interest in our African boy Mahommah. He says he will try to get an Arabic Bible for him, and thinks that if the A.B.F.M. Society should not be able to establish a mission in Soudan in connection with this young man, that the English Baptists will undertake it.[32] Mahommah is advancing in English. He has explained to us a good many particulars of his escape from prison, etc. He wishes to express thanks to those kind friends in New York and Boston, who so kindly assisted him.

3.
Mrs. [Nancy]³³ A. L. Judd to C. P. Grosvenor,
Delavan Temperance Hall, Port-au-Prince, 24 March 1848³⁴

... I must now speak of the *good news*, that I promised, though I fear you may be disappointed, as it is only the conversion of one more precious soul (though we hope of others) but that one, is our dear Mahomah. Yes, dear brother, we think we have undoubted proofs, that he has "passed from death unto life." I scarcely ever witnessed a conversion where better evidence was given, or one that so rejoiced my heart.—He has succeeded in entwining himself strongly in the affections of us all, and I do think we feel most grateful to God for so soon granting us the desire of our hearts in his conversion. I scarcely think

---

31. The name is misprinted as "Pebley" here, but given correctly as "Webley" later in the letter; i.e., W.H. Webley, a missionary of the English Baptist Missionary Society, based at Jacmel on the south coast of Haiti.

32. The English Baptists already had a mission in West Africa, at Douala in Cameroun.

33. Name misprinted in the original as "Mary."

34. Printed in *Christian Contributor and Free Missionary*, 17 May, 1848, under the title, "Letter from Mrs. Judd."

I could rejoice more in the conversion of our only child. Oh! That I might know whether I should or not. Will not you and our dear brethren at home, pray earnestly that our son (who is nearly nine years old,) may soon be converted? I should then have no object between me, and perishing [in] Haiti, to labor and pray for, as he and Mahomah have been on my mind so much that other objects were almost crowded out. But you wish to know some circumstances of this conversion. How I wish I could give it to you, and your readers, as we have received it. But that is impossible.

About the time of receiving your very welcome letter (which I design to speak of presently) we received one from Mr. Elias Smith, (the gentleman who aided in the escape of the Brazilian slaves from prison) informing us of the arrival of sister Young in New York,[35] and of his visiting her to make particular inquiries concerning them. He expressed a very warm interest for them, and especially for Mahommah, that God would give him a "good heart". He had learned the expression from sister T.[36] we presume, as that was the term we made use of, to convey to his mind the idea of the new birth. Mr J.[37] explained to him the contents of the letter, as well as he could, and particularly that Mr. S. prayed for Mahomah, that he might have a "good heart." This seemed to affect him considerably, and he appeared to study upon it much. The next day, or within two or three days, we received your letter, together with a number of others from our friends, in which he was remembered, and Mr. J. again explained to him that Mr. Grosvenor prayed for him, that he might have a "good heart." I wish you could have seen the grateful expression of his countenance. Though one of the most grateful creatures I ever saw, for every little favour, yet there is nothing that he appears so very grate-

35. Sister Young was a member of the Baptist Free Mission in Haiti, whose role in Baqua-qua's conversion is mentioned later in this letter. She had returned to the U.S.A. because of ill-ness, and died soon after: see ABFMS, Sixth Annual Meeting, Charlestown, Massachusetts, 2 May 1849.

36. Sic: presumably misprinted for "Y.", i.e., Young.

37. Presumably = her husband William Judd, rather than (as in no. 1 above) Mr. Jones.

ful for as prayer, and the next is, for instruction in learning to read. Perhaps I may mention, that a few days before, having felt unusually anxious for him and my little son that morning, as I went into the kitchen, where he was at work, he observed that I had been weeping. He anxiously inquired the cause. I told him I felt bad for him—feared he had got a bad heart, and did not love God—that I wanted he should have a "good heart", and love God & all men, &c. I did not say a great deal to him, but he seemed to reflect upon it, and feel disturbed in his mind, and not long after he went to my sister[38] to inquire what Madam meant. She tried to explain to him that it was not anything in partic- ular that he had done to me, (as he rarely needs a chiding word;)[39] but that he needed a good heart. And now to hear about one and another, praying for him in New York, and hearing the same thing often, from all of us in family worship, as we frequently called his name, as he understands English yet so imperfectly, we endeavored to adapt the language to his understanding. All these things have been pondered over in his mind, when about three weeks since, he was thoroughly aroused to a sense of his dangerous condition, and began to cry in earnest for salvation. About this time, there was one young brother (by the name of Preisar) staying with us for a few days to help us, and he frequently conversed with M. and manifested much anxiety for him. One day, as our little son was singing "The Old Church Yard," "O sinner you will tremble," &c., our young brother seized upon the circumstance, to introduce the subject of future punishment, and of the dreadful state of those who died in their sins. This we had as yet not attempted to do, as we considered his mind not sufficiently enlightened for this especially as his knowledge of the English lan- guage was so limited, we feared we might convey some erroneous impression. But this simple hearted brother, it seemed, was not afraid

38. Electa Lake, who ran a school for the Mission in Port-au-Prince.
39. Contrast the admission in the *Biography*, p. 58, that, prior to his conversion, he was sometimes "abusive" to and would "fight" with Mrs. Judd. But this may refer to Baquaqua's subsequent behavior, in the time between his original conversion and his acceptance for bap- tism, as described by the Rev. Mr. Judd in a later letter (no. 4).

to preach terror even, in the best manner he could, and as M. had already begun to feel himself a sinner, and having so often heard of the goodness of God, and now to hear about his great hatred of sin, and the awful punishment awaiting the guilty, he began to feel the deepest concern. As he sat at the supper that evening I soon observed that something was the matter, as he said but little, and had none of his pleasantry, and humor with which he often interested and amused us. In the course of the evening Mr. Judd who had been to town that day returned, and I overheard them conversing together, when some thing he said interested me to go down and speak with him myself. (Being very busy I had not sought an opportunity immediately after supper.) I accordingly went out to the kitchen, where he and this brother were, and seating myself by him I tenderly inquired why he appeared so sad? If anything had been said to grieve him? (He is extremely sensitive.) He shook his head mournfully, and said—"O madam—Mahommah wants a good heart." O brother Grosvernor,— I can not describe to you the feelings these words gave me. It is only the words that I can imperfectly give you, but the manner can not be described. After conversing a few minutes with him, I asked him if he wished us to pray for him? When he replied, "O yes—thank you." We all three knelt down and our brother prayed first—then I tried to pray for him and express his desires as well as I could: when I requested *him* to pray, which he did in language something like the following:

"O Lord, give me a new heart. O Lord, clean my heart. O make me love God. O Lord, give me a good heart, Amen." In short, it seemed to amount to about the same as the Publican's prayer, "God be merciful to me a sinner," and both responded a hearty "Amen."—I now bid them good night and retired, leaving them together. The next day he appeared much distressed, and for several days he was so anxious that he ate and slept but little, and could hardly work enough to get our ordinary meals (he is our cook) so that our brother assisted him some. As you may judge, we all felt the most intense anxiety. As he seemed to express his feelings the most freely to Brother P., we inquired frequently about him. He expressed to P. that he thought his

(P.) sins had been small in comparison of his own. He says, "God very good for Mahomah (meaning him) Mahomah sin so much, O too much," (his expression often for very much) referring to his sins in Africa as well as since. After a few days I observed a change in his countenance, and his whole appearance; when I ventured to ask him, if he loved God? He replied with an animated smile, "O yes, me love God much—me love Jesus Christ—O, much, too much." I then inquired about his feelings towards men, when he replied, "O yes, me love all all." In order to satisfy myself fully, I put the test question— and do you love Captain De Cost?[40]—when with a face beaming with heavenly love, he said, "O yes, me love Captain De Cost me pray for Captain De Cost, for God give him a good heart."[41] As my heart was about full, I asked no more questions, but left him to pursue his work—while I hastened to my chamber, with a heart palpitating with hope and joy. My sister, also, soon began to make inquiries about his loving God, though we both carefully avoided hinting to him that we began to hope he was a Christian, as we thought he might find *that* himself, or that the Lord might reveal it to him in his own time and way. She had a few evenings previous told him that, when God gave him a new heart, he would feel that he loved him in his heart. In conversing with her, he expressed a strong desire to love God more—he felt he loved him "too much" (very much: this expression we have since corrected) but he wanted to love him all all, (meaning as we suppose, loving him according to the first commandment.) Not long after, brother P. came, who had been away the night before. My sister inquired of him, if he had seen M. when he said, he just saw him. "Ah, then you have heard the good news." "No, I only just spoke with him as I came along.["] She then told him that we began to hope M. was converted. He could eat no more then (having sat down to the table a few minutes before) but hastened out to learn for himself. A short time after, he returned with great satisfaction and told us some

40. Cf. n.1 5 above.
41. Cf. *Biography*, p. 43.

things he said. He told us M. wanted to know certain that he had a good heart and loved God all: then he wanted to be *baptized*. (I don't know but he is some related to the Eunuch, as there had not been a word said on this subject) and then he wanted to die the same day. (But we hope he won't though, don't you?) On Friday morning he inquired if it was not the day for the meeting (our evening prayer meeting). When we told him it was, he seemed impatient for the hour to arrive; he wanted to go and meet the Christians and talk to them. Accordingly, in the evening he got up and spoke, expressing a desire to love God and Jesus Christ, and to sin no more (which he often expressed) and to go to Heaven when he died, &c. On the Sabbath he attended meeting—appeared rather sad; and, after our return home, my sister inquired the cause. But he declined telling her, saying— "by-and-by, Miss Lake". The next morning he told her he had been thinking about *Africa*; and how bad the people were there. (This he would never admit until lately.[)] "Now I see the people *very* bad in Africa." It seems his mind had been so troubled about it the night before, that he sat up a long time and reflected upon it, and when he finally fell asleep, he *dreamed* of being there, and with an old play-mate, the 'President's son' as he calls him, with whom it seems he was quite intimate,[42] and who, he says, was very wicked. (By the way, we are convinced from many circumstances and instances, which he has related from time to time, that their [sic] parents, particularly his mother, were related or some way connected with the prince, or chief of the country where he lived.)[43] For the first time since he has lived with us, he expressed a desire to go back to Africa, to tell them about Jesus Christ. O how many, many deeply interesting circumstances, I have gathered already of his former history, if I had time to write and you room to publish, whichI feel could not fail to be read with the

---

42. Presumably this was a son of the local ruler in whose service Baquaqua was employed immediately prior to his enslavement, according to the *Biography*, pp. 31–34. His use of the term "President" evidently reflects the republican constitution currently in force in Haïti (although in 1849, the Haitian President Faustin Soulouque proclaimed himself "Emperor").

43. Cf. *Biography*, p. 31.

deepest interest. But I must hasten to close this already too long letter soon, or I shall not get it on board the last vessel bound for New
York for near a fortnight. It is now about three weeks since we first
began to hope for him, and every day seems to develope [sic] some
new Christian grace in his character and conduct.—He manifests
great care and anxiety for his comrade who was companion in prison
and slavery,[44] both for his temporal wants, and for his salvation. He is
probably several years younger (I should think at least six) than
David, but he cares for him as if he were so much older.—The truth
appears to be that David's spirits were broken and subdued by slavery, while Mahomah's never were. It seems, by what he has informed
us lately, that he was several years a slave in Africa,[45] but though he
so affectingly spoke of his dreadful feelings on being separated from
his friends, especially his mother whom he often speaks of with great
affection,[46] and whom he was often flattered he should see again,
being told that she would send the money to redeem him:[47]—but, said
he, "my mother not know where Mahomah was, and I see her no
more:" yet his sufferings and degradation were comparatively nothing, to what they were after he was taken to the coast and sold the
white man.[48] His description a few evenings since, of the scene when
he was taken on board the ship exceeded any thing I ever listened to.
His broken English and expressive gesticulation, only serving to
heighten and interest, to the most painful intensity. Though you and
your readers have all read such accounts until any thing of the kind
appears stale, (if that is the expression) yet I trust I shall be pardoned

44. Named in the next sentence as David; but referred to in accounts of the judicial proceedings in New York in 1847 by the Portuguese name, José da Rocha.

45. Cf. no. 4 below. Contradicted by Mrs. Judd's earlier letter of 8 October 1847 (above),
as well as by the later *Biography*, pp. 35–42, which state that he was taken to the coast directly after his enslavement; for discussion of this contradiction, see Introduction.

46. Cf. n. 24 above.

47. The *Biography*, pp. 35, 39, refers to his hopes of regaining freedom during his journey
south to the coast, but the wording there implies that he hoped to escape, rather than to be redeemed.

48. Cf. *Biography*, p. 25 (though there presented as a general observation, rather than with
reference to Baquaqua's own experiences).

for relating one or two circumstances, though it is utterly impossible to give the vividness of an eye witness to the scene.

After detailing briefly the manner of chaining and getting them on board, and of the heart-rending cries of distress from old and young, and of his hearts "dying" as he expressed it, (but how impossible to give his expression of it) he spoke in particular of one man, who it seemed was madened to perfect desperation, who broke loose in some way, like the "Demoniac of Gadara," and seizing a large knife, or dirk rushed upon his tormentors with perfect fury, with the design, probably, of selling his life as dearly as possible, and I think he said it took six strong athletic men to disarm, and bind him. This they finally did, when they stript him of his clothes sufficiently to expose his back—they then took a knife and cut the flesh into deep gashes and then filled them with Cayene pepper. In this dreadful condition he lingered two days, and though he was still alive, they finally took him up and threw him into the sea....[49]

But to go on with Mahomah. He had firmly resolved to *never* return to Brazil, and he awaited the decision of his fate there in New York with such feelings as but few among white, or perhaps even colored persons ever realized.—When David expressed apprehensions that they were to be killed and eaten, he replied, "well—then we shall not have to go back to Brazil."—From my knowledge of his firmness and decision, when his mind is made up to any thing, I have no kind of an idea, that he ever would have returned to Brazil, and I very much doubt whether Capt. Decosta would, if he had attempted to carry him back, unless he had kept him firmly and constantly bound. But O with what horror does he look upon his wicked designs, upon his own and his master's life now.[50] And his deep, deep gratitude to God for his not suffering him to commit the awful deed seems to

49. Cf. *Biography*, p. 43.
50. The *Biography*, pp. 46, 53, refers to two occasions when Baquaqua contemplated killing his master and then himself, once (which seems to be the occasion referred to here) during the voyage to New York with Captain Costa, and once earlier in Pernambuco (when he was owned by a different person).

know no bounds for this, as well as his so often sparing him, when there was "but a step between him and death." Five times he speaks of, as being rescued from the jaws of death.[51] I will mention one as a specimen. While a slave in Rio Janeiro (if I have not forgotten) his master came in one day in a rage about something and was going to reek [sic: = wreak] his vengeance upon his poor slave (which happens to be a common thing, I believe, especially among civilized white people) when his sudden terror was such, that he ran and leaped into the sea. He was immediately carried out by a wave, and sank twice, when a man who it seems saw him, came and rescued him just as he was sinking the third time, and he was taken to the shore very nearly senseless.[52] When speaking of some of these narrow escapes, he says, with his peculiarly expressive manner, "Ah! God very good for Mahomah—not let him die." Indeed gratitude seems to be a prominent characteristic of his moral feelings. Never does he receive a favor from any one without thanking them for it, in a manner that makes you feel it. A few evenings since he was speaking of his first coming to live with us—"I come to Mr. Judd's with Mr. Jones—I not know any thing—Miss Young tell me," (as sr. Young was detained at home from feeble health most of the time she had more opportunities then for hearing and instructing him than the rest of us, and we often heard interesting things of him, in return for our news about the good meetings,) "Mr. Judd tell me" &c., naming all. "I learn little, little," (and you would often be amused at our various expedients to learn

51. The *Biography* mentions clearly only three occasions on which Baquaqua narrowly escaped death, his attempted suicide in Pernambuco (which Mrs. Judd goes on to mention here) and twice at sea, first on the voyage from Rio Grande do Sul to Rio de Janeiro (p. 49) and the second on the voyage from Rio to New York (p. 52) when the ship was in danger of foundering. However, he may also have had in mind two experiences in West Africa: in Daboya, where he was caught up in a local war and captures (p. 30); and at "Efau" on his passage to the coast after enslavement, when he feared that he might be sacrificed in a religious ceremony (p. 38). He may also have counted the time in Rio de Janeiro when he fell into the water while boarding ship after a drunken spree, but he himself says the water was shallow, so he was in no danger (pp. 50–51).
52. Cf. *Biography*, p. 46, but this places this incident not during his period of residence in Rio de Janeiro, but in Pernambuco earlier.

him "little little,"[)] "by and by I understand" and summing it all up
he says, "O very good—God pay you all." Of Mr. Smith he said, as
reference was made to the expense he had been at to save them—"by
and by I go work—get the money—go pay him," and then added,
"but God pay Misser Smith." But for fear you will become wearied
out with my endless details—I will now close....

4.

*Rev. W. L. Judd to C. P. Grosvenor, Maison de Campagne,
Commune du Port-au-Prince, 21 July 1848*[53]

...since the 16th of April, we have not been able to accomplish
much. We, however, commenced again as soon as practicable, and
have maintained public worship regularly ever since, both in French
and English.—The congregations have, however, been small, but are
somewhat increasing at this time. There has appeared to be a greater
religious interest for two or three weeks past than for some time
before.—This, I hope has been increased by the baptism of Mahommah last Sunday morning.[54] This young exile from Africa is a noble
specimen of his race. We judge him to be about eighteen years of
age,[55] from the city of KACHNA, (or he pronounces it *Kasheenah*) in
Soudan.[56] Says, he was a slave for some time on the coast of Africa;[57]
afterwards nearly two years in Brazil:[58] has many a time well nigh lost
his life; but out of all the Lord has delivered him; and, we trust, he is

53. Printed in the *Christian Contributor and Free Missionary*, 23 August 1848, under the
title "Letter from Br. Judd:—Baptism of Mahommah." The second paragraph of the extract
included here was reproduced in Foss and Mathews, *Facts for Baptist Churches*, 393; and from
there also in the *Biography*, pp. 59–60.
  54. I.e., 16 July.
  55. Cf. n. 5 above.
  56. I.e., Katsina; cf. n.18 above.
  57. Cf. n. 45 above.
  58. Implying that he was transported from Africa to Brazil in 1845; see further discussion
in annotation to the main text, n. 215.

now the Lord's freeman. From the time of his arrival at Port-au-Prince, I was seized with an irrepressible desire that he should receive religious instruction, with the view of his being returned to his people in Africa. And, though at the time I had not the least necessity for him, I could not avoid the impression that it was my positive duty to receive him into my family. Since it has turned out that he has been very profitable to us. Our hopes, however, have been nearly blasted several times, as there were so many to lead him in the downward road to which his own natural heart was too much inclined;[59] and it required no small exercise of faith to believe that he might yet become a missionary to Africa. But God heard our prayers and touched his heart much sooner than we could reasonably expect, considering his feebleness in the language.

His experience before the church was very affecting. Several persons present, not professors of religion, wept on hearing it.—He is endowed by nature with a soul so noble that he grasps the world at a stroke, in the movements of his benevolent feelings. And the expression of such noble feelings in a style so simple and broken as his, is truly affecting. He now seems filled with the most ardent desire to labor for the salvation of souls: talks much of Africa, and prays ardently that her people may receive the gospel. Dreams often of visiting Kachna,[60] accompanied by a "good white man," as he calls a missionary, and being kindly received by his mother.[61] He had been asking for baptism a considerable time, which I felt that I could not refuse to him any longer. We repaired to the sea-side very early in the morning, accompanied by a mixed congregation. After singing and praying in French, I delivered a discourse of perhaps twenty minutes, mostly extemporaneous upon (Les usages pratiques de l'ordonnance du bapteme) the practical usages of baptism, founded on Romans vi: 4. After this, [I] prayed in English for the special benefit of

59. Cf. *Biography*, p. 58, referring to his getting drunk and abusing and quarreling with Mrs. Judd, prior to his conversion; see also n. 39 above.

60. Misspelled "Kaskua" in the *Biography*, p. 59.

61. As stated in no. 2 above, his father was already dead; cf. also n. 24 above.

Mahommah. In passing down the gentle descent to reach a sufficient depth of water, I asked him, if he wished now to devote himself entirely to God and to the good of the world. He replied, "*O yes,* Mr. Judd—*I want to do all for God, all for good.*" In the waters of the great deep, which in their eternal freedom rolling, bathe Africa as well as Haiti, I buried him with Christ in baptism, hoping that he may yet be borne upon their surface, as a messenger of mercy to the dark land of his birth....

5.

Mrs. Nancy A. L. Judd to C. P. Grosvenor, Maison de Campagne, Commune du Port-au-Prince, 21 July 1848[62]

Although Mr. Judd has written you a long letter, yet as the vessel does not sail until tomorrow morning by which we expect to send the present communications, I will add a few words with your permission. Last evening we attended our weekly prayer meeting, which was unusually interesting ... Last evening we felt to rejoice with one who was "going on his way rejoicing," after being baptized, like one of his ancient countrymen. See Acts viii.39. We had an interesting time, and Mohammah after trying to express the joy and thankfulness of his heart by singing—praying and talking in English all that he could, suddenly paused and said—"O God can understand me," and he broke out in a strain of eloquence in his native tongue. The effect was thrilling. O how I wished, that you and some others of our dear brethren could have heard his earnest and impassioned manner. At Mr. J's request he tried to give us a little of the subject of it in English. It seems he was admiring the wonderful providence of God in his dealings with him, from his early childhood, how he had guarded and

---

62. Printed in *Christian Contributor and Free Missionary,* 30 August 1848, under the title, "Letter from Sister Judd."

led him on, from the time he was captured as a slave, near his paternal home—his being sent to Brazil—and the singular preservations
he had there—how anxious he was to have his master sell him—and
his using means to provoke and discourage [sic] him to do it[63]—but
there "God not let him sell him"—but he must be taken to New York
and there rescued, and sent on to Boston—and from there to Port-au-
Prince—and finally he was brought to live with Mr. Judd, and there
taught about Jesus Christ—and he should finally have the happiness
of being baptized—and he felt such a love of God and all men as was
wholly inexpressible. I do not know as I ever saw one, who seemed
more powerfully to recognize the overruling hand of God in all that
had befallen him, than he does. And yet he seems to recognize with
unusual clearness the agency, and accountability of man.[64]—He
appears to have an increasing desire for Africa, which we feel to
encourage. But he seems anxious to labor for those within his reach
now. He talks and labors with David whenever he has an opportunity. One little circumstance will illustrate his disposition on this subject. Directly opposite our little chapel room, there lived for a time, a
Spanish gentleman and his wife, who were Catholics. M. used to frequently call on them, and as the Portuguese and Spanish language is
nearly the same, he could converse with him considerably on the subject of religion. He tried to persuade him (the Spaniard) to attend our
meetings and hear Mr. Judd, when he preached in French, as he
understood that language too. But he declined the invitation. M.
inquired of him if he loved God? when he replied that he did, and
drew from his bosom a small wooden crucifix, and said "here is my
God," and said he prayed to his God every day, "O no" said M. "do
not say so," and expressed much uneasiness that the man should worship a wooden God. Soon after he left him at that time, but could not
feel satisfied without making an other effort to convince him of his

---

63. Cf. *Biography*, p. 46.
64. Despite their regular invocation of providential divine intervention, the Free Mission
Baptists rejected the Calvinist doctrine of predestination, believing instead in "free will," and
hence were often referred to as Free Will Baptists.

wickedness and folly. Accordingly in a few days he called again, when in a short time the subject was renewed. They had now quite a long conversation on the subject, in the course of which he requested him to let him take the crucifix in his hands. This he at first rather declined to do: but finally drew it out and suffered Mohammah to take it in his hands, though he still retained the cord or chain around his neck. He now examined it, and said—"this God wood, eh? You take e little wood—go make e fire—cook e dinner, very good, eh? You take e wood—build e house make e all e all—very good. Well you take e little wood—make a God—go pray for God, eh? Well I pray for your God." Then assuming an air of mock gravity, he commenced—"O Lord, give me clean heart—make me good, make me love every body—give me good to eat, go heaven when I die. Oh! Your God not say e nothing."—Then after turning it round, and thumping it slightly with his finger nail, he let it drop from his hand, with an air of mingled pity and contempt. The man then returned it to his bosom, not without an air of offended pride and chagrin. He attempted to get away from his awkward position, by saying that the cross made him think of God, and so it was useful to him, in reminding him of God and his duty to pray to him. But said M., there is Mr. Judd: he pray for God every day—pray very much, and he no have wooden God. I love God very much—pray for God *every* day, think of God very much—much—I *think* of God all the time—every day— and I no have e *nothing*. Good people all pray for God. God understand all. O Mr.—*very bad*, [to] have wooden God. God not like it."

He was evidently much disturbed, for he told M. not to talk so, and if he loved him, he begged him to say no more on the subject. I think this was the last conversation that Mohammah had with him, for in a short time after he removed to Jamaica …

6.

Mrs. Nancy A. L. Judd to C. P. Grosvenor,
Port-au-Prince, 13 November 1848[65]

It is an old saying, that "when we mount our hobbies, we are apt to jade our friends." I do not know but I shall be apt to do this in regard to Mahommah, not sufficiently considering that every one can not feel the same interest in him that I do. But as you are at liberty, you know, to withhold whatever your more impartial judgement shall see is not of sufficient general interest, to be put into your columns, I write with perfect freedom to you. I feel, at least, that you will make all due allowance for one who has an only child, (as I now consider him),[66] over whose temporal interest, and spiritual "budding intellect" I am left to watch from day to day, with all the solicitude of a mother … But I will say but little this time myself, but enclose some of his own words, in a letter to a friend of his, a gentleman who takes much interest in him, and for whom he feels the most anxious solicitude for his salvation.—But the letter will speak for itself. I had the curiosity to copy it verbatim and I enclose it to you spelling and all.[67] He has improved in spelling considerably, since then, although it seems difficult for him to get hold of the sounds of the letters. If I was by your side, how many little interesting circumstances (interesting to me and I believe they would be to you) concerning him, I should love to relate. I will mention just one. Some time since, while reading the account of Abraham's being called to offer up Isaac, (He is reading the Bible by course:) I watched his countenance with anxious interest, to see what effect it had upon him. After explaining and simplifying the language to him, so as to have him be sure and comprehend it, I paused and said to him, what do you think of that? He looked

---

65. Printed in *Christian Contributor and Free Missionary*, 27 December 1848, under the title, "Letter from Sister Judd."

66. Mrs. Judd's own son was now in the U.S.A., having been sent home from Haiti earlier in 1848.

67. See no. 1 in Appendix 3.

thoughtfully a few moments, and then said to me inquiringly, "Abraham good man, eh?" Yes. "Isaac good man?" Yes. "O well— very well—very good, if God say so; yes, I think so." There was one of the sweetest expressions of faith—of perfect filial confidence on his countenance at this moment, that I ever saw. I could scarcely keep from weeping. Truly, I thought, you are a "son of Abraham," possessor of "like precious faith."…

APPENDIX 3

Letters of Mahommah Gardo Baquaqua, 1848–54

1.

To Mr. Hepburn, undated [November 1848][1]

My Dear Misser Hebburn (Hepburn)[2]

I lovee [sic] you very much. I want you every Sunday not sell any thing.[3] God say not work Sunday. God make all in six days. God not work Sunday.[4] I want you every day pray God for make you a new heart—make you love God—love to do all God say. I [a]fraid Misser Hebburn not got good heart. I feel very sorry. By-and-by you die. If you not love God—not love Jesus Christ you can't go to he[a]ven when you die. I think he[a]ven very happy place God there—Jesus Christ—all good people go there when they die. I not see Misser Hebburn any more in this world. I die in Africa—go he[a]ven.—Go

---

1. This and the following letter were printed together in the *Christian Contributor and Free Missionary*, 13 December 1848, under the title, "Two Letters from Mahommah, the Fugitive from Brazilian Slavery." Although this letter is printed second, it was written earlier, some time before 13 November 1848: see letter of Mrs. Judd to Cyrus Grosvenor, editor of the *Christian Contributor*, 13 November 1848 (no. 5 in Appendix 2, above). Mrs. Judd explains that she copied the letter for despatch to Grosvenor, preserving the spelling of the original; the words in brackets are evidently explanatory glosses added by her.

2. Not identified, beyond the explanation in Mrs. Judd's covering letter that he was "a gentleman who takes much interest in [Mahommah], and for whom he feels the most anxious solicitude for his salvation." He is referred to in Rev. Judd's covering letter (dated 14 December 1848, printed together with Baquaqua's letter) as "Mahommah's friend Mr. H" (letter of 14 December 1848).

3. Presumably Hepburn was a shopkeeper or trader in Port-au-Prince.

4. Although this is most naturally read as referring to the necessity for sabbath observance, it is possible that the issue was rather which day of the week should be regarded as the sabbath. A minority among the Baptists took the view that Saturday rather than Sunday should be the sabbath. The issue was discussed in the *Christian Contributor and Free Missionary* in the late 1840s, and one of the missionaries of the American Baptist Free Mission in Haiti, the Rev. William Jones, was forced to resign in 1850 when he adopted "seventh day" views: ABFMS, Seventh Annual Meeting, Bristol, Ontario, 5–7 June 1850.

to very bad place. O I want very much *much* Misser Hebburn you go he[a]ven when you die. I think he[a]ven very happy place God there—Jesus Christ there—all good people go there when they die. By-and-by may-be God make me go back Africa. I not see Misser Hebburn any more in this world. I die in Africa—go he[a]ven—what if I not see Misser Hebburn there? What if I see him go that bad place bible call hell? Misser Hebburn very good [man]. [He] give me close (clothes)[.] I feel very good (thankful) for Missee [sic: Misser?] Hebburn. I very glad you feel sorry for my poor mother, and for all the pe[o]ple in Africa. (Mr H. had expressed much sympathy for him for his mother and friends whose case he had represented in his own pathetic manner) who have got no bible—no one to tell them how Jesus Christ die for sinners. I pray for my poor mother and for pe[o]ple in Africa every day. I pray for Misser Hebburn for God make him good man. I want you not feel bad (offended) for me for I write so.

Your friend, Mahommah

2.

To Cyrus P. Grosvenor, Port-au-Prince, 14 November 1848[5]

My Friend Mr Grosvenor:
I want to see you very much. The Brazilian Consul said if he saw me in New York again, that he would send me to Brazil for a slave.[6]

5. A covering letter from Nancy Judd, 15 November 1848, notes that, unlike no. 1, this letter was sent to the *Christian Contributor and Free Missionary* as written "from his own pen." The circumstances of composition are explained as follows: "As you see, our Mahommah has written to you himself. This he spoke to me about doing several days ago, and wished me to assist him some about *spelling*. But as I was quite busy writing myself, the considerate child did not like to interrupt me. So he got sister Cushman to help him occasionally with a word he was at a loss about." "Sister Cushman" was the wife of a missionary of the Foreign Evangelical Society, who arrived in Haiti around this time, and stayed with the Judds while her husband was away looking for a place to settle, as reported in W.L. Judd, 19 November 1848, in *Christian Contributor*, 13 December 1848.

6. The Brazilian Consul-General in New York, Luiz Henrique Ferreira d'Aguiar, had supported Baquaqua's owner Captain Costa in the legal case arising from Baquauqa's attempted escape in New York in 1847: cf. *Biography*, p. 56.

I want him to love God. I want all the good people in New York to pray to God for him to give him a new heart. I want them to pray for me too. I want to love God very much more—I want all the people that love God to pray for my mother and brother and sisters in Africa. I want to go to the United States very much, and go to school and learn to understand the Bible very well.

By-and-by I want to go back to Africa and see my friends and tell all the people about Jesus Christ.—May be God give them new hearts.

Mahommah

3.
To [W. Walker?] Freetown,[7] 28 September 1850[8]

Dear Brother, Sir: —

I feel thankful to God, and I try to pray to God for he his [sic] helps. O my Christian friends we must remember our Saviour Jesus Christ, who died for our sins, he pray for enemies, pray for them, and pray for poor and needs [?= needy]. Dear beloved Brethren, your suffering, our suffering, for the poor negro. God made one blood all nations, but foolish men say his no God, and they dost serve Christ and dost believe naything [= nothing] good, they believe devil, and they love everythings bads, we must pray for them, if they believe in the Bible and read it, they cannot do so, the first book of Genesis. In the beginning God created the heaven, and the earth, and the earth was without form, and void, and darkness was upon the face of the deep, and the Spirit of God moved upon the face of the waters, and

7. More properly Freetown Corners, as in no. 4; about six miles south of McGrawville, where Baquaqua was now attending New York Central College. It is not indicated what he was doing in Freetown Corners, but a later letter (no. 11) mentions that he was friends with a white girl who belonged to the Baptist Church there.

8. Printed in *The American Baptist*, 10 October 1850, under the title "Mahommah".

God said, let there be light, and there was light, and God saw the [light], that it was good. And God divided the light from the darkness he called night, and he created male and female, and he created everything we can see in this world. God made one blood all nation, we must love one another, and pray for one another to[o]. I believe the church of Christ, the church of Jesus Christ, they love one anothers, and pray one for anothers to[o], and I found so many kind of the churches here, some of them preach the gospel, dost care [for] the poor slave, they dost pray for them, and they believe slavery is good, they are Christians, Sir, I cannot believe that, never, never, NEVER can be so. I believe Christian pray for poor slave and preach against slavery. I hear they come after the slave here,[9] if we had only city here, no bodys trouble negro here[10] but I am very glad if we had, but you must look all it,

from your friend,
Mahommah G. Baquaqua

4.
*To [W. Walker?], Freetown Corners,
21 February 1851*[11]

My Dear Brother: —
I have received a letter from sister Josephine Cushman Bateman.[12] She gave me one dollar, and her friend one dollar. She lives a great way off, but she remembers me. I am happy to see some feel so to the

---

9. Alluding to the Fugitive Slave Act, enacted in 1850; cf. also no. 4 below.
10. Baquaqua appears to suggest that blacks were more vulnerable in the countryside than in the city.
11. Printed in *The American Baptist*, 6 March 1851, under the title, "Letter from Mahommah."
12. Wife of a missionary in Haiti, whom Baquaqua had known there: cf. n. 4 above.

poor negro. I am a poor negro myself; I have no father, or mother, or sister. But I thank God, he gives me a great many friends.

Chap. xxiii, Deut. 15,[13] "Thou shall not deliver unto his master the servant which is escaped from his master unto thee; he shall dwell with thee, even among you, in that place which he shall choose, in one of the gates where it liketh him best: thou shall not oppress him."

In 2d Samuel xxiii, chapter 3, and 4, God said: "He that ruleth over men, must be just, ruling in the fear of God. And he shall be as the light of the morning without clouds."

Now if the rulers of this country ruled in the fear of God, they would not make such wicked laws. The fugitive slave law says, The fugitive shall be delivered up to his master, God says, Thou shalt not deliver him to his master. Which is right, to obey God or man?

Pray for me, that God will help me in my studies, and send me back to Africa, that I may tell my poor friends about the saviour who died for our sins, and rose again.

from your friend,

Mahommah G. Baquaqua

5.
*To Mrs. Smith,[14] McGrawville,
20 October 1851.[15]*

My dear Sister

I have heard some thing to day about brother Smith, but I did not

13. Chap. xxiii, Deut. 15–16.

14. I.e., wife of Gerrit Smith, to whom nos. 14–15 are addressed. As one of Baquaqua's letters (no. 15) implies, he had visited the Smiths' home in 1851, perhaps more than once. He had been in Peterboro to attend the semi-annual meeting of the American Baptist Free Mission Society in 1851, which Smith had hosted in his home; see *The American Baptist*, 11 September 1851.

15. This letter and nos. 14–15 are preserved in the Gerrit Smith Collection, Arents Research Library, Syracuse University, Syracuse, New York.

believe. I think can not be so. I hear he was in prison,[16] I feel so bad to day, I [do not?] know what to do. Sister write to me as soon as you can. I should like hear all about it. I wish I was[?] at Petterbro,[17] if they come after him I will go with him, indeed, O I can not tell how I feel today, and some other I have heard to[o]. I am very sorry the p[e]ople so prejudice against [pe]ople and against God. I try to pray for my friends in prison that God will deliver them.

I can not write any more for pleasnt [= present] remember me in your prayer, and give my love to all friends there, I did not write good to night at all. I feel don't well[?] [i.e. = I don't feel well?]

Mahommah G. Baquaqua

6.

To George Whipple,
Brooklyn, 10 August 1853[18]

Dear Bro

I made my mand [= mind] to go to Africa this fall, if I can. I did

---

16. Apparently the reference is to the so-called "Jerry Incident," in which Gerrit Smith was involved. Smith and other abolitionists who were attending the Liberty Party convention in Syracuse in October 1851 successfully stormed the local jail to free the fugitive slave, Jerry McHenry, who was spirited across Lake Ontario to Kingston, Canada West. Smith and other leaders of the Liberty Party were indicted for "treason" and had to appear in court in nearby Auburn, although it does not appear that Smith was actually imprisoned. The case against Smith dragged on for a year before it was dropped; see Horton and Horton, *In Hope of Liberty*, 255; and Henrietta Buckmaster, *Let My People Go: The Story of the Underground Railroad and the Growth of the Abolition Movement* (Boston, 1941): 211 13.

17. To be identified with Peterboro, the village near Syracuse where the Smith mansion was located. The village was named after Gerrit Smith's father, Peter.

18. This and the following seven letters are preserved in manuscript in the American Missionary Society Archives, Amistad Research Center, Tulane University, New Orleans, nos. 81288, 81296, 81308, 81322, 81343, 81362, 81457, 81449. They all relate to Baquaqua's application to serve in the Society's Mendi Mission, in Sierra Leone, led by George Thompson. Baquaqua had apparently been in contact with the Association, whether by letter or personally, before writing this letter, since it seems to be responding to questions put to him.

not think that my friends will do anything in my Mission.[19] They want me rise about $5,000, I think I can never do it in 2 years.[20] I did not like to stay in this County Country; I feel I may do more good in Africa than I can here. I not gone [= going ?] to say nothing about you or any body else to my friends.[21] I know how to make all come right. I did not expect to say much about, at all. Dear Br—pray that God will direct. I will work with Geo. Thompson, if God will. I will live [= leave ?] here Monday. And I like you writ[e] to me as soon as you can. If I get home I will try to get ready. I will write to you again. I believe in one ~~Chru~~ Church.[22] I have so much to say but I must stop. Remember me in your prayers. I will do the same for you. If you write to me sent [= send] to McGrawville, Cortland, Co., N.Y.[23] I should like to have you give me the nebers [= numbers], and Street if I come so [I] know neast [= next ?] to go.[24]

Your in Christ,

M.G. Baquaqua

19. This probably reflects Baquaqua's conclusion that the American Baptist Free Mission Society would not, after all, deliver on its promise to send him as a missionary to Africa; however, an alternative meaning might be that he did not think the Free Mission would allow the funds which Baquaqua had collected for them to be used to finance his joining the Mendi Mission (cf. no. 8 below).

20. From June 1853, Baquaqua had been involved in fund-raising for the Free Mission, for its projected mission to Africa in which Baquaqua was intended to serve: letter of A.L. P[ost], in *American Baptist*, 28 July 1853; ABFMS, Eleventh Annual Meeting, Albany, New York, 7–8 June 1854.

21. Presumably Whipple had asked whether the Free Mission knew of Baquaqua's approach to the American Missionary Association. He evidently insisted that Baquaqua should tell them: cf. no. 10 below.

22. I.e., he was not concerned with denominational differences within Christianity. Since the American Missionary Association was a Congregationalist body, and at least nominally Calvinist in doctrine, Whipple had probably asked whether Baquaqua, as a "Free Will" Baptist, was willing to operate with it. Our thanks for advice on this question to David Bebbington.

23. Baquaqua had lived at Freetown Corners for some time in early 1853, but had moved back to McGrawville: cf. *Biography*, p. 64.

24. Presumably to meet Whipple personally.

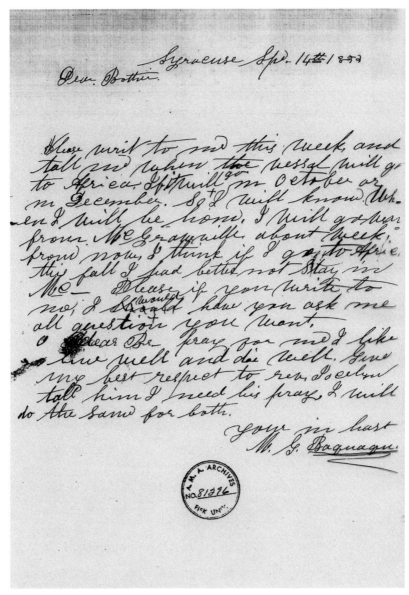

PLATE 25. Letter from Baquaqua, apparently to George Whipple: 'tell me when the vessal will go to Africa', 14 September 1853 (American Missionary Association Archives, Amistad Research Center, Tulane University, New Orleans).

7.

To George Whipple, Syracuse, 14 September 1853

Dear Brother,

Please writ[e] to me this week, and tell me when the vessal will go to Africa. If it will go in October or in December. So I will know when I will be hom[e]. I will go [a]way from McGrawville about week from now, I think if I go to Africa this fall I had better not Stay in Mc——— Please if you write to me, I would have you ask me all questions you want.

O dear Br pray for me I like to live well and die well. Give my best respect to rev. Jocelyn[25] tell him I need his pray, I will do the same for him.

Your in hast

M.G. Baquaqua

8.

To unnamed recipient, New Berlin, 18 September 1853

Dear Br

I have wrote a few lines to Br Whipple list [= last] week. I did not he[a]red from him yet. I should like you tall [= tell] him I did not think that my friends will let me have the money which I corlated [= collected ?].[26] I should be very happy if thus will, I will tall [= tell] to them be and be [= by and by] may be they will pay my passage. But if they did not I hope some friends will pay. I should like to labor with Geo. Thompson. Remember me in your prayer. Please writ[e] to me

25. Perhaps A. S. Joslyn, who had been pastor of the Baptist Church at Elgin, New York, in 1850: cf. letter of J. Scott, 22 January 1850, in *Christian Contributor and Free Missionary*, 7 March 1850.

26. Cf. n. 20 above.

direct your letter to McGrawville[.] I go there this week,[27] I came here to get somethings.

Your in hast

M.G. Baquaqua

9.
To [George Whipple?], New Berlin, 25 September 1853

Dear Brother,

I have wrote one to you and I did not hear from you. I should like you tell me if you please, if I go with Br. Thompson do you think we can try to found [= find] my Mother and Sister[28] and Brother in Africa. Write to me this week and sent to New Berlin N.Y. If vessel ready to go to Africa I am ready to go.

Your in hast

M. G. Baquaqua

10.
To George Whipple, McGrawville, 8 October 1853

Dear Brother,

I have just returned home and found a letter from you. I have consulted some of my friends and no objections have been made as yet, to my going to Africa in connexion with the Mendi Mission.[29]

I have just heard that Brother Thompson has returned to the United

27. He was in fact still at New Berlin a week later, but was back at McGrawville by 8 October: cf. nos. 9–10 below.

28. The handwriting is unclear, and this could be "sisters"; it should be noted that Baquaqua states in the *Biography* (p. 26) that he had three sisters.

29. Cf. n. 21 above.

States on account of his wife's illness.

If that is true, will you not inform me, and where I may direct a letter to him. I know very well that I should be better prepared to go.[30] I ought to have been in school last summer, but my friends thought best, that I should go round and see what I could get to aid me on my mission.[31] I think I can improve my mind some yet, but the English Language has been very hard for me to understand and speak.

I think I shall not remain in the United States long, unless the prospect opens for me to return to my native land. I do not wish to burden your Society. If I could do good by going I should be happy indeed to go but if not I think I shall go to Canada, and then I fear I shall give up going entirely.[32] Please my good brother write me immediately, for I will stay here till I hear from you. I thank you kindly for your good advice and will try and do the best I can. Pray for me my brother that God will direct my steps. This is my prayer.

Your obligde friend and brother,

M.G. Baquaqua

11.
To [George Whipple?], McGrawville, 26 October 1853

Dear Bro.

I did not like to have you think that I have been doing some things very bad. But I did not. This Lady they spoke of, She was very good friends to the colored people. I got acquainted with her about three years ago. She very good friend to me, about four months ago they began to talk about her and I, that we going to get marry. Her Mother

---

30. Implying that Whipple had queried his qualifications for service in the mission, perhaps especially his competence in English, as implied later in this letter: cf. also no. 13 below.

31. Cf. n. 20 above.

32. Presumably (since he continued his efforts to return to Africa until at least 1857) this means only that he would give up hope of joining the Mendi Mission specifically.

did not allow me to come to her house, so I want [= went] one day
and told her that I never say to her daughter that I should like to get
Marry with her, but She did not believe me.[33]

I member in the Baptist Cruch [= Church] in Freetown[34] also this
Lady. I long time ago I should like to take my letter from that Cruch,[35]
I did not agree with they, in count of slavery. They have a covena[n]t
meeting last Sat[ur]day and I expect to go after my letter Sunday
Morning,[36] and I Expect to live [= leave] McGrawville Monday morning for Canada.[37] Sunday morning I ready to go to Freetown meeting,
and some my friend came up and told me I had better not go to
Freetown to day. I said why, he said I hea[r]d that you going to get
marry to day in Freetown. I said bless my body to day, something
I did not know nothing about it, he said if they see I going they will
think truth, so I give up going. And I do thank God I did not go; if
I go they will do very bad to me indeed, about four or five carriages
went before I did, they thought I gone, from McGrawville to Freetown, about 6 miles. I have to be very careful, I dont go out much.
I studys my books, this all.[38] I have a great trouble with these wickit
[= wicked] people.

33. This was shortly after the Allen-King affair, as discussed in the Introduction. Professor
Allen was driven out of Phillipsville, near Fulton, on 30 January, after visiting the home of one
of his students, Mary King. The couple fled to England after marrying in New York City in late
March. As discussed in the Introduction, there was considerable press coverage in upstate New
York, much of it hostile. Baquaqua's problems are to be interpreted in this context.

34. Although Baquaqua was now resident in McGrawville, he had lived in Freetown
Corners earlier in 1853: cf. n. 12 above

35. I.e., to transfer his membership to another church. The "letter" would be requested from
the first church so that it could be presented to another by the bearer to testify that he had been
a member in good standing (i.e., on the membership roll and not under discipline for some
moral offense); he would then be admitted without further enquiry into his background. Our
thanks for elucidation of this point again to David Bebbington.

36. The covenant meeting would be a meeting restricted to church members for the renew-
al of the church covenant, often held annually. As it was a meeting for business, it would have
the authority to issue a letter of recommendation.

37. Although his departure for Canada on this occasion was evidently deferred, he probably went there soon after: cf. *Biography*, p. 64. But he was back in McGrawille in January 1854,
prior to leaving definitively for Canada: cf. nos. 12–13.

38. Baquaqua seems to have resumed his schooling at this point: cf. no. 13, with n. 45
below.

Forget not the voice of thine Enemies; The tumult of those that rise up against thee increaseth continually. Psalms. 74, 23. Save me, O God; for the water[s] are come in unto my soul, Dear Bro—I deed [sic] your prayer. Psalms. 69, 1.

Please let Mr Smith[39] see the letter I send to you before you return to me aga[i]n. I should like to tall [= tell] you all this matter, but I feel very bad, the people use me so, this make me feel bad. give my best respect to Bro. J———[40] and all my friend.

Your Bro in Christ,

M.G. Baquaqua

bismi'llah al-ra[hman] [in Arabic script][41]

PS. If you see Geo- Thompson tell him if he think I can do some good in Africa, I had better go with him. if I can not teach I will be cook to him than I go cook to my master, I had better cook for Missionary than slavehold[er].[42] Mahommah

12.
To [George Whipple?], McGrawville, 6 January 1854

My dear Br

Some thing which is nescesary for me to let you know. I should

---

39. Possibly Elias Smith, who had assisted Baquaqua to escape from New York in 1847: cf. letter of Nancy Judd, 24 March 1848 (no. 3 in Appendix 2 above), or perhaps Gerrit Smith, the benefactor of Central College.

40. Presumably the Rev. Mr. Jocelyn, as in no. 7 above.

41. The Arabic phrase is an incomplete version of the Quranic rubric, *bismi'llah al-rahman*, "In the name of God, the merciful ...". Allan Austin's suggestion (*Transatlantic Stories*, 169) that its inclusion here might indicate that Baquaqua was contemplating returning to Islam if he got back to Africa seems improbable; more likely, it was intended to demonstrate his knowledge of Arabic, and thus his potential usefulness as an interpreter for missionary work.

42. A reference to the fact that he had served as steward to his Brazilian owner Captain Costa, prior to his escape in New York (see *Biography*, p. 48), as well as to the Judds in Haiti.

like to know, if I will go to Africa, this year or next year, Because I have to work in the farm in Spring, I board myself here above two years. I use to hire one acre of land, this reason I should like to know.

Your in Christian love,

M.G. Baquaqua

13.
To [George Whipple?], McGrawville, 22 January 1854

Dear Bro,

Yours of the 14th is received, I now take my pen to ad[r]ess you, in regard to your request, my anxiety to go to Africa is this that God send me in this country to know the way of Salvation, And now I think my duty to go, if God open the way for me to go, and teach my fellow country-men, I have been think[ing] about it, pray[ing] about it, But my duty [is] to forsak[e] all for Christ, and go. Now how can I go without have been sent, Romans 10, Chapter 8.18.[43] I believe I am disciple of Christ. I have a great many trials. But my pray[er] is all may [be] heard, If I go I should like to be interpreter, I understand Arabic and Zogoo[44] languages. I will abide with your Mission, if I am not sick as death. I wish I understand English language more than I dose now. I do not wish to be under great restraint, the outher [other] members of the Miss[ion] -You say that they want a good man to go there, but I did not know how good I am, but I love God and try to do which is right. Please write to me again.

Your sincer[e]ly,

M.G. Baquaqua

43. *Romans* Chapter 10, verse 8: "But what saith it? The word is nigh thee, even in thy mouth, and in thy heart: that is, the word of faith, which we preach"; and *Romans* Chapter 10, verse 18: "But I say, Have they not heard? Yes verily, their sound went into all the earth, and their words unto the ends of the world."

44. Djougou, i.e., presumably Dendi.

I have so much to say but nost [now is ?] school time,[45] I must suf[f]er, remember me in your prayer, I will do the same for you. Your in hast. M

PLATE 26. Gerrit Smith: 'I do not exspected to write to you to Washington' (Letter to Smith, Chatham, Canada West, 25 May 1854), referring to Smith's election to Congress as a radical abolitionist; photograph in Octavius Brooks Frothingham, *Gerrit Smith: A Biography* (New York, 1909), frontispiece.

14.
To Gerrit Smith,
Chatham,[46] *25 May 1854*

My dear Brother in Christ,

I do not exspected to write to you to Washington.[47] I am very sorry to inform you that the free Mission has kill[ed] the Africa Mission.[48] And kill[ed] Mahommah to[o] but I must live before I die. Now[?] dear Brother, I should like to get a peace [=

45. Implying that he had resumed schooling, although where is not clear. Austin, *Transatlantic Stories*, 168, assumes that he returned to Central College; more likely, he was attending a lower-level school, as he had done earlier in 1853 (then at Freetown Corners).

46. Located in southwestern Ontario, near Detroit; see Farrell, "Negro Community in Chatham."

47. Gerrit Smith had been elected to Congress in 1852, but resigned his seat in August 1854; see Harlow, *Gerrit Smith*.

48. Alluding to the failure of the ABFMS to realize its projected mission to Africa, in which Baquaqua was to have served. The Board of the Society, in its report to the Annual Meeting in June 1854, reported its continuing failure to find a minister to undertake the mission, but also implicitly criticized Baquaqua for failing to raise the requisite funds: ABFMS, Report of Tenth Annual Meeting, Utica, New York, 1–2 June 1854. The strained relations between Baquaqua and the Free Mission Society coincided with the decline in the influence of the ABFMS in Canada West; see Introduction. In 1854, for example, the Mission was expelled from the black community at Dawn, to the north of Chatham, which it had been administering for two years; see Winks, *Blacks in Canada*, 231.

PLATE 27. Chatham, Canada West: 'I was kindly treated by all classes wherever I went' (Biography, p.4); King Street, looking west from 5th Street, 1860, Courtsey of the Chatham-Kent Museum, 85.27.2.15, N674, Bk. 2#15.

piece] of land,[49] but I have nothing to begin with. I should be very happy to have you give me advice. If you can help me if you will puy [= buy] me a land in Canada,[50] or in the stat[e] of New York.[51] Remember my Mother, Sister, Brother, and Friends in Africa pray for us. God bless you. If you have a little please write to me dire[c]t to

49. This seems to imply that, having failed to secure his return to Africa, Baquaqua now contemplated settling permanently in North America; but if so this was clearly only a passing mood, since he continued his efforts to get to Africa thereafter, at least down to 1857: see Introduction.

50. Probably referring to the community of Buxton, a few miles south of Chatham, which was founded with the understanding that settlers would purchase land; see Allen P. Stouffer, *The Light of Nature and the Law of God: Anti-Slavery in Ontario, 1833–1877* (Montreal and Kingston, Ont., 1992): 82–101; and Victor Ullman, *Look to the North Star: A Life of William King* (Boston, 1969): 129–61.

51. In 1846, Smith pledged 120,000 acres of land in upstate New York for the settlement of free blacks and eventually issued over 3,000 land titles for 40–60 acre tracts to blacks; see James Oliver Horton and Lois E. Horton, *In Hope of Liberty: Culture, Community and Protest among Northern Free Blacks, 1700–1860* (New York, 1997): 243.

Chatham, Canada West. The Free Mission did not do right by me at this time. I am not able to inform you all matter. I will remember you in my humble[?] prayer.

15.
To Gerrit Smith, Detroit,[52] *4 July 1854*

My dear Bro in Christ

I taking walk to day in this city. I call in the store and I saw a newspaper. I take and look it. I found a some thing about you in that paper. And I feel bad about it. I tell Rev. William[53] He say not so. And I feel a little better. I hea[r]d some thing like this, that when you year you are very good Abbolition[ist], And now you in Washington, and you gone [= going] to be a souther[ner].[54] They say a great many things about you in that paper which I not able to tell you all of it. If the paper belong to me I will sent to you. do you recolete [= recollect] what I have told you in Pettrbro befor you go to Washington. I hope you don[t] forget it. I pray to God for you. Will you write to me direct to Chatham Canada W [55]

I received your last[?] letter I know that you give to the poor.[56] I think you give more than receive. I read your hand writing very well indeed. God bless you.

Your in love

---

52. As explained in the postscript to this letter, Baquaqua was visiting Detroit to arrange the publication of his *Biography.*

53. Unidentified, but possibly the Rev. William King, the founder of the all-black community at Buxton, near Chatham. For the career of William King and the community at Buxton, see Ullman, *Look to the North Star.*

54. Possibly a reference to the fact that Smith, an avowedly radical abolitionist, had voted in favor of annexation of Cuba on the belief that slavery could be confined to that island and hence abolished on mainland North America; see Harlow, *Gerrit Smith.*

55. Where Baquaqua was now resident: cf. no. 14 above.

56. Presumably this was in response to Baquaqua's earlier letter to Smith (no. 14) requesting help to purchase land; the wording implies that Smith had responded negatively.

M.G. Baquaqua

P.S. my narrative ready for the press. this reason I come here, but cause [= cost] too much to printed [= print it]. I have no more to pay for it[.] it will be very interest[ing] book. English man wrote it for me.[57] I pay him for do it. I should be very happy to have you lend me $200. to printed [sic]. and I will pay you about 6 Month. I may pay you before that time soon the books come up [as] soon [as] I can not help geting [sic] money.[58]

Your truly

Mahommah Gardo Baquaqua

57. Referring to Samuel Moore, the editor of the *Biography* (who was actually Irish, not English).

58. Whether Smith provided any financial assistance is not known, but Baquaqua was able to get the printing done within a few weeks of this letter, by August 1854: see Introduction.

APPENDIX 4

Review of the *Biography*, published in *The American Baptist*, 2 November 1854[1]

Biography of Mahommah G. Baquaqua

This is a pamphlet of some 65 pages[2]—an autobiography, but revised and prepared for publication by Samuel Moore, Esq.,[3] and printed at the Tribune office,[4] in Detroit.—The subject of the narrative is a native of Zoogoo, in the interior of Africa, whence he was kidnapped and sold into slavery. He spent some years as a slave, first in Africa,[5] and afterwards in Brazil. Accompanying his Brazilian master in a voyage to New York, he escaped from the vessel, but was arrested and imprisoned. By the interposition of sympathizing friends he found himself at liberty; and, making his way to Haiti, became acquainted with Mr. Judd, and was converted to the Christian faith. For some years past he has been receiving instruction in this country; and hopes, at some future time, to aid in giving the gospel to his countrymen. The pamphlet is sold for twenty-five cents.

1. Probably written by the editor of *The American Baptist*, Warham Walker.
2. Sic: actually, 66.
3. For discussion of this assessment of the authorship of the *Biography*, see Introduction.
4. I.e., the *Detroit Tribune*, which was published by George E. Pomeroy, the printer of Baquaqua's book.
5. The *Biography* mentions only a period of "several weeks" spent in servitude in Africa (at "Efau," apparently in northern Dahomey), as opposed to transit to the coast. Conceivably, the reviewer is recalling statements in earlier published accounts of Baquaqua, which refer to a substantial period spent by Baquaqua in slavery in Africa: e.g., Foss & Mathews, *Facts for Baptist Churches*, 392. For discussion of this question, see Introduction.

GLOSSARY[1]

Place Names

Zoogoo, Zoozoo	Djougou
Bergoo, Berzoo	Borgu [=Nikki]
Sa-ba	[source of salt, unidentified]
Sal-gar	Salaga
Da-boy-ya	Daboya
Zar-ach-o	? Yarakeou

"Gates [Quarters] of Zoogoo"

u-boo-ma-co-fa	yobume (lit. "behind the market")
fo-ro-co-fa	Foro-[Magazi] (lit. "farm of the Magazin")
Bah-pa-ra-ha-co-fa	Bakparakpey
Bah-too-loo-co-fa	Batoulou
Bah-lah-mon-co-fa	Ba-Leman, i.e., imam; probably the ward now known as Limamande
Ajaggo-co-fa	unidentified

Journey to the coast

Ar-oo-zo [?=Ar-oo-go]	? Alejo
Chir-a-chur-ee	Krikri
Cham-mah	Tchamba
Efau	"Fon," i.e., Dahomey; referring to a town in the north of the kingdom
Dohama	Dahomey
Gra-fe	Glehue (Ouidah)

1. We wish to thank Nassirou Arifari Bako, Albarka Soulleymane, Alfa Houssane Djarra, Sani Alaza, and Zakari Dramani-Issifou for discussing Baquaqua's text with us and for their suggestions on interpretation of specific terms. We also consulted Petr Zima, *Lexique Dendi (Songhay) (Djougou, Bénin)* (Köln, 1994).

253

Personal Names/Titles

Gardo	Mahommah's middle name	Gado, son born after twins (Dendi and Hausa)
Baquaqua	Mahommah's last name	unidentified
Sa-bee	form of addressing king	*sabeni*, majesty (Dendi)
Ma-ga-zee	senior title, from Hausa, *magaji*	e.g., ward head in Djougou
Wa-roo	name	see Woo-roo
Woo-roo	name of fellow slave	Woru, first-born son (Dendi)
massa-sa-ba	title of rulers of neighboring towns subordinate to Djougou	*massasawa* = title of ruler of Soubroukou[2]

Words and Phrases

gui-ge-rah	place of Muslim worship	*dyì?gìré*, mosque (Dendi)
sarrah	sacrifice at end of Ramadan	*sárà*, alms (Dendi), *salla*, prayer; ceremony at end of Ramadan (Hausa)
yah-quim-ta-ca-ri	large elephant	*térékúnté*, elephant (Dendi)
yah-quin-ta-cha-na	small elephant	elephant + *tyéénè*, small (Dendi)
ka-fa	elephant tusk musical instrument	possible Hausa derivation (*kafo* = horn)
bon-ton	type of tree	*bántàn*, the silk cotton tree (Dendi)
cofa	gate	*kofa*, gate (Hausa)[3]
bah	father	*ba*, father (Baatonu); *bààbá*, father (Dendi)
bah-she	antelope	*béésè* (Dendi)
harnee	corn	*háánì*, millet (Dendi)
harnebee	"fine grain"	*háánì bi*, "black corn," sorghum (Dendi)
gan-ran	"fruit" = kola	*goro*, kola (Hausa)

2. According to informants in Djougou.

3. According to informants, *kofa* designates the bush beyond the town limits in Dendi, but it is not in Zima, *Lexique Dendi*. The word for "ward" in Dendi is *frani*, and the word for gate, *fúù méè*.

my-ache-ee-ah-dee-za-in-qua-hoo-noo-yo-haw-coo-nah	"the bride and groom are coming out today" —invitation to marriage	"my-ache-ee" = Mahiachi, personal name "ah-dee-ze" = Adiza, personal name "hoo-noo" = *hùnú* = go out (Dendi) "haw" = *hó?* = today (Dendi)
nya-wa-qua-foo	house where bride lodges prior to marriage	not identified, but includes *fúù*, house (Dendi)
unbah	medicine man [non-Muslim]	unidentified
wal-la	writing board	*allo*, writing board (Dendi and Hausa)
che-re-choo	bodyguard	*tyiriku*, royal slave (Baatonu)
loch-a-fau	measure of distance, "mile"	unidentified
bah-gee	alcoholic drink	*bádyi*, beer (Dendi)
goo-noo	"leopard" in "Efau" = ?Fon	*gúnnù*, lion (Dendi)
gardowa	command for Baquaqua	Baquaqua's middle name + some command[4]

4. Perhaps a corruption of Dendi *káá* (take away, remove).

BIBLIOGRAPHY

Archives
American Baptist Samuel Colgate Historical Library, Rochester, New York
- Reports of the Annual Meetings of the American Baptist Free Mission Society

American Missionary Association Archives, Amistad Research Center, Tulane University, New Orleans

Arquivo Histórico Diplomático do Itamaraty, Rio de Janeiro

Bibliothèque de Centre du Recherches Africaines, Paris
- Fonds Person, Yves Person, "Zugu, ville musulmane"

Chatham-Kent Museum, Chatham, Ontario

Detroit Public Library
- Burton Historical Collection

Cortland County Historical Society, Cortland, New York
- New York Central College Collection
- Miscellaneous Scrapbook & McGraw Schools and Central College, vol. 108

Lamont Memorial Free Library, McGraw, New York
- *Facts, Fotos and Folklore of McGraw*, 1976
- *McGrawville Centennial*, 1969
- *Cortland County Sesquicentennial*, 1958
- *McGraw, N.Y. Illustrated*

Parliamentary Papers, U.K. (PP)
- Correspondence relating to the Slave Trade 1840-60

Public Record Office, Kew (PRO)
- FO 84/886, Slave Trade Correspondence, Journal of Louis Frazer, 30 July 1851
- FO 97/434, Niger Expeditions, No. 19, Baikie to Lord Russell, 22 March 1862

Syracuse University Library, Special Collections, Syracuse, New York
- Gerrit Smith Papers

Newspapers
The American Baptist
Christian Contributor and Free Missionary
Church Missionary Gleaner

Church Missionary Intelligencer
Cortland County Express
Detroit Tribune
Diário do Pernambuco
Diário do Rio de Janeiro
Illustrated London News
Kent Advertiser
The Liberator
National Anti-Slavery Standard
New York Daily Tribune
New York Express
New York Herald
Oswego Daily Times
Provincial Freeman
Springfield Gazette
Syracuse Star

Unpublished Theses and Papers

Bako, Nassirou Arifari. "La Question du peuplement dendi dans la partie septentrionale de la République du Bénin: le cas du Borgou'." Mémoire de maîtrise, Université Nationale du Bénin, 1989.

Berberich, Charles William. "A Locational Analysis of Trade Routes of the Northeast Asante Frontier Network in the Nineteenth Century." Ph.D. diss., Northwestern University, 1974.

Brégand, Denise, "Anthropologie historique et politique du Borgou; Wangara et Wasangari." Thèse de Doctorat Nouveau Régime, Université de Paris 8, 1997.

Costa e Silva, Alberto da. "Buying and selling Korans in nineteenth century Rio de Janeiro." Paper presented at the conference, "Rethinking the African Diaspora: The Making of a Black Atlantic World in the Bight of Benin and Brazil," Emory University, Atlanta, 1998.

Debourou, Djibril Mama. "Commerçants et chefs dans l'ancien Borgu (des origines à 1936)." Thèse de Doctorat du 3e cycle, Université de Paris I, 1979.

Farrell, John Kevin Anthony. "The History of the Negro Community in Chatham, Ontario." Ph.D. diss., University of Ottawa, 1955.

Hanchett, Catherine M. "New York Central College and its three Black professors, 1849–1857." Paper presented at the conference, "A Heritage Uncovered: the Black Experience in New York State," Elmira, N.Y., 22 April 1989.

Hanchett, Catherine M. "'Dedicated to equality and brotherhood'": New York Central College, C.P. Grosvenor, and Gerrit Smith." Paper presented at the Madison County Historical Society, Oneida, N.Y., 16 February 1989.

Hanchett, Catherine M. "New York Central College students." New York Central College Collection, Cortland County Historical Society, Cortland, N.Y., 1997.

Hanchett, Catherine M. "After McGrawville: The later careers of some African American students from New York Central College." Paper presented before the Cortland County Historical Society, 26 February 1992.

Idris, Musa Baba. "The role of the Wangara in the formation of the trading diaspora in Borgu." Paper presented at the Conference on Manding Studies, SOAS, London, 1972.

Lovejoy, Paul E. "Slavery and memory in an Islamic society: Whose audience? Which audience?" Paper presented at the conference, "Historians and their Audiences: Mobilizing History for the Millennium," York University, Toronto, 13–15 April 2000.

Ouorou-Coubou, Osséni. "L'Islam en pays baatonu au XIX siècle." Memoire de Maîtrise en Histoire, Université Nationale du Bénin, 1997.

Vergolino, José Raimundo Oliveira. "A demografia excrava no nordeste do Brasil: o caso de Pernambuco—1800/1888" (texto para discussão No. 383, Departamento de Economia, Universidade Federal de Pernambuco, March 1997).

Published Books and Articles

Anon. "A Native of Bornoo." *The Atlantic Monthly*, 19 (October 1867), 485–95.

Anon. *Dendi Cine tila Bukatante/Livre du dendi pratique* (n.d.).

Allen, William G. *The American Prejudice against Colour: An Authentic Narrative, showing how easily the Nation got into an Uproar.* London: W. and F.G. Cash, 1853.

Andrews, William L. *To Tell a Free Story: The First Century of Afro-American Autobiography.* Urbana: University of Illinois Press, 1986.

Andrews, William L., ed. *African American Autobiography: A Collection of Critical Essays.* Englewood Cliffs, N.J.: Prentice Hall, 1993.

Andrews, William L., Frances Smith Foster, and Trudier Harris, eds. *The Oxford Companion to African American Literature.* New York: Oxford

University Press, 1997.

Appiah, Kwame Anthony, and Henry Louis Gates, eds. *Microsoft Encarta Africana 2000.* Redmond, Wash.: Microsoft Corporation, 2000.

Austin, Allan. *African Muslims in Antebellum America: Transatlantic Stories and Spiritual Struggles.* New York: Garland Publishing, 1997.

Austin, Allan. *African Muslims in Ante-Bellum America: A Sourcebook.* New York & London: Garland Pub., 1984.

Bako, Nassirou Arifari. "Routes de commerce et mise en place des populations du Nord du Bénin." In *Le sol, la parole et l'écrit. Mélanges en hommage à Raymond Mauny,* vol. 2, 655–72. Paris, 1981.

Baquaqua, Mahommah Gardo, *Biografia e narrativa do ex-excravo afrobrasileiro* (trad. de Robert Krueger, Brasília: Hedições Humanidades, 1997).

Bassett, Thomas J., and Philip W. Porter, "'From the best authorities': The Mountains of Kong in the cartography of West Africa." *Journal of African History* 32 (1991): 367–413.

Bargery, G.P. *A Hausa-English Dictionary and English-Hausa Vocabulary.* London: Oxford University Press, 1934.

Barth, Heinrich. *Travels and Discoveries in North and Central Africa, being a Journal of an Expedition undertaken under the auspices of H.B.M.'s Government in the Years 1849–1855,* 3 vols. London and New York, 1859.

Bell, Howard H. "Introduction," in M.R. Delany & Robert Campbell, *Search for a Place: Black Separatism and Africa, 1860.* Ann Arbor: University of Michigan Press, 1969.

Bell, Howard H. "The Negro emigration movement, 1849–1854: A phase of Negro nationalism." *Phylon* 20 (1959): 132–42.

Bethell, Leslie M. *The Abolition of the Brazilian Slave Trade: Britain, Brazil and the Slave Trade Question 1807–1869.* Cambridge: Cambridge University Press, 1970.

Blackett, R.J.M. "William G. Allen: The Forgotten Professor." *Civil War History* 26 (1980): 39–52.

Blassingame, John W., ed. *Slave Testimony: Two Centuries of Letters, Speeches, Interviews, and Autobiographies.* Baton Rouge: Louisiana State University Press, 1977.

Borghero, Francesco. "Relation sur l'établissement des missions dans le Vicariat du Dahomé" (1863), in *Journal de Francesco Borghero, premier missionnaire au Dahomey (1861–1865),* edited by Renzo Mandirola & Yves Morel. Paris: Karthala, 1997.

Bowdich, T.E. *Mission from Cape Coast Castle to Ashantee.* London: J. Murray, 1819.

Bowen, T.J. *Central Africa: Adventures & Missionary Labours.* London: Cass, 1857.

Brégand, Denise. *Commerce caravanier et relations sociales au Bénin: les Wangara du Borgou.* Paris: L'Harmattan, 1998.

Buckmaster, Henrietta. *Let My People Go: The Story of the Underground Railroad and the Growth of the Abolition Movement.* New York: Harper & Brothers, 1941.

Burton, Richard. *Mission to Gelele, King of Dahome.* London: Tinsley Brothers, 1864.

Castro de Araújo, Ubiratan. "1846: Um ano na rota Bahia-Lagos: Negócios, negociantes e outros parceiros." *Afro-Ásia* 21–22 (1998–99): 83–110.

Carretta, Vincent, ed. *Unchained Voices: An Anthology of Black Authors in the English-Speaking World of the Eighteenth Century.* Lexington: University of Kentucky Press, 1996.

Carretta, Vincent. "Olaudah Equiano or Gustavus Vassa? New light on an eighteenth-century question of identity." *Slavery and Abolition* 20, no. 3 (1999): 96–105.

Carvalho, Marcus J.M. de. "Le 'Divin Maître': Esclavage et liberté à Recife dans les années 1840." In *Pour l'histoire du Brésil,* edited by François Crouzet and Denin Rolland, and P. Bonnichon: pp. 435–49. Paris: l'Harmattan, 2000 .

_____. "Os Caminhos do Rio: Negros Canoeiros no Recife na Primeira Metade do Século XIX." *Afro-Ásia* 19–20 (1997): 75–93.

_____. *Liberdade: Rotinas e Rupturas do Escravismo, Recife, 1822–1850.* Recife: Universitária da UFPE, 1998.

Castelnau, Francis de. *Renseignements sur l'Afrique Centrale et sur une nation d'hommes a queue qui s'y trouverait, d'après le rapport des Négres du Soudan, esclaves a Bahia.* Paris: P. Bertrand, Libraire-Éditeur, 1851.

Clapperton, Hugh. *Journal of a Second Expedition into the Interior of Africa.* London: J. Murray, 1829.

Conrad, Robert Edgar, ed. *Children of God's Fire: A Documentary History of Black Slavery in Brazil.* Princeton, N.J.: Princeton University Press, 1984.

Conrad, Robert Edgar. *World of Sorrow: The African Slave Trade to Brazil.* Baton Rouge: Louisiana State University Press, 1986.

Curtin, Philip D., ed. *Africa Remembered; Narratives by West Africans from the Era of the Slave Trade.* Madison: University of Wisconsin Press, 1967.

Delany, Martin R. & Robert Campbell. *Search for a Place: Black Separatism and Africa, 1860.* Ann Arbor: University of Michigan Press, 1969.

Delany, Martin. *The Condition, Elevation, and Destiny of the Colored People of the United States, Politically Considered.* Philadelphia, 1852.

Delany, Martin. *Official Report of the Niger Valley Exploring Party* (Leeds, 1861), reprinted in Delany & Campbell, *Search for a Place*, 23–148.

Delval, Raymond. *Les Musulmanes au Togo.* Paris: Publications orientalistes de France, 1980.

Diouf, Sylviane A. *Servants of Allah: African Muslims Enslaved in the Americas.* New York: New York University Press, 1998.

Douglass, Frederick. *Narrative of the Life of Frederick Douglass, an American slave, written by himself.* Boston: Published at the Anti-slavery office, 1845.

Drew, Benjamin. *A North-Side View of Slavery. The Refugee: or the Narratives of Fugitive Slaves in Canada, Related by Themselves, with an Account of the History and Condition of the Colored Population of Upper Canada.* Boston: J. Jewett and Company, 1856.

Duncan, John. *Travels in Western Africa in 1845 & 1846.* 2 vols. London: Richard Bentley, 1847.

Dunn, Seymour B. "The early academies of Cortland County." *Cortland County Chronicles* 1 (1957): 57–76.

Dupuis, Joseph. *Journal of a Residence in Ashantee.* London: H. Colborn, 1824.

Eisenberg, Peter L. *The Sugar Industry in Pernambuco: Modernization without Change, 1840–1910.* Berkeley: University of California Press, 1974.

Eltis, David. *Economic Growth and the Ending of the Transatlantic Trade.* Oxford: Oxford University Press, 1987.

Eltis, David, Stephen D. Behrendt, David Richardson and Herbert S. Klein, *The Trans-Atlantic Slave Trade: A Database on CD-ROM.* New York: Cambridge University Press, 1999.

Eltis, David, and Stanley Engerman. "Fluctuations in sex and age ratios in the transatlantic slave trade, 1663–1864." *Economic History Review* 46 (1993): 308–23.

Equiano, Olaudah, *The Life of Olaudah Equiano, or Gustavus Vassa, the African, written by himself.* London: Published by author, 1789.

Falola, Toyin, and Paul E. Lovejoy, eds. *Pawnship in Africa: Debt bondage in historical perspective.* Boulder, Colorado: Westview Press, 1994.

Ferrez, Gilberto. *Photography in Brazil*. Trans. Stella de Sá Rego. Albuquerque: University of New Mexico Press, 1984.

Forbes, Frederick E. *Dahomey and the Dahomans, being the Journals of Two Missions to the King of Dahomey and Residence at his Capital in the Years 1849 and 1850*. 2 vols. London: Longman, Brown, Green and Longmans, 1851.

Forbes, Frederick E. *Six Months' Service in the African Blockade, from April to October, 1848*. London: Richard Bentley, 1849.

Foss, A.T., and Edward Mathews. *Facts for Baptist Churches*. Utica, NY: American Baptist Free Mission Society, 1850.

Frothingham, Octavius Brooks. *Gerrit Smith: A Biography*. New York: [1909] Negro University Press, 1969.

Fyfe, Christopher. *A History of Sierra Leone*. London: Oxford University Press, 1962.

Gates, Henry Louis, Jr., ed. *The Classic Slave Narratives*. New York: New American Library, 1987.

Gomez, Michael. *Exchanging Our Country Marks: The Transformation of African Identities in the Colonial and Antebellum South*. Chapel Hill: University of North Carolina Press, 1998.

Harlow, Ralph Volney. *Gerrit Smith, Philanthropist and Reformer*. New York: H. Holt and Company, 1939.

Hazard, Samuel. *Santo Domingo Past and Present with a Glance at Hayti*. New York: Harper & Brothers, 1873.

Hogg, Peter C. *The African Slave Trade and its Suppression: A Classified and Annotated Bibliography of Books, Pamphlets and Periodical Articles*. London: Frank Cass, 1973.

Horton, James Oliver and Lois E. Horton. *In Hope of Liberty: Culture, Community and Protest among Northern Free Blacks, 1700–1860*. New York: Oxford University Press, 1997.

Hunwick, John. "'I wish to be seen in our land called Afrika': Umar b. Sayyid's appeal to be released from slavery (1819)." Forthcoming.

Hurston, Zora Neale. "Cudjo's Own Story of the Last African Slaver." *Journal of Negro History* 12, no. 4 (1927): 648–63.

Johnson, Marion. "News from Nowhere: Duncan and Adofoodia." *History in Africa* 1 (Waltham, Mass.: African Studies Association, 1974): 55–66.

Jones, Howard. *The Mutiny on the Amistad: The Saga of the Slave Revolt and its Impact on American Abolition, Law and Diplomacy*. Revised ed. New York: Oxford University Press, 1988.

Karasch, Mary. *Slave Life in Rio de Janeiro 1808–1850*. Princeton, N.J.:

Princeton University Press, 1987.

Kirk-Greene, Anthony and Paul Newman, eds. *West African Travels and Adventures: Two Autobiographical Narratives from Northern Nigeria.* New Haven, Conn.: Yale University Press, 1971.

Klein, Herbert S. *The Atlantic Slave Trade.* Cambridge and New York: Cambridge University Press, 1999.

Klose, Heinrich. *Le Togo sous drapeau allemand (1894–1897).* Trans. Phillippe David. Lomé: Karthala, 1992.

Koelle, Sigismund Wilhelm. *Polyglotta Africana.* Graz: Akademische Druck- u. Verlagsanstalt, 1963 [1854].

Krueger, Robert. "Milhões de Vozes, umas Pàginas Preciosas. As Narrativas dos Escravos Brasileiros." In *Imàgenes de la Resistencia Indígena y Esclava,* edited by Roger Zapata. Lima: Editorial Wari, 1990.

Kuba, Richard. *Wasangari und Wangara: Borgu und seine Nachbarn in historische Perspectif.* Hamburg, Germany: Lit., 1996.

Lander, Richard. *Records of Captain Clapperton's Last Expedition to Africa.* London: Colburn and Bentley, 1830.

Lander, Richard, and John Lander. *Journal of an Expedition to Explore the Course and Termination of the River Niger.* London and New York: Harper & Brothers, 1832.

Lara, Silvia Hunold. "Biografia de Mahommah G. Baquaqua." *Revista Brasileira de História—São Paulo* 16 (1988): 269–84.

Law, Robin. "Between the sea and the lagoons: the interaction of maritime and inland navigation on the pre-colonial Slave Coast." *Cahiers d'études africaines* 29 (1989): 209–37.

Law, Robin. *The Horse in West African History.* Oxford and New York: Published for the International African Institute by Oxford University Press, 1980.

Law, Robin. "On pawning and enslavement for debt on the pre-colonial Slave Coast." In *Pawnship in Africa: Debt bondage in historical perspective,* edited by Toyin Falola & Paul E. Lovejoy. Boulder, Colorado: Westview Press, 1994.

Law, Robin. *The Oyo Empire c.1600–c.1836.* Oxford: Clarendon Press, 1977.

Law, Robin. "'Central and eastern Wangara': an indigenous West African perception of the political and economic geography of the Slave Coast, as recorded by Joseph Dupuis in Kumasi, 1820." *History in Africa,* vol. 22. Waltham, Mass.: African Studies Association, 1995.

Law, Robin. "Further light on John Duncan's account of the 'Fallatah

Country' (1845)." *History in Africa*, vol. 28. Waltham, Mass.: African Studies Association, 2001.

Law, Robin. "The evolution of the Brazilian community in Ouidah." *Slavery & Abolition* 22 (2001): 22–41.

Law, Robin, and Paul Lovejoy. "Borgu in the Atlantic slave trade." *African Economic History* 27 (1999): 69–92.

Levtzion, Nehemiah. *Muslims and Chiefs in West Africa*. Oxford: Clarendon Press, 1968.

Leyburn, James G. *The Haitian People*. Westport, Conn.: Greenwood Press, 1966.

Lockwood, Charles. *Manhattan Moves Uptown: An Illustrated History*. Boston: Houghton Mifflin, 1976.

Logan, Rayford W., and Michael R. Winston, eds. *Dictionary of American Negro Biography*. New York: Norton, 1982.

Lombard, Jacques. "Aperçu sur la technologie et l'artisanat bariba." *Etudes dahoméennes* 18 (1957): 7–55.

Lombard, Jacques. *Structures de type "féodal" en Afrique noire: étude des dynamismes internes et des relations sociales chez les Bariba du Dahomey*. Paris: Mouton, 1965.

Lovejoy, Paul E. "Background to rebellion: The origins of Muslim slaves in Bahia." In *Unfree Labour in the Development of the Atlantic World*, edited by Paul E. Lovejoy and Nicholas Rogers. London: Frank Cass, 1994.

Lovejoy, Paul E. "Biography as source material: towards a biographical archive of enslaved Africans." In *Source Material for Studying the Slave Trade and the African Diaspora*, edited by Robin Law. Stirling, Scotland: Centre of Commonwealth Studies, University of Stirling, 1997.

Lovejoy, Paul E. *Caravans of Kola: The Hausa Kola Trade, 1700–1900* Zaria, Nigeria: Ahmadu Bello University Press, 1980.

Lovejoy, Paul E. "Cerner les identités au sein de la diaspora africaine, l'islam et l'esclavage aux Amériques." *Cahiers des Anneaux de la Mémoire* 1 (1999): 249–78.

Lovejoy, Paul E. "The 'coffee' of the Sudan: Consumption of kola nuts in the Sokoto Caliphate in the nineteenth century." In *Consuming Habits: Drugs in History and Anthropology*, edited by Jordan Goodman, Paul E. Lovejoy, and Andrew Sherratt. London: Routledge, 1993.

Lovejoy, Paul E. "Ethnicity, religion and the mirage of identity: Mahommah Gardo Baquaqua's journey to the Americas." In *Liberté, identité, intégration et servitude*, edited by Mohammed Ennaji and Paul E. Lovejoy. Rabat, forthcoming.

Lovejoy, Paul E. "Jihad e Escravidão: As Origens dos Escravos Muçulmanos de Bahia." *Topoi: Revista de História* 1 (2000): 11–44.

Lovejoy, Paul E. "The Kambarin Beriberi: The formation of a specialized group of Hausa kola traders in the nineteenth century." *Journal of African History* 14, no. 4 (1973): 633–51.

Lovejoy, Paul E. "Polanyi's 'Ports of Trade': Salaga and Kano in the nineteenth century." *Canadian Journal of African Studies* 16 (1982): 245–78.

Lovejoy, Paul E. "The role of the Wangara in the economic transformation of the Central Sudan in the fifteenth and sixteenth centuries." *Journal of African History* 19, no. 2 (1978): 173–93.

Mabee, Carleton. *Black Education in New York State*. Syracuse, N.Y.: Syracuse University Press, 1979.

Mathews, Edward. *The Autobiography of the Rev. E. Mathews, The "Father Dickson," of Mrs. Stowe's "Dred."* London: Houlston and Wright, 1853.

Mercier, P. "Histoire et légende: la bataille d'Illorin." *Notes africaines* 47 (1950): 92–95.

Moore, Samuel, ed. *An Interesting Narrative. Biography of Mahommah G. Baquaqua, A Native of Zoogoo, in the Interior of Africa (A Convert to Christianity,) with a Description of That Part of the World; including the Manners and Customs of the Inhabitants*. Detroit: George Pomeroy and Company, 1854.

Muir, Ramsay. *A History of Liverpool*, 2nd ed. London: University Press of Liverpool, 1907.

Nash, Gary B. *Forging Freedom: The Formation of Philadelphia's Black Community, 1720–1840*. Cambridge, Mass.: Harvard University Press, 1988.

Neufeld, Ernest, ed. *The Renascence of City of Hall; Commemorative Presentation Rededication of City Hall, The City of New York, July 12, 1956*. New York: New York Department of Public Works, 1956.

Newsome, M.T., ed. *Arguments, Pro and Con, on the Call for a National Emigration Convention, to be held in Cleveland, Ohio, August, 1854, by Frederick Douglass, W.J. Watkins, and James M. Whitfield, With a Short Appendix of the Statistics of Canada West, West Indies, Central and South America*. Detroit: George Pomeroy and Company, 1854.

Nunez, Benjamin. *Dictionary of Afro-Latin American Civilization*. Westport, Conn.: Greenwood Press, 1980.

Palmer, Friend. *Early Days in Detroit*. Detroit, Mich.: Hunt & June, 1906.

Pescatello, Ann M., ed. *The African in Latin America*. New York: Knopf, 1975.

Perham, Margery, and Mary Bull, eds. *The Diaries of Lord Lugard.* Evanston, Ill.: Northwestern University Press, 1959.

Pomeroy, Albert A. *Geneology of the Pomeroy Family.* Toledo, Ohio: Franklin Printing and Engraving Co., 1912.

Ripley, C. Peter, ed *The Black Abolitionist Papers. Volume I. The British Isles, 1830–1865.* Chapel Hill: University of North Carolina Press, 1985.

_____. *The Black Abolitionist Papers. Volume II. Canada, 1830–1865.* Chapel Hill: University of North Carolina Press, 1985.

Sanneh, Lamin. *Abolitionists Abroad: American Blacks and the Making of Modern West Africa.* Cambridge: Harvard University Press, 1999.

Schön, James Frederick. *Magána Hausa. Native Literature, or Proverbs, Tales, Fables and Historical Fragments in the Hausa Language, to which is added a Translation in English.* London: Society for Promoting Christian Knowledge, 1885.

Schön, James Frederick and Samuel Crowther. *Journals of the Rev. James Frederick Schön and Mr Samuel Crowther, who ...accompanied the Expedition up the River Niger in 1841.* London: Hatchard and Son, 1842.

Sherman, Joan R. "James M. Whitfield: Poet and Emigrationist: A Voice of Protest and Despair." *Journal of Negro History* 57, no. 2 (1972): 169–76.

Short, Kenneth R. "New York Central College: A Baptist experiment in integrated higher education, 1848–61." *Foundations: A Baptist Journal of History and Theology* 1 (1962): 250–56.

Smith, Robert. "The canoe in West African history." *Journal of African History* 11, no. 4 (1970): 515–24.

Spradling, Mary Mace, ed. *In Black and White. Supplement: A Guide to Magazine Articles, Newspaper Articles, and Books Concerning More Than 6,700 Black Individuals and Groups.* 3rd ed. Detroit: Gale, 1980.

Stanley, Brian. *The History of the Baptist Missionary Society, 1792–1992.* Edinburgh: T. & T. Clark, 1992.

Stewart, Marjorie H. *Borgu and its Kingdoms: A Reconstruction of a Western Sudanese Polity.* Lewiston, N.Y.: E. Mellen Press, 1993.

Stouffer, Allan P. *The Light of Nature and the Law of God: Anti-Slavery in Ontario, 1833–1877.* Baton Rouge: Louisiana State University Press, 1992.

Taylor, Yuval, ed. *I Was Born a Slave: An Anthology of Classic Slave Narratives.* 2 vols. Chicago: Lawrence Hill Books, 1999.

Thomas, Hugh. *The Slave Trade: The History of the Atlantic Slave Trade 1440–1870.* London: Picador, 1997.

Trimingham, J. Spencer. *Islam in West Africa.* Oxford: Clarendon Press, 1959.

Turner, Richard Brent. *Islam in the African-American Experience.* Bloomington: Indiana University Press, 1997.

Ullman, Victor. *Look to the North Star: A Life of William King.* Boston: Beacon Press, 1969.

Verger, Pierre. *Flux et reflux de la traite des Nègres entre le Golfe de Bénin et Bahia de Todos os Santos du XVIIe au XIXe siècle.* Paris: LaHaye, Mouton, 1968.

Walvin, James. *Black Ivory: A History of British Slavery.* London: HarperCollins, 1992.

Wayne, Michael. "The Black population of Canada West on the eve of the American Civil War: A reassessment based on the manuscript census of 1861." In *A Nation of Immigrants: Women, Workers, and Communities in Canadian History, 1840s–1960s,* edited by Franca Iacovetta, Paula Draper, and Robert Ventresca. Toronto: University of Toronto Press, 1998.

Whitfield, James. *America, and Other Poems.* Buffalo: Leavitt, 1853.

Wilks, Ivor, ed. "Abu Bakr al-Siddiq of Timbuktu." In *Africa Remembered,* edited by Philip D. Curtin. Madison: University of Wisconsin Press, 1967.

Wilks, Ivor. *Asante in the Nineteenth Century.* Cambridge: Cambridge University Press, 1975.

Wilks, Ivor. *Wa and the Wala.* Cambridge: Cambridge University Press, 1989.

Winch, Julie. "'You Know I am a Man of Business': James Forten and the factor of race in Philadelphia's antebellum business community." *Business and Economic History* 26, no. 1 (1997): 213–28.

Winks, Robin. *The Blacks in Canada.* Second edition. Montreal & Kingston, Ont.: McGill-Queen's University Press, 1997.

Wolf, W. "Dr Ludwig Wolfs letzte Reise nach Barbar (Bariba oder Borgu)," *Mitteilungen aus den Deutsche Schutzgebieten,* 4 (1891), 1–22.

Woodson, Carter G., ed. *The Mind of the Negro as Reflected in Letters Written during the Crisis, 1800–1860.* New York: Russell and Russell, 1969.

Wright, Albert Hazen, ed. *Cornell's Three Precursors: I. New York Central College.* Studies in History No. 23, Pre-Cornell and Early Cornell VIII, Ithaca: New York State College of Agriculture, 1960.

Zima, Petr. *Lexique Dendi (Songhay) (Djougou, Bénin).* Köln: Rüdiger Köppe Verlag, 1994.

INDEX